Power, Construction and Meaning in Festivals

Whether through education, sport or festivity, events form the basis on which we attribute cultural meaning, significance and value to our lives. In this light, community events have the potential to create positive and negative social, cultural, economic and environmental impacts within the community across a wide variety of genres and platforms.

This book offers a deeper and more critical insight into the relationships, dynamics and planning processes of festivals and events and the impact this has upon authenticity, cultural consumption and the local communities they serve. It does so by looking at a range of key debates in power theory, event planning and design, event construction, experience and meaning, authenticity, sustainability, social inclusion, accessibility and sponsorship engagement. International case studies are embedded within the chapters, examining the role of stakeholders, local communities, organisers, local governments and infrastructure.

This critical event studies text is interdisciplinary and will make valuable reading for students and researchers who are interested in the relationships and dynamics involved in the construction and planning of festivals and events, their immediate impact and their significance for the future.

Allan Jepson, PhD, is an ex festival practitioner, a Nottingham Forest supporter and currently a senior lecturer and researcher in critical event studies (CES) at the University of Hertfordshire, United Kingdom. Allan has contributed widely to critical event studies literature within the realm of community festivals and events and has two key texts in this area (*Exploring Community Festivals and Events* and *Managing and Developing Communities, Festivals and Events*, both with Alan Clarke, University of Pannonia, Hungary). Allan's current research interests include the role of inclusive/exclusive and sub-cultures within festivals and events, the cultural relationships of festival stakeholders and in particular local community(ies), the role of stakeholders in event production/construction and how these impact upon the consumption of cultural events and festivals, power, hegemony and decision making in local community festivals and events, the role of festivals and events as a catalyst for integrating culturally diverse communities, psychology and events; self and group efficacy and how this effects community engagement in event planning and consumption, knowledge management in events, community festivals and events and their impact on the quality of life (QOL) of individuals and families; and more recently arts participation and memory creation amongst the over 70s. Allan is currently collaborating in research with colleagues from the following Universities; AUT University, New Zealand; and Leeds Beckett University, United Kingdom. Email: a.s.jepson@herts.ac.uk.

Alan Clarke works at the University of Pannonia in the Tourism Department of the Faculty of Business and Economics. He is a co-director of the Balaton Tourism Research Institute (known as BATUKI in Hungary) and works with stakeholder groups around the Lake and in the Balaton Highlands to promote the development of sustainable tourism in the region. He continues to work on critical events studies and hospitality. He is delighted that he has the Veszprém International Festival on his doorstep, which keeps him in touch with world-class organisation and world-class performers. He is also a visiting professor at the University of Derby in the United Kingdom and continues working on European projects, having just joined the launch of 'The Wine Lab' with partners from both the study of and the production of wine throughout Europe. Alan continues to publish widely, developing long-standing interests in sustainability and community development. He has contributed to many journals but is now taking on the responsibility of editor in chief for the recently launched *International Journal of Spa and Wellness*. His love of Sheffield Wednesday continues and confidence is at a new high as his subscription to a Hungarian channel showing Premiership Football demonstrates. But the true loves of his life, Ruth, Jamie, Dan and Alex, continue to delight and amaze as they grow older. Email: alanhungary@hotmail.com

Routledge Advances in Event Research Series
Edited by Warwick Frost and Jennifer Laing
*Department of Marketing, Tourism and Hospitality,
La Trobe University, Australia*

For a full list of titles in this series, please visit www.routledge.com/tourism/series/RAERS

Commemorative Events: Memory, identities, conflict
Warwick Frost and Jennifer Laing

Power, Politics and International Events: Socio-cultural analyses of festivals and spectacles
Edited by Udo Merkel

Event Audiences and Expectations
Jo Mackellar

Event Portfolio Planning and Management: A holistic approach
Vassilios Ziakas

Conferences and Conventions: A research perspective
Judith Mair

Fashion, Design and Events
Edited by Kim M. Williams, Jennifer Laing and Warwick Frost

Food and Wine Events in Europe: A stakeholder approach
Edited by Alessio Cavicchi and Cristina Santini

Event Volunteering: International perspectives on the event volunteering experience
Edited by Karen Smith, Leonie Lockstone-Binney, Kirsten Holmes and Tom Baum

The Arts and Events
Hilary du Cros and Lee Jolliffe

Sports Events, Society and Culture
Edited by Katherine Dashper, Thomas Fletcher and Nicola McCullough

The Future of Events and Festivals
Edited by Ian Yeoman, Martin Robertson, Una McMahon-Beattie, Elisa Backer and Karen A. Smith

Exploring Community Events and Festivals
Edited by Allan Jepson and Alan Clarke

Event Design: Social perspectives and practices
Edited by Greg Richards, Lénia Marques and Karen Mein

Rituals and Traditional Events in the Modern World
Edited by Warwick Frost and Jennifer Laing

Battlefield Events: Landscape, commemoration and heritage
Edited by Keir Reeves, Geoffrey Bird, Laura James, Birger Stichelbaut and Jean Bourgeois

Events in the City: Using public spaces as event venues
Andrew Smith

Event Mobilities: Politics, Place and Performance
Edited by Kevin Hannam, Mary Mostafanezhad and Jillian Rickly-Boyd

Approaches and Methods in Events Studies
Edited by Tomas Pernecky

Visitor Attractions and Events: Locations and linkages
Adi Weidenfeld, Richard Butler and Allan Williams

Critical Event Studies: A Guide for Critical Thinkers
Karl Spracklen and Ian R. Lamond

The Value of Events
John Armbrecht, Erik Lundberg, Tommy D. Andersson, Don Getz

Festival Encounters
Theoretical Perspectives on Festival Events
Michelle Duffy and Judith Mair

Legacies and Mega Events
Facts of Fairy Tales?
Edited by Ian Brittain, Jason Bocarro, Terri Byers and Kamilla Swart

Exhibitions, Trade Fairs and Industrial Events
Edited by Warwick Frost and Jennifer Laing

Power, Construction and Meaning in Festivals
Edited by Allan Jepson and Alan Clarke

Power, Construction and Meaning in Festivals

Edited by
Allan Jepson and Alan Clarke

LONDON AND NEW YORK

First published 2018 by Routledge

2 Park Square, Milton Park, Abingdon, Oxon OX14 4RN
605 Third Avenue, New York, NY 10017

Routledge is an imprint of the Taylor & Francis Group, an informa business

First issued in paperback 2022

Copyright © 2018 selection and editorial matter, Allan Jepson and Alan Clarke; individual chapters, the contributors

The right of Allan Jepson and Alan Clarke to be identified as the authors of the editorial material, and of the authors for their individual chapters, has been asserted in accordance with sections 77 and 78 of the Copyright, Designs and Patents Act 1988.

All rights reserved. No part of this book may be reprinted or reproduced or utilised in any form or by any electronic, mechanical, or other means, now known or hereafter invented, including photocopying and recording, or in any information storage or retrieval system, without permission in writing from the publishers.

Notice:
Product or corporate names may be trademarks or registered trademarks, and are used only for identification and explanation without intent to infringe.

Publisher's Note
The publisher has gone to great lengths to ensure the quality of this reprint but points out that some imperfections in the original copies may be apparent.

British Library Cataloguing-in-Publication Data
A catalogue record for this book is available from the British Library

Library of Congress Cataloging-in-Publication Data
A catalog record for this book has been requested

ISBN: 978-1-138-06322-8 (hbk)
ISBN: 978-1-03-233937-5 (pbk)
DOI: 10.4324/9781315161181

Typeset in Sabon
by Apex CoVantage, LLC

This book is dedicated to my beautiful wife Joanna, and our three wonderful young children: Henry (nearly 5), Freddie (3) and Ellie (1 ½) who bring surprises, love and laughter into our life every day.

I would also like to dedicate this book to Dr Andrew Francis, a courageous, determined and supportive academic who always showed great faith in me.

I am thankful for; and gratefully acknowledge the support for research at the University of Hertfordshire: in particular Celeste Jones and Professor Damian Ward, and the amazingly supportive Tourism, Hospitality and Events Management academic group, and finally, my continuing friendship with Alan Clarke.

Contents

List of figures xi
List of tables xiii
List of contributors xv

1 Introducing power, meaning and authenticity 1
ALLAN JEPSON AND ALAN CLARKE

2 A q-study of organisers' perspectives on factors of festival success in Crete 5
DIMITRIOS P. STERGIOU, EIRINI PEHLIVANIDOU AND DAVID AIREY

3 "I don't think they give a monkey's about me": exploring stakeholder power and community alienation at Glastonbury Festival 21
ZOE WHITE AND RAPHAELA STADLER

4 Event evolution and the planning process: the case of the Finnish housing fair 35
KARINE DUPRE

5 The sporting and heritage festival of Landsmót in Iceland: identity expressions and performances of nation, gender and rurality 49
SUSANNA HELDT CASSEL

6 Personal networks in festival, event and creative communities: perceptions, connections and collaborations 65
DAVID JARMAN

7 Innovation in rural festivals: are festival managers disempowered? 91
GRZEGORZ KWIATKOWSKI AND ANNE-METTE HJALAGER

8	The effects of supply chain management (SCM) activities and their impact upon festival management and the customer experience W. GERARD RYAN AND STEPHEN KELLY	109
9	The importance of the stakeholder relationship for the success of an event: the case of Montreal MOHAMED REDA KHOMSI	129
10	'Power wrestling': the life and (untimely) death of the Real Food Festival TRUDIE WALTERS	139
11	Religion and politics – event, authenticity and meaning: A dialogical approach RUTH DOWSON AND IAN LAMOND	153
12	Commemoration, celebration, and commercialisation: akaroa's French Festival JOANNA FOUNTAIN AND MICHAEL MACKAY	169
13	Managing community stakeholders in rural areas: assessing the organisation of local sports events in Gorski Kotar, Croatia JELENA ĐURKIN AND NICHOLAS WISE	185
14	Concluding remarks on power authenticity and meaning ALAN CLARKE AND ALLAN JEPSON	201

Index   205

Figures

4.1	Locations of Finnish housing fairs since 1970	42
4.2	Yearly visitors (in thousands), according to housing fair attendance	43
4.3	List of housing fair themes 1991–2016	43
4.4	A wordle diagram to demonstrate the major themes of the Finnish housing fairs	44
5.1	The Icelandic Horse	56
5.2	Landsmót a national sport and heritage festival	56
6.1	Network wheel sociogram for 'ego A'	78
6.2	Network wheel sociogram for 'ego B'	78
6.3	Ego A's network with the ego-alter tie lengths adjusted to reflect the strength of tie	81
6.4	Ego B's network with the ego-alter tie lengths adjusted to reflect the strength of tie	82
6.5	Employing E-NET's 'spring embedding' algorithm to reposition the nodes on the sociogram graph (ego A)	83
6.6	Employing E-NET's 'spring embedding' algorithm to reposition the nodes on the sociogram graph (ego B)	83
8.1	Simple diagram of activities and firms in a supply chain	111
8.2	Multi-directional flow within a supply chain	111
8.3	Macro supply chain representation for a large outdoor music festival	115
8.4	Micro supply chain representation for a large outdoor music festival	116
8.5	Organisations, primary research and communication points within the supply chain	117
8.6	Kraljic's (1983) Portfolio purchasing model	121
8.7	Kraljic's (1983) portfolio model (adapted).	122

Tables

2.1	Statements which received highest positive and negative scores in the Pragmatic/Traditional Management perspective	12
2.2	Statements received highest positive and negative scores in the Communitarian/Person-oriented perspective	14
3.1	Stakeholder objectives of Glastonbury Festival	28
6.1	Alter attributes	79
6.2	Perceived tie strengths	82
6.3	Structural holes data	84
7.1	Number of organizations involved in the festival as collaborating partners apart from the main responsible organization	98
7.2	The Pearson correlation between the number of involved organizations and several distinctive characteristics of the examined festivals	98
7.3	Connectivity index (by up to three main variables in the festival)	99
7.4	The Pearson correlation between the purpose of the festival and the number of involved organizations	101
7.5	A Pearson correlation between the festivals' assessed impacts and the number of involved organizations	102
13.1	List of sport event stakeholders	188
13.2	Limitations, challenges and issues facing rural communities based on the findings from this study	191

Contributors

David Airey is emeritus professor of the University of Surrey. In 2006, he received the United Nations World Tourism Organization's Ulysses Prize. He co-edited the first book on tourism education and has recently co-edited the 500-page Routledge handbook on the same topic. Email: d.airey1@btinternet.com

Susanna Heldt Cassel is a professor of human geography, head of department of human geography, and director of the Centre for Tourism and Leisure Research at Dalarna University, Sweden. She has published widely in tourism geography in the *Scandinavian Journal of Tourism and Hospitality Management, Tourism, Culture and Communication* to name but a few. Her research investigates the role of gender, rurality migration patterns and photography in leisure, tourism and events. Email: shc@du.se

Alan Clarke works at the University of Pannonia in the Tourism Department of the Faculty of Business and Economics. He is a co-director of the Balaton Tourism Research Institute (known as BATUKI in Hungary) and works with stakeholder groups around the lake and in the Balaton Highlands to promote the development of sustainable tourism in the region. He continues to work on critical events studies and hospitality. He is delighted that he has the Veszprém International Festival on his doorstep, which keeps him in touch with an world-class organisation and world-class performers. He is also a visiting professor at the University of Derby in the United Kingdom and continues working on European projects, having just joined the launch of 'The Wine Lab' with partners from both the study of and the production of wine throughout Europe. Alan continues to publish widely, developing long-standing interests in sustainability and community development. He has contributed to many journals but is now taking on the responsibility of editor in chief for the recently launched *International Journal of Spa and Wellness*.

His love of Sheffield Wednesday continues, and his confidence is at a new high as his subscription to a Hungarian channel showing Premiership Football demonstrates. But the true loves of his life, Ruth, Jamie,

Dan and Alex, continue to delight and amaze as they grow older. Email: alanhungary@hotmail.com

Ruth Dowson is an events practitioner with 30 years' experience in the strategic development, management and delivery of events, in UK public/private sectors. Since 2007, Ruth has been a senior lecturer and researcher in event studies at Leeds Beckett University, United Kingdom. Dowson was as a priest in the Church of England in 2013. She co-authored *Event Planning and Management* (Kogan Page). Email: r.dowson@leedsbeckett.ac.uk

Jelena Đurkin, PhD, is a senior assistant and researcher in the Faculty of Tourism and Hospitality Management at University of Rijeka, Croatia. She is interested in topics of community entrepreneurship and community-based tourism. Jelena completed her PhD in 2015 and has previously conducted research and published work on Gorski Kotar in Croatia. Email: jelenad@fthm.hr

Karine Dupre, PhD, is an associate professor, a French architect and planner and head of the architecture program at Griffith University, Australia. An enthusiast about cross-disciplinary approaches and partnerships, her main research project is currently about the impact of Chinese tourism on cities. Other research interests include cities and tourism, tourism and urban development and building heritage and identity. Email: k.dupre@griffith.edu.au

Joanna Fountain, PhD, is a senior lecturer in the Tourism in the Environment, Society and Design Faculty at Lincoln University. She has broad research interests in cultural heritage tourism and rural tourism and festivals and events. A specific focus of her research is the production and consumption of wine and other gastronomic tourism experiences. Email: Joanna.Fountain@lincoln.ac.nz

Anne-Mette Hjalager is a professor at the Institute of Entrepreneurship and Relationship Management at University of Southern Denmark. Her areas of research include economic development and innovation in rural areas, tourism management and planning. She has published articles in several leading journals including *Tourism Management*, *Journal of Travel Research* and *Journal of Sustainable Tourism*. She is an editor in chief of the *Journal of Gastronomy and Tourism*. Email: hjalager@sam.sdu.dk

David Jarman, since 2007, after his final summer working with the Edinburgh Festival Fringe, has been programme leader of Edinburgh Napier University's BA (Hons) International Festival and Event Management. His publications focus on the application of social network analysis methods to festivals and events, including a chapter in *Critical Event Studies* (2016). Email: dsrjarman@gmail.com

Allan Jepson, PhD, is an ex-festival practitioner, a Nottingham Forest supporter and currently a senior lecturer and researcher in CES at the University of Hertfordshire, United Kingdom. Allan has contributed widely to critical event studies literature within the realm of community festivals and events and has two key texts in this area (*Exploring Community Festivals and Events* and *Managing and Developing Communities, Festivals and Events*, both with Alan Clarke, University of Pannonia, Hungary). Allan's current research interests include the role of inclusive/exclusive and sub-cultures within festivals and events; the cultural relationships of festival stakeholders and in particular local community(ies); the role of stakeholders in event production/construction and how these impact upon the consumption of cultural events and festivals, power, hegemony and decision making in local community festivals and events; the role of festivals and events as a catalyst for integrating culturally diverse communities, psychology and events; self and group efficacy and how this effects community engagement in event planning and consumption, knowledge management in events, community festivals and events and their impact on the QOL of individuals and families; and, more recently, arts participation and memory creation amongst the over 70s. Allan is currently collaborating in research with colleagues from the following Universities; AUT University, New Zealand; and Leeds Beckett University, United Kingdom. Email: a.s.jepson@herts.ac.uk.

Stephen Kelly, PhD, is a senior lecturer in the School of Business, Leadership and Economics at Staffordshire University in the United Kingdom, where he teaches and researches in purchasing and supply management, operations management and project management. He is currently working on an EU ERASMUS+ funded project – PEREFCT – developing a harmonised pan-European purchasing curriculum with the Universities of Dortmund, Mainz, Twente and Lappeenranta. His current research focuses on supplier perceptions of buying processes, the supply chains of festivals and purchasing and supply management education. He is the co-founder and organiser of the annual IPSERA (International Purchasing and Supply Education and Research Association) Educator's Conference and is an IPSERA executive committee member. He has a PhD in management science from Lancaster University, a member of the Chartered Institute of Procurement and Supply, a senior fellow of the Higher Education Academy and a reviewer for the *Journal of Purchasing & Supply Management*. Before his academic career, he worked for over ten years in a variety of purchasing and supply chain roles for organisations such as Siemens, GEC and the NHS. Email: stephen.kelly@staffs.ac.uk.

Mohamed Reda Khomsi, PhD, is a professor in the Department of Urban Studies and Tourism, School of Management, Université du Québec à Montréal. His research focuses on governance models, assessment of the hallmark tourist event and smart destinations. Mohamed is the author of over a dozen articles and book chapters on these topics, including an article on new models of destination governance entitled (in french): Le nouveau modèle de gouvernance du secteur touristique québécois (2017). In *Les contrats de destination*, Spindler, J; Bédé, S (eds). Harmattan, Paris. Email: khomsi.mohamed_reda@uqam.ca.

Grzegorz Kwiatkowski, is an adjunct at the Koszalin University of Technology in Poland. He hold a PhD in business administration from the University of Southern Denmark. His core field of research focusses on event and festival management, participatory placemaking and rural development. He has published articles in several journals including *Event Management, Scandinavian Journal of Hospitality and Tourism*, and *International*. Email: gregory.pl.kwiatkowski@gmail.com

Ian Lamond, PhD, is a performer, writer and arts practitioner turned academic/activist with almost 30 years of either treading the boards or tapping the computer keys. Since 2012, Lamond has been a senior lecturer and researcher in event studies at Leeds Beckett University, United Kingdom. He is co-author of *Critical Event Studies* and co-editor of *Protests as Events* and *Critical Event Studies: Approaches to Research*. Email: i.lamond@leedsbeckett.ac.uk.

Michael Mackay, PhD, is senior lecturer in rural studies in the Environment, Society and Design Faculty at Lincoln University. His research and teaching interests include rural tourism, rural social change, entrepreneurship, interpretive sociology and qualitative research methods. He is also engaged in social impact assessment and policy development regarding recreation and tourism in the New Zealand countryside. Email: Michael.Mackay@lincoln.ac.nz

Eirini Pehlivanidou, holds an MSc in tourism management from the Hellenic Open University. She is also a certified tourist guide. She has worked as an administrative assistant in both the public and private sectors. Email: pechl_eirini@yahoo.gr

W. Gerard Ryan EdD was the events manager at the Cavern Club in Liverpool before taking on a post in education. Prior to that, Gerard was the development manager for the Merseyside Music Development Agency, the first of its kind in the United Kingdom. Gerard spent the early years of his career as a professional musician. More recently, Gerard has written extensively, with publications that include book chapters and journal articles with a variety of conference papers, reports and international academic projects in areas of events management, the creative industries and other training support materials. Email: w.g.ryan@salford.ac.uk

Raphaela Stadler, PhD, is a senior lecturer in event management at the University of Hertfordshire, United Kingdom. She has published on knowledge management/transfer in festival organisations, power, community cultural development and event attendance and family QOL. She is currently involved in a research project on arts participation and memory creation amongst the over 70s. Email: r.stadler@herts.ac.uk.

Dimitrios P. Stergiou holds a PhD from the University of Surrey. Currently he is assistant professor of tourism management at the Hellenic Open University. He has over ten years of experience in teaching, learning and research in the wider areas of tourism education and tourism management. Email: dstergiou@eap.gr

Trudie Walters, PhD, wrote her chapter while working at the University of the Sunshine Coast in Australia. She is now a lecturer at the University of Otago in Dunedin, New Zealand. Her event studies research agenda centres on how events are utilised, perceived and valued, particularly in a non-economic sense. Email: trudie.walters@otago.ac.nz

Zoe White is an event management graduate from the University of Hertfordshire, United Kingdom. With a strong interest in music festivals, she completed her dissertation on the topic of Glastonbury Festival, exploring the impact it has on the host community. She is currently working as a fundraising assistant for the Tusk Trust, an African Wildlife Conservation charity based in Dorset. Email: zoelouisawhite@hotmail.co.uk

Nicholas Wise is senior lecturer in tourism and events management at Liverpool John Moores University. His research focuses on sport, events and tourism, looking specifically at social regeneration, sense of place and community. His research focuses primarily on cases in the Balkans (Croatia and Serbia) and Latin America (Dominican Republic and Brazil), addressing community change and local impacts. Email: nwise5@kent.edu

1 Introducing power, meaning and authenticity

Allan Jepson and Alan Clarke

Our book contains contributions from 20 researchers, all of which are intrigued by the prospect of what events can achieve positively for their stakeholders', and the ways in which power, meaning and authenticity are central concepts to achieving potential positive outcomes in the creation of events.

We begin in Chapter 2 with "A Q-study of Organisers' Perspectives on Factors of Festival Success in Crete" by Dimitrios P. Stergiou and Eirini Pehlivanidou, from the Hellenic Open University, Greece and David Airey, from the University of Surrey, United Kingdom. They observe that regional events play an important role in the Cretan tourism product with many communities hosting regional festivals. Exploring these from a managerial perspective, the authors note that these festivals provide a range of entertainment and activities and identify many factors that determine their success. The study used Q-methodology to uncover festival success factors based on the subjective perceptions of festival organisers in Crete and identify clusters of participants sharing common viewpoints. The Q-analysis identified two factors representing different perspectives of festival organizer opinion about success factors in the Cretan festival market: A Communitarian/Person-oriented focus and a Pragmatic/Traditional Management focus.

In Chapter 3 Zoe White and Raphaela Stadler from the University of Hertfordshire, United Kingdom raise some interesting challenges to what is seen as one of the most successful events. The chapter is entitled "I Don't Think They Give a Monkey's about Me": Exploring Stakeholder Power and Community Alienation at Glastonbury Festival", and they argue that it is becoming more and more recognised that the needs of the host community need to be met and satisfied in order to ascertain their support for future music festivals. Empowering the host community, including them in the decision-making process, or co-creating the event experience with them have all been found to be essential elements of the planning process and in ensuring the long-term success of a festival.

Moving on, Chapter 4 takes us to Australia, as Karine Dupre, from Griffith University, Australia, presents a study entitled "Event Evolution and the Planning Process: The Case of the Finnish Housing Fair". She observes the Finnish housing fair is an event that promotes the quality of housing and living conditions in Finland by displaying building products and buildings in a different city across the country each year. For five years, it has attracted more than 110,000 visitors. The study details how this community event is planned, constructed and valued. The focus on processes shows that early strategy, flexibility and adaptation are the key elements to ensure long-term sustainability. Overall, this case study provides a greater understanding into the relationships, dynamics and planning processes of festivals and events and the impact this has with the local communities they serve.

In Chapter 5, Susanna Heldt Cassel from Dalarna University, Sweden offers a powerful analysis of performances of nation, gender and rurality in the sporting and heritage festival of Landsmót in Iceland. She argues that events and festivals celebrating national identity or the uniqueness of the cultural and traditions of a specific region or place may be interpreted as arenas where identities of both people and places are staged and performed. Sports and cultural events may enhance and play with identities, such as the co-construction of gender identities and national identities, as a part of the event or festival itself. These co-constructions and expressions of identity discourses as part of events and festivals are not least reinforced with the impact of social media and the posting of images by many other actors than the organisers and managers of the event.

David Jarman, from Edinburgh Napier University, United Kingdom, offers an intriguing analysis entitled "Personal Networks in Festival, Event and Creative Communities: Perceptions, Connections and Collaborations" in Chapter 6. This chapter introduces the application of ego network analysis methods to the study of perceived personal networks in the festival, event and creative industries. From an opening critique of traditional stakeholder analyses, which it is argued lack the detail necessary to adequately reflect the experiences of individuals in these industries, two case studies are used to introduce and apply this form of social network analysis. Examination and comparison of the cases reveals compositional and structural elements of the two networks, providing evidence of the individuals' social capital and brokerage potential. The potential for network analysis to reveal a person's power within their community is considered.

"Innovation in Rural Festivals", Chapter 7, offers a discussion of innovation and empowerment, or rather disempowerment by Grzegorz Kwiatkowski, from Koszalin University of Technology, Poland and Anne-Mette Hjalager, from the University of Southern Denmark. Based on an empirical survey among 315 Danish rural festivals, this chapter addresses the opportunities for the management of festivals to provide continuous innovations. Taking into account that festival management is largely a bottom-up process occurring in a multi-actor environment, the authors conclude that local and external collaboration tend to limit an innovative capacity, and festivals' management needs to proceed gently with more radical categories of changes. The chapter distinguishes between self-empowerment, community

Introducing power, meaning and authenticity 3

empowerment and bridging empowerment aiming finally to establish a collective innovative orientation.

Chapter 8 by W. Gerard Ryan, from the University of Salford, United Kingdom, and Stephen Kelly, from Staffordshire University, United Kingdom, take the focus in "The Effects of Supply Chain Management (SCM) Activities and Their Impact Upon Festival Management and the Customer Experience". They observe that as the number of festivals and the need to provide more satisfying customer experiences continue to grow, the challenges faced by festival managers have become more complicated than ever. For them, this means that festival organisers are becoming progressively more reliant on their inter-organisational/delivery partners to sustain and improve their ongoing operational activity. Supply Chain Management (SCM) provides a new dimension to a traditional perspective on the management of festivals, as collective co-operation can lead to the provision of superior value to customers. Through data collected from multiple semi-structured interviews with directors and employees at UK-based music events and festival suppliers, this chapter offers insights into how the effective and efficient management of SCM carries additional benefits to festival delivery.

For Chapter 9, our attention is drawn to Canada by Mohamed Reda Khomsi from the University of Quebec, Canada. Montreal was the first Canadian city to host major international events such as the World Fair of 1967 and the Olympic Games of 1976. The impact of these two events remained very limited or even negative if we consider skepticism observed among citizens regarding the hosting of major events. Unlike these two events, the celebrations of the 350th anniversary of the city celebrated in 1992 will be shown to have important spin-offs for the city. This chapter aims to explain how an event with lower value, cost and international influence can generate greater benefits for the host community than hallmark events and is called "The Importance of the Stakeholder Relationship for the Success of an Event; The Case of Montreal".

In Chapter 10, Trudie Walters, from the University of Otago, New Zealand addresses themes central to this collection in a contribution entitled "'Power Wrestling': The Life and (Untimely) Death of the Real Food Festival" (which is a title the editors would have loved to have come up with first!) The author notes that the life cycles of local community events and festivals and the attendant role of power in these life cycles is not well understood, particularly when a festival ceases to exist. This chapter examines the evolution of a local community food festival in Southeast Queensland, Australia, and investigates the changing nature of power relations during its existence. 'Power to' (as an enabling force) was explicitly implicated in the conceptualising and creation of the festival, whilst 'power over' (as a constraining force) shaped its life course and contributed to its (untimely) death.

Ruth Dowson and Ian Lamond from Leeds Beckett University, United Kingdom, turn their attention to religion and politics in "Event, Authenticity and Meaning: A Dialogical Approach", Chapter 11. This chapter transgresses the old adage, 'never discuss religion or politics'. Taking a dialogical approach, the similarities and differences in how we can understand the articulation of events within church and social movement communities are discussed. Adopting the format of a conversation, the authors' examine their differing conceptual positions and practical experiences, establishing points of similarity and difference. They argue that contemporary social movement and religious discourses and practices frequently find expression through formal and informal events, and they conclude that maybe the two are not as far apart as we may have first thought.

Joanna Fountain and Michael Mackay, from Lincoln University, New Zealand offer "Commemoration, Celebration, and Commercialisation: Akaroa's French Festival" as Chapter 12. They explore how the township of Akaroa has held a community festival celebrating the French heritage of the town for more than two decades. In 2015, the festival was larger than ever before, marking 175 years since the first French settlers arrived. Based primarily on in-depth interviews, this chapter explores the meanings this festival holds for a range of festival stakeholders. The analysis reveals that different stakeholders attribute varied meanings to the event, ranging from the largely commercial to the personally significant, with a clear distinction evident between meanings framed around 'celebration and spectacle' and those centred on remembering the region's cultural heritage.

Jelena Đurkin, from the University of Rijeka, Croatia, and Nicholas Wise, from Liverpool John Moores University, United Kingdom, take us to Croatia for Chapter 13 in their chapter titled "Managing Community Stakeholders in Rural Areas" by assessing the organisation of local sports events in Gorski Kotar, Croatia. This chapter explores the complexity of organising small-scale sport events in rural areas by analysing important characteristics of rural areas and the overlapping of stakeholder categories. These findings are supported by empirical evidence from a case study and new insights on distrust and different desired social and economic outcomes of local organisers have come to light.

In the final contribution in Chapter 14, the editors return to reflect on the contributions contained in the volume and defending the cause for greater research of the kinds found here. They argue that there is still much work to do in deepening our understanding of the forces behind festivals and events.

We very much hope that you will enjoy reading this collection as much as we did working with the contributors. The chapters are thought provoking and tease out many of the themes which contribute to a critical understanding of festivals and events.

2 A q-study of organisers' perspectives on factors of festival success in Crete

Dimitrios P. Stergiou, Eirini Pehlivanidou and David Airey

Introduction

The Greek island of Crete has witnessed remarkable levels of tourism growth over the last 40 years. In 2015, more than 3.5 million tourists visited Crete, and the island had 167,540 hotel beds, the largest concentration of bed supply in the country (Hellenic Chamber of Hotels, 2016; SETE, 2015). Moreover, it has been estimated that tourism acts as the most important contributor to the added value of the products of Crete (40.34%) and that approximately 40% of the local population are involved in tourism activities, either directly or indirectly (Andriotis, 2008; Region of Crete, 2012). As a result, tourism is considered today to represent the largest economic activity of the island.

Crete provides tourists with a wide variety of activities, events and destinations to enjoy (Andriotis et al., 2007). An important point to address in this context is that residents of Crete take particular pride in their island and communities. Each community in Crete has its own history, customs and sense of pride. In many regional districts of Crete, therefore, one common occurrence is the regional festival with the island hosting over 60 regional events and festivals each year (Department of Festivals and Cultural Events, 2016). Festivals have been defined by Janiskee (1980: 97) as 'formal periods or programs of pleasurable activities, entertainment, or events having a festive character and publicly celebrating some concept, happening or fact'. Festivals represent a cultural practice through which community values, ideologies and identity are celebrated (Getz, 2010). Accordingly, festivals play a significant role in the Cretan tourism product, bringing locals and visitors together to celebrate different occasions while at the same time encouraging preservation of the customs and traditions of the place (Region of Crete, 2016).

Even though statistics related to the economic contribution of festivals to the Cretan economy are not available, festival tourism is pronounced by local authorities as a strategy to assist in extending the destination's life cycle (Greek National Tourism Organisation, 2003). If festivals are being used by tourism organisations such as regional tourism councils to attract tourists or visitors to a destination, then it is imperative that relevant research and evaluation is undertaken to provide appropriate information for festival management. However, despite a recent movement toward more formal organisation and planning of tourism, initiated mainly at the level of local authorities (Andriotis, 2003), to the best of the authors' knowledge no research has been undertaken on the many festivals hosted in regional Cretan communities. As a result, there appears to be a lack of awareness of the information needs for festival management, not only in Crete but also across the Greek festival industry.

From a managerial perspective, festivals in Crete provide a wide range of entertainment and activities. Each festival possesses certain factors that make it a success, whether this is defined against economic, social, cultural or other objectives. From this, it follows logically that each festival may take different roads to success and each festival organiser may define success in a different way. However, regional festivals are often developed in a manner that may not meet with the success originally envisioned by organisers (Lade and Jackson, 2004). It is therefore necessary for festival organisers to have a clear understanding of why the events exist, what their goals are, and for whom they are being organised (Allen et al., 2011). These are concerns that every event organiser must plan and identify in order to maximise the potential benefits associated with the festival (Shone and Parry, 2013). In response to these issues, the purpose of this study is to use views of festival organisers to identify perceptions of key factors contributing to festival success in Crete. The nature of the study is exploratory and its methodological framework resides in the use of Q-methodology to focus on the subjective insights of research participants.

Literature review

The proliferation of events staged around the world towards the latter half of the twentieth century was prompted by, among other factors, an increase in leisure time and discretionary income, socialisation needs and the growth of an economy driven by the consumption of experiences (Allen et al., 2011; Getz, 2008). Subsequently, over the first decade of the twenty-first century, participation in events has become an important aspect of the contemporary tourism experience (O'Sullivan et al., 2009). In the context of tourism, events comprise a key element in both the origin and destination areas, demonstrating a capacity to act as a motivator of tourism and subsequently contribute to the economic and social well-being of a destination (Bowdin et al., 2011; Connell et al., 2015). As the event phenomena flourished in recent decades, academic interest in understanding their contribution has risen accordingly with event studies representing today an important and growing area of tourism research. In fact, a recent review article of event tourism research published in *Tourism Management*, reports a literature base of over 10,000 items as a conservative estimate (Getz and Page, 2015).

Within event studies, festivals have emerged as a distinct sub-field, with the universality and popularity of festival experiences attracting the attention of scholars in many disciplines (Getz, 2010). While this literature is characterised by a multiplicity of perspectives and disciplinary approaches, previous literature reviews may be used to identify core areas of research and publication. Formica (1998) found that, from the 1970s through to the 1990s, the dominant themes of festival-related research were economics or financial impacts, marketing, profiles of festivals or events, sponsorship, management, and trends/forecasts. Getz (2000), based on an analysis of articles appearing in the journal *Event Management* from 1993 to 2000, concluded that economic development and impacts, followed by sponsorship and event marketing at the corporate level, were the most frequently studied topics. Other management topics and general marketing were also well-established themes.

Moscardo (2007) asserted that the existing academic tourism literature on festivals is most obviously associated with the evaluation of economic benefits, but also acknowledged a growing recognition of a wider set of potential impacts of festivals on host regions. In her overview of literature, Quinn (2009) identified two dominant themes: management-related literature and studies with socio-cultural investigative foci. More recently, Getz (2010), from a large-scale review of 423 research articles, asserted that the body of festival studies literature is dominated by three broad strands – namely, the roles, meanings and impacts of festivals in society and culture, festival tourism with a particular concern on the assessment of economic impacts, and festival management. What seems to emerge from this brief examination of previous overviews of research on festivals is a dichotomy between the management/economics literature and those other literatures whose engagement with the study of festivals has developed from an interest on place, society, or culture.

As a sub-field of festival studies, research on determinants of festival success has, to a certain extent, tended to reflect this dichotomy, producing mixed results. For example, researching critical success factors at a major music festival, Manners et al. (2012) concluded that general management was the most important factor for a memorable visitor experience. On the other hand, Schuster (2001) has written about how successful festivals and events are those that are embedded in contextual environments, of interest to local populations and driven by local agendas. Space precludes further commentary of individual studies here. However, even a cursory review of this literature reveals several factors that may be perceived as immediate reasons for festival success, such as sense of place, community involvement, community well-being, social interaction, revenue, budget, visitor numbers, theme, qualified and experienced staff, measurable objectives, and market orientation (see, for example, the overviews in Jepson and Clarke, 2013; Kinnunen and Haahti, 2015; Leenders et al., 2015; Manners et al., 2012). Resembling Quinn's (2009) dominant themes in festival studies, these factors, it may be argued, pertain to socio-cultural and management perspectives. Lade and Jackson (2004) have reached a similar conclusion, arguing that the key contributing success factors considered by researchers can be organised into three categories: community involvement and support, management functions, and marketing. Also pointing to this issue, Kinnunen and Haahti (2015) have asserted that research on key success factors for festivals is characterised by a diversity of approaches and priorities, with academics predominantly focusing on measures of economic success and to a lesser extent on social, cultural and environmental considerations.

While economic and managerial values have undoubtedly been an overt driver of research in the field of festival success factors, other researchers have adopted a broader perspective of success. Dwyer and colleagues (2000) have stressed how the success of an event or festival should not only be measured by direct economic contributions, but it should also incorporate impacts concerned with the socio-cultural, physical, and political environments of an event. Similarly, Pasanen et al. (2009) have made the point that while economic considerations have always prevailed, social and cultural perspectives are also essential for the success of events and festivals. Quinn (2009) sees the embedding of festivals in particular locales as fundamental to fully understand the relationships between the socio-cultural environment of festivals and the tangible dimensions related to managing and measuring outcomes for "success". This broader perspective is also reflected implicitly in Mykletun's (2009: 147) definition of festival success as 'the ability of a festival to attract an increasing number of participants, balance its economy, be appreciated by local people and develop as a hallmark event for the region'.

To a large degree, these broader conceptions of festival success mirror the breadth of the festival experience, involving as it does different meanings attached to it. As Getz (2010) explains, people create festivals for different purposes, and one's experience of a festival provides meaning at the individual level. This implies that 'festivals may be understood as meaning different things to different people' (Dayan, 2000: 26). Festivals, as Dayan (2000) noted, are themselves loci for different interpretations – from stakeholders, participants, audiences, organisers, and so on. To fully understand and create knowledge about festivals, therefore, 'it is necessary to consider who produces them and why, how they are planned and managed, why people attend, their outcomes on multiple levels, and the dynamic forces shaping individual festivals and festival populations' (Getz, 2010: 20).

In view of this last point on the need to ensure the presence of multiple "voices" in festival research, studies on the success of festivals are almost exclusively based on the views of community residents and festival attendees. They are, therefore, of limited scope because they are confined to an "outsiders" examination of the festival experience – i.e., they 'evaluate the festival from the outside' (Kinnunen and Haahti, 2015: 253). To this end, this chapter takes an interest in broadening the scope of these earlier studies.

It does so, by focusing on insider (as opposed to outsider) perspectives, using Q-methodology to uncover festival success factors based on the subjective views of festival organisers. The purpose is to identify clusters of participants sharing common viewpoints, with a view to shed light on the long list of success factors found in festival research from a largely neglected angle.

Methodology

Q-methodology is a research technique that is used to systematically investigate human subjectivity and the lived experiences of individuals (Brown, 1980). The methodological details of this approach have been extensively reported elsewhere (see, for example, Brown, 1980) and are only addressed briefly here. In this method, respondents (the P-sample) rank order (Q-sort) a set of statements (the Q-sample) according to a specified condition of instruction. This activity allows the researcher to obtain a relatively precise ranking of large sets of items without overwhelming participants. "Inverted" factor analysis (Q-factor analysis [QFA]) is then applied, using the participants as the variables and the set of measurements as the sample. In this way, the unit of analysis becomes the individual rather than a population. This process groups participants who sorted the Q-sample in a similar way, identifying areas of consensus and conflict, and assisting in developing shared views. Given this ability to identify and differentiate perspectives within a group, Q-methodology is most often deployed to explore complex and contested concepts and subject matters (Watts and Stenner, 2012). It, therefore, fitted very well to the contested nature that surrounds research on festival success factors, as manifested by the differing notions of success suggested from the review of the literature.

This study used a 37-statement Q-sample of festival success factors collected from journal articles, professional publications, and conference proceedings. This number of statements is considered sufficient for exploratory purposes and not overwhelming for the respondents (McKeown, 1990). The selection of statements followed an "unstructured" approach, because the researchers were not theory testing, but rather allowing the perceptions of the festival organisers to emerge. This is in contrast to Q-samples "structured" by a factorial design, which focus the researcher on specific topics necessary to investigate a theory (McKeown and Thomas, 1988). Privileging respondents' voices in this way, this study operationalised success in accordance with Lade and Jackson's (2004: 3) view, as 'the accomplishment of the festival organisers' predetermined aims'.

For the purposes of this study, festival organisers were defined as those 'dealing directly with the development and/or management of festivals' (O'Sullivan et al., 2009: 25). Accordingly, and in the absence of any official information, respondents were identified through Internet searches of websites, publications, and agencies associated with the development, management, and promotion of festivals in Crete. This process resulted in

33 potential cases for this study. Their roles and willingness to participate were confirmed either with a personal telephone call or email message. Of these, 29 indicated consent for participation, with the understanding that no personal information or information about their festivals would be collected as part of the Q-study, no attempt would be made to associate individuals/festivals with responses, and that the Q-sort procedure would not be time consuming. Whilst this number of respondents might be considered small by quantitative standards, the aim of Q-methodology is to explore the subjective meaning that items have for respondents, rather than to ascertain the numerical incidence and demographic correlates of such opinions (Stergiou et al., 2008). Consequently, a large sample is not necessary. In fact, typical Q-studies range from 20 to 60 respondents, which are considered adequate for assessing the diversity and structure of the available viewpoints on a topic (Phi et al., 2014).

Upon consenting to participate, respondents gained access to a web application that replicated the features of a physical Q-sort (see Hackert and Braehler, 2007). In this exercise, festival organisers were asked to sort the 37 statements based on their personal perceptions regarding their importance or unimportance for achieving festival success. To accomplish the sort they entered the numbers of the statements on a score sheet with nine columns, numbered from −4 (most unimportant) to +4 (most important), with rows arranged in a triangular distribution as follows: 2–3–4–5–9–5–4–3–2. In the final stage of the sorting procedure, respondents were invited to indicate their willingness to participate in a follow-up telephone interview where they would be asked to comment on any issue they felt strongly about, so as to capture any diversity in viewpoints that was not already captured in the Q-sorts. In this way, interviews were used to increase the validity of the Q-study by 'illuminating the quantitative interpretation of respondents' views through qualitative analysis' (Stergiou and Airey, 2011: 316). Data collection took place in June 2015.

Data analysis was conducted with the use of PQMethod, a statistical program for the analysis of Q-sort data (see Schmolck, 2014). Following standard procedures (see Brown, 1980), the completed Q-sorts were first intercorrelated to determine the degree of agreement or disagreement of viewpoints among individual participants. The data was submitted to QFA using a Principal Component method and Varimax rotation to arrive at two Q-factors in the output. To facilitate the interpretation of results, factor arrays were calculated. In essence, the factor array gives an "idealised" Q-sort for each factor, representing the group of subjects who load significantly on that factor. The aim of factor interpretation is to 'uncover, understand and fully explain the viewpoint captured by the factor and shared by the significantly loading participants' (Watts and Stenner, 2012: 181). Having the same level of mathematical rigor as quantitative research and an interpretive component comparable to that of qualitative methodology,

Q-methodology is often thought to provide a bridge between the two (Sell and Brown, 1984).

Results and overview of the studied festivals

The study concentrated on 29 regional festivals all around Crete. As already indicated, no festival information was obtained from respondents themselves. However, some general profile characteristics about these festivals were compiled during the process of identifying potential respondents. These are briefly presented here to provide some sense about the context of this research. The oldest festival in the sample was founded in 1995 and the newest in 2014. The majority were organised by "private entities", such as cultural associations (4), companies (5), non-profit organisations (5) and individuals or groups of individuals (4), the remaining being projects of local government. Sixteen festivals charged visitors an entrance fee ranging from 10 to 25 euros. All but two of the festivals have been held consecutively on an annual basis. Only three festivals had a specific theme with the vast majority offering multi-themed activities, focused mainly on Cretan music, dancing, and history/culture. The festivals generally lasted several days, though their duration varied from one day to two weeks. Almost all festivals were held during the spring and summer months, with only two festivals taking place in autumn.

Q-factor interpretation

The analysis identified two factors which were interpreted as different perspectives of festival organizer opinion about success factors in the Cretan festival market. The factor array corresponding to each factor was interpreted by studying how the 37 statements were arranged. These overall ranking patterns are understood to explain the distinct perception held by each group of respondents. The initial interpretation was developed by placing emphasis on 'high salience statements' (Vincent and Focht, 2008: 168) – i.e., those statements assigned at the extremes of the sort, because they indicate what respondents felt most strongly about. This was refined by considering areas of agreement (consensus statements) and divergence (distinguishing statements) across all perspectives. Finally, the interpretation was supported by examining the interview responses (if applicable) of those festival organisers who loaded significantly on each factor.

The Pragmatic/Traditional Management perspective

This perspective indicates a strong focus on the traditional activities and concerns of festival organisers, with the highest scores being given to management and economic-related statements. According to Table 2.1, four of

Table 2.1 Statements which received highest positive and negative scores in the Pragmatic/Traditional Management perspective

Most important (+4)	Being profitable in economic terms The ability of the organiser to co-ordinate all management activities
(+3)	Sound financial planning There is a strong leadership from the organiser Set specific and measurable objectives
Important: other distinguishing statements	Attract new crowds Have a loyal base of visitors Address new tastes in the market Identify consumer needs and respond accordingly
(-3)	Corporate sponsorship Utilise know-how from local authorities Network with other festivals and create partnerships
(-4) Most unimportant	Engage local communities within the planning process Collect data on the festival's environmental impacts
Unimportant: other distinguishing statements	Inject a percentage of revenues into the local economy Community representation on the management team

Source: Authors, 2017

the five most important factors dealt with, what Getz (2010: 14) called, 'standard management functions' applied to festivals; co-ordinating, financing, leadership, and goal-setting, demonstrating a top-down approach to the management of the festival. The other most important factor concerned the desire for economic success, which, according to one respondent, 'is in reality the only factor that can establish a festival as a successful one'. This perspective also demonstrated an emphasis on the importance of taking a market orientation, by identifying and responding to customer needs and market trends. This is related to being able to retain existing and attract new visitors and enjoy economic benefits. One festival organiser commented in relation to this: 'It is the ability of the festival to penetrate a market in the first instance that brings economic success and legitimises it. If the festival is able to attract and retain its visitors, then it is successful'. Table 2.1 highlights the management perspectives which received the highest positive and negative scores as a result of our analysis.

Festival organisers in this perspective tended to favour management autonomy and reject the importance of active local engagement with the management aspects of festivals. This distinctive view is best summarised by the following comments: 'Autonomy of management is necessary in order to run the festival on business lines, make quick decisions and take prompt actions' and 'The interference of local community interests and politics impair the efficient administration of a festival'. They also dismissed the importance of collaborations with other festivals, local authorities and corporate sponsors because '[they] impose expectations of conformity and compliance, which run the risk of losing the separate identity of the festival'. At the same time, they did not seem to embrace sustainable strategies, as they considered assessing environmental impacts and providing a portion of their profits to local communities to be unimportant for festival success. However, it has to be pointed out that the practice of redistributing profits might actually be unattainable and not necessarily undesirable. As one respondent explained, 'We have limited turnovers and make very modest profits. Increasing regional income is not, and could not be, an aim of our festival. Local communities can benefit from visitor spending'.

The Communitarian/Person-oriented perspective

This Q-perspective is characterised by an emphasis on the social and cultural significance of festivals for the towns and regions hosting them. In this connection, protecting local traditions, building pride and a sense of belonging in the community were among the success factors receiving the highest scores of importance. On the other hand, the Communitarians held sceptical views towards the importance of adopting a market orientation. A comment illustrating this scepticism was as follows: 'A successful festival is one that is connected to the locality and promotes socio-cultural values. Opening the festival to external trends might threaten local traditions and diminish its importance for the local people'. Commenting on the same issue, another respondent brought a different perspective, focusing attention on cost considerations:

> Developing and maintaining a high level of market orientation is associated with high costs which may outweigh the possible benefits to be gained by the festival. In this case the resource investments required to adopt market-oriented behaviours would be better employed elsewhere.

On these views, then organising the festival around customer needs and new market preferences to attract niche markets and new crowds were deemed unimportant for festival success. As a comparison to the management perspectives outlined in Table 2.1; Table 2.2 provides the highest positive and negative scores from our analysis of a Communitarian or Person-orientated perspective.

Demonstrating some correlation to the Pragmatic/Traditional Management factor, respondents in this perspective indicated a strong focus on the economic success of the festival, which is necessary 'to cover at least the costs of the festival and to gain a certain surplus to secure its survival'. Also sharing common ground with the Pragmatists, they seemed to reject the importance of collecting data on the festival's environmental impacts to festival success. However, a distinguishing point is their distrust of top-down

Table 2.2 Statements received highest positive and negative scores in the Communitarian/Person-oriented perspective

Most important (+4)	Develop a high level of pride among the locals
	Create a sense of belonging to the community
(+3)	Being profitable in economic terms
	The organisational structure is people-centric
	Protect the traditions of local communities
Important: other distinguishing statements	Experienced employees with practical knowledge
	Engage local communities within the planning process
	Have a strong local volunteer corps
	Financial support from local government
(−3)	There is a strong leadership from the organiser
	The ability of the organiser to co-ordinate all management activities
	Collect data on the festival's environmental impacts
(−4) Most unimportant	Address new tastes in the market
	Target niche markets
Unimportant: other distinguishing statements	Identify consumer needs and respond accordingly
	Attract new crowds

Source: authors, 2017

management and leadership. Instead, they stressed the importance of a people-centric organisational culture, valuing success factors related to the employees and volunteers involved in the festival and the engagement of local communities within the planning process. As one respondent indicated, 'Command-and-control approaches inhibit trust and creativity. Success is about getting everyone involved'. Another respondent reported, 'There is always too much work to do to wait for someone to give orders. Even if the ideas come from the management team, it's the people "on the ground" who will make things happen'. Finally, getting local government grants was important for them, but they did not wish to elaborate further on this issue during the telephone interviews.

Conclusions

The objective of the study reported earlier was to explore the insights of festival organisers in Crete about the importance of suspected factors in festival success. Q-methodology was used for this purpose as it draws on both qualitative and quantitative techniques. By using follow-up interviews to illuminate the perspectives gained from the sorting procedure, it allows for a multi-method approach which can be used as a means of exploring the complexities of festival management that cannot be satisfactorily addressed using single methods (Phi et al., 2014).

Indeed, the management of festivals is a complex and multifaceted activity. A variety of perceptions and attitudes exists on what is essential, desirable, or appropriate to the success of a festival. The research literature mirrors this complexity through the presence of a large number of suspected success factors and differing notions of success. Using Q-methodology to identify clusters of festival organisers' opinion with respect to festival success factors, the findings presented here bring a different angle to this literature by providing insights from a much neglected research population.

Evidently there are, among study participants, two different perspectives of festival success factors. The first perspective emphasises autonomy in the management of festivals, driven by the ability of organisers to make and act upon decisions independently and free of interventions from third parties. In this context, emphasis is placed on the top-down implementation of management functions used to promote a strong market orientation. The second perspective, on the other hand, presents a different picture. Particularly it stresses the importance of getting support from local authority revenues and favours a people-oriented organisational culture, which values the social and cultural aspects of festivals instead of following market trends. Within this diversity, two common factors are worth addressing. First, in both perspectives economic performance was selected as a leading indicator of festival success, which is in line with authors who maintain that the desire for economic gains drives the majority of festivals (e.g. Andersson and Getz, 2008; Lade and Jackson, 2004). Second, environmental evaluation does not seem to be an issue of concern for the respondents. Why this is the case cannot be identified from the results obtained here. Perhaps this could be attributed to the major gaps that exist in methodology pertaining to environmental impact studies and the high costs associated with obtaining relevant measures (Getz et al., 2010). However, given that the environmental impacts of festivals have generally been neglected by festival scholars (Sherwood, 2007), further research is required to explore this issue.

Taken at their face value, these findings are not particularly surprising. It is not unexpected that respondents with a market-oriented approach to festival organisation take an interest in management functions. As Andersson and Getz (2008: 206) point out, with particular emphasis on festival management, 'a marketing orientation is primarily a philosophy or value set, which has to be manifested in various management strategies'. Nor is it in any way odd for regional festivals, which may rely mainly on local and regional audiences, that their success may be defined in terms of social and cultural goals. After all, not all festivals need to be tourism or market-oriented; festivals also have other important roles to play, from providing new recreational opportunities to establishing a community identity, and from cultural development to preserving traditions (Getz, 2010). However, a closer examination of the respective positions of the identified Q-factors reveals a distinction in perceptions of success, which resembles the dichotomy that exists in the literature between studies emphasising economic/managerial values and those with socio-cultural investigative foci. As such, they also give rise to wider issues of festival success that extend beyond the sample of practitioners and the types of festivals examined in this study.

As already discussed, a number of scholars have called for a broader conception of festival success, seeking to merge apparently dichotomic streams of research. Very much like triple-bottom-line approaches to festival management (see Hede, 2007), these calls seem to forward the underlying assumption that managerial, socio-cultural and environmental perspectives are equally important with regard to festival success. Findings of this Greek research and results of previous studies, however, suggest that this is not the case for all festivals. As Getz (2008, 2010) acknowledges, festivals have many actors and stakeholders. They often depend on external sources of funding and are subject to high public scrutiny. Many are in the not-for-profit sector, run by volunteers and exist for purposes other than economic gains. Consequently, 'attention to critical success factors for festivals might reveal different forces and issues at work' (Getz, 2002: 217). For example, given the evidence provided previously by Andersson and Getz (2008), the objectives of festivals with strong funding and support from local government are generally focused on culturally or socially oriented outcomes, with less emphasis placed on economic impacts. On the other hand, those festivals dependent mostly on paying customers have no choice but to increase marketing efforts. Each festival, therefore, may have 'its own set of objectives, whether it is in relation to achieving economic, social, cultural or long-term tourism outcomes' (Lade and Jackson, 2004: 2).

The directions for future festivals research identified by this study, as emerging from the aforementioned issues, are quite clear – more research on the socio-cultural and environmental factors of festival success is needed, along with a better understanding of the relationship between festival management, perceptions of success and the different types of festivals. In this connection, a larger study that employs a multi-festival, international, and perhaps a quantitative, approach would be highly informing to the festival sector and its researchers. Future studies may also evaluate the long-term efficacy of specific practices and approaches to festival organisation in different cultural and political contexts.

As is the case with all forms of research, this study is subject to some limitations. First, the fact that it is based solely on the experience of festival organisers in Crete means that the findings are specific to this research context. Second, it was not possible to identify the whole population of potential respondents, and therefore it may be the case that those not participating in this study would have provided different viewpoints to those reported here. Finally, the number and nature of the success factors used in the Q-sorting was limited to those selected through a review of the literature. It has to be acknowledged that the studies reviewed for the purposes of this analysis do not constitute a truly random sample in the sense that another reviewer could have identified a somewhat different sample of studies and factors. These limitations apart, it is hoped that this chapter will contribute to critical discussions about the determinants of festival success and serve to progress the research agenda in this field.

References

Allen, J., O'Toole, W., Harris, R. and McDonnell, I. (2011). *Festival and Special Event Management* (5th edn). Brisbane: Wiley.

Andersson, T.D. and Getz, D. (2008). Stakeholder management strategies of festivals. *Journal of Convention and Event Tourism*, 9(3): 199–220.

Andriotis, K. (2003). Local authorities in Crete and the development of tourism. *Journal of Tourism Studies*, 13(2): 53–62.

Andriotis, K. (2008). Integrated resort development: The case of Cavo Sidero, Crete. *Journal of Sustainable Tourism*, 16(4): 428–444.

Andriotis, K., Agiomirgianakis, G. and Mihiotis, A. (2007). Tourist vacation preferences: The case of mass tourists to Crete. *Tourism Analysis*, 12(1/2): 51–63.

Bowdin, G., Allen, J., O'Toole, W., Harris, R. and McDonnell, I. (2011). *Events Management* (3rd edn). Oxford: Butterworth-Heinemann.

Brown, S.R. (1980). *Political Subjectivity: Applications of Q Methodology in Political Science*. New Haven, CT: Yale University Press.

Connell, J., Page, S.J. and Meyer, D. (2015). Visitor attractions and events: Responding to seasonality. *Tourism Management*, 46: 283–298.

Dayan, D. (2000). Looking for Sundance: The social construction of a film festival. In: I. Bondebjerg (ed.), *Moving Images, Culture and the Mind*. London: University of Luton Press (pp. 43–52).

Department of Festivals and Cultural Events (2016). Festivals in Greece 2015. Available at: http://festival.culture.gr/%CE%B1%CF%81%CF%87%CE%B5%CE%B9%CE%BF%CF%86%CE%B5%CF%83%CF%84%CE%B9%CE%B2%CE%B1%CE%BB%CE%B5%CF%80%CE%B9%CE%BA%CF%81%CE%B1%CF%84%CE%B5%CE%B9%CE%B1%CF%83-2015/ [accessed 22/11/2016] [in Greek].

Dwyer, L., Mellor, R., Mistilis, N. and Mules, T. (2000). A framework for assessing 'tangible' and 'intangible' impacts of events and conventions. *Event Management*, 6(3): 175–189.

Formica, S. (1998). The development of festivals and special event studies. *Festival Management and Event Tourism*, 5(3): 131–137.

Getz, D. (2000). Developing a research agenda for the event management field. In: J.J. Allen, R. Harris, L.K. Jago and Veal, A.J. (eds.), *Events Beyond 2000: Setting the Agenda, Proceedings of Conference on Event Evaluation, Research and Education*. Sydney: Australian Centre for Event Management, University of Technology (pp. 10–21).

Getz, D. (2002). Why festivals fail. *Event Management*, 7: 209–219.

Getz, D. (2008). Event tourism: Definition, evolution, and research. *Tourism Management*, 29: 403–428.

Getz, D. (2010). The nature and scope of festival studies. *International Journal of Event Management Research*, 5(1): 1–47.

Getz, D., Andersson, T. and Carlsen, J. (2010). Festival management studies: Developing a framework and priorities for comparative and cross-cultural research. *Festival Management Studies*, 1(1): 29–59.

Getz, D. and Page, S.J. (2015). Progress and prospects for event tourism research. *Tourism Management*, 52: 593–631.

Greek National Tourism Organisation (2003). Strategic planning for the promotion of the sustainable tourism development in the Region of Crete. Available at: www.gnto.gov.gr/sites/default/files/files_basic_pages/meleti_B_fasi_kriti.pdf [accessed 23/11/12016] [in Greek].

Hackert, C. and Braehler, G. (2007). FlashQ Software. Available at: www.hackert.biz/flashq/home/ [accessed 22/08/2016].

Hede, A.M. (2007). Managing special events in the new era of the triple bottom line. *Event Management*, 11: 13–22.

Hellenic Chamber of Hotels (2016). Number of hotel establishments, rooms and beds. Available at: www.grhotels.gr/GR/BussinessInfo/library/DocLib/2015-HOTELS_REGIONS.pdf [accessed 22/11/2016] [in Greek].

Janiskee, R. (1980). South Carolina's harvest festivals: Rural delights for day tripping urbanities. *Journal of Cultural Geography*, 1(Fall/Winter): 96–104.

Jepson, A. and Clarke, C. (2013). Events and community development. In: R. Finkel, D. McGillivray, G. McPherson and Robinson, P. (eds.), *Research Themes for Events*. Wallingford: CABI (pp. 6–15).

Kinnunen, M. and Haahti, A. (2015). Visitor discourses on experiences: Reasons for festival success and failure. *International Journal of Event and Festival Management*, 6(3): 251–268.

Lade, C. and Jackson, J. (2004). Key success factors in regional festivals: Some Australian experiences. *Event Management*, 9: 1–11.

Leenders, A.M., van Telgen, J., Gemser, G. and Van der Wurff, R. (2015). Success in the Dutch music festival market: The role of format and content. *The Journal on Media Management*, 7(3/4): 148–157.

Manners, B., Kruger, M. and Saayman, M. (2012). Managing the beautiful noise: Evidence from the Neil Diamond show. *Journal of Convention & Event Tourism*, 13(2): 100–120.

McKeown, B.F. (1990). Q methodology, communication, and the behavioral text. *Electric Journal of Communication/ La Revue Electronique de Communication*, 1(1). Available at: www.cios.org/EJCPUBLIC/001/1/00111.html [accessed 24/12/2016].

McKeown, B.F. and Thomas, D.B. (1988). *Q Methodology*. Newbury Park, CA: Sage Publications Ltd.

Moscardo, G. (2007). Analysing the role of festivals and events in regional development. *Event Management*, 11(1/2): 23–32.

Mykletun, R.J. (2009). Celebration of extreme playfulness: Ekstremsportveko at Voss. *Scandinavian Journal of Hospitality and Tourism*, 9(2/3): 146–176.

O'Sullivan, D., Pickernell, D. and Senyard, J. (2009). Public sector evaluation of festivals and special events. *Journal of Policy Research in Tourism*, 1(1): 19–36.

Parent, M.M. (2008). Evolution and issue patterns for major-sport-event organizing committees and their stakeholders. *Journal of Sport Management*, 22, 135–164.

Pasanen, K., Taskinen, H. and Mikkonen, J. (2009). Impacts of cultural events in Eastern Finland: Development of a Finnish event evaluation tool. *Scandinavian Journal of Hospitality and Tourism*, 9(2/3): 112–129.

Phi, G., Dredge, D. and Whitford, M. (2014). Understanding conflicting perspectives in event planning and management using Q method. *Tourism Management*, 40: 406–415.

Quinn, B. (2009). Festivals, events and tourism. In: T. Jamal and Robinson, M. (eds.), *The Sage Handbook of Tourism Studies*. London: Sage Publications Ltd. (pp. 483–503).
Region of Crete (2012). Economic facts 2012. Available at: www.crete.gov.gr/attachments/article/1891/Economic%20Facts%20Crete.pdf [accessed 22/11/2016].
Region of Crete (2016). Traditional festivals: In Crete people celebrate all year round. Available at: www.incrediblecrete.gr/traditional-festivals/ [accessed 21/11/2016].
Schmolck, P. (2014). The Qmethod page. Available at: http://schmolck.userweb.mwn.de/qmethod/ [accessed 12/04/2016].
Schuster, J.M. (2001). Ephemera, temporary urbanism and imaging. In: L.J. Vale and Warner, S.B. (eds.), *Imaging the City: Continuing Struggles and New Directions*. New Brunswick, NJ: CUPR Books (pp. 361–397).
Sell, D.K. and Brown, S.R. (1984). Q-methodology as a bridge between qualitative and quantitative research: Application to the analysis of attitude change in foreign study programme participants. In: J.L. Vacca and Johnson, H.A. (eds.), *Qualitative Research in Education*. Kent, OH: Kent State University (pp. 79–87).
SETE (2015). International arrivals at main Greek airports, November 2015 provisional data. Available at: http://sete.gr/el/statistika-vivliothiki/statistika/ [accessed 22/11/2016].
Sherwood, P. (2007). A triple bottom line evaluation of the impact of special events: The development of indicators. *Doctoral Dissertation*. Melbourne: Victoria University, Centre for Hospitality and Tourism Research.
Shone, A. and Parry, B. (2013). *Successful Event Management: A Practical Handbook* (4th edn). Andover: Cengage Learning EMEA.
Stergiou, D. and Airey, D. (2011). Q-methodology and tourism research. *Current Issues in Tourism*, 14(4): 311–322.
Stergiou, D., Airey, D. and Riley, M. (2008). Making sense of tourism teaching. *Annals of Tourism Research*, 35(3): 631–649.
Vincent, S. and Focht, W. (2008). US higher education environmental program managers' perspectives on curriculum design and core competencies: Implications for sustainability as a guiding framework. *International Journal of Sustainability in Higher Education*, 10(2): 164–183.
Watts, S. and Stenner, P. (2012). *Doing Q-Methodological Research: Theory, Method and Interpretation*. Los Angeles, CA: Sage Publications Ltd.

3 "I don't think they give a monkey's about me"

Exploring stakeholder power and community alienation at Glastonbury Festival

Zoe White and Raphaela Stadler

Introduction

As one of the main stakeholders affected by music festivals, it is becoming more and more recognised that the needs of the host community need to be met and satisfied in order to ascertain their support for future music festivals. Empowering the host community, including them in the decision-making process, or co-creating the event experience with them have all been found to be essential elements of the planning process and in ensuring the long-term success of a festival (Derrett, 2003; Clarke & Jepson, 2011; Rogers & Anastasiadou, 2011; Stadler, 2013; Jepson & Clarke, 2016).

Glastonbury Festival is the largest Greenfield Music and Performing Arts Festival in the World (Glastonbury Festival, 2016) and provides an interesting case study to explore and examine the perspective of the host community with regards to their relationship with other key stakeholders and subsequent socio-cultural impacts imposed by the festival. In-depth interviews with members of the host community and festival volunteers were conducted in order to investigate whether Glastonbury Festival creates either community pride or community alienation. Findings from this study show that although participants appreciated the excitement and local pride generated and the improvement of facilities provided by Glastonbury Festival, they perceived the festival as a "political minefield" where the event organisers hold power over other stakeholders. There is little to no engagement with the host community throughout the festival planning process.

The purpose of this chapter is to use a Critical Management approach in order to explore how power relationships between event organisers, the host community and other key stakeholders shape different perceptions of meaning. It is argued here that the lack of a shared vision is a major factor alienating the host community, making them feel powerless and hence threatening the long-term success of the festival. The chapter concludes with a set of recommendations for festival organisers to build on the well-established community pride, but to go beyond the allocation of free tickets in order to positively "engage" the host community.

Event stakeholder power

The concept of power and stakeholder power more specifically has been explored and applied to events and festivals in a number of different ways (see, for example, Macleod & Carrier, 2010; Clarke & Jepson, 2011; Reid, 2011; Stadler, 2013; Batty, 2016). A central argument is that power does not simply exist, but is created through and shaped by relationships between different stakeholders (Church & Coles, 2006). In this sense, power can be a source of authority on the one hand, but it can also produce meaning, knowledge and discourse (Gramsci, 1971; Weber, 1978; Foucault, 1978; Clegg, 1998). Clegg (1998) further argued that power is the result of particular hierarchical structures of organisations. These structures imply certain rules and procedures which need to be followed, although often unspoken. Power, according to Clegg (1989), therefore needs to be analysed in terms of relationships and networks within an organisation that shape action, authority, rules and control, but can also change power relations between different stakeholders over time.

In a festival and events context, Clarke and Jepson (2011) identified "power brokers" and argued that the Festival Steering Committee held direct power over the festival and its construction. Weber's (1978) view on power can directly be applied to this situation in that one group of people will obey the rules of the game defined by another group exercising authority. The power relationship between the different stakeholders in this case can be a source for repression, discipline or control.

Reid (2011) identified power relations between different event stakeholders in a rural and regional context. She found that the largest stakeholder group or the one that has been involved in the event production for a long time is the one with the highest level of power. In many cases, this also depends on individual personalities. Reid (2011) further discussed a range of issues and challenges in managing these complex stakeholder power relations, such as lack of commitment, skills and knowledge, particularly in a rural context where the event organising committee tends to be voluntary in nature. Along similar lines, Batty (2016) explored issues of power within a community sport event organisation in New Zealand and discussed questions of legitimacy. She found that although many stakeholders have legitimacy to make decisions and be involved in the event production process due to their hierarchical position as assigned by the event organiser, certain stakeholders or stakeholder groups – such as the local or host community – often perceive their actual level of power to be different. This is in part due to pre-existing relationships between individual stakeholders who may have worked together in other contexts or other events.

In a rare example highlighting the positive use of power, Stadler (2013) applied the Foucauldian concept of power/knowledge (1978) to a festival context and analysed the power relations between festival organisers and members of the community within a community cultural development project. Through working *with* the community rather than imposing ideas upon them, new forms of knowledge were created, power relations were reshaped and the community felt a sense of empowerment. Stadler (ibid) argued that a shared meaning between different stakeholders of what the organisation is about, what is important and why, can not only shape positive action and give a sense of direction but also empower certain groups of people who might not have power in a traditional sense.

With the exception of the last example on how power can be used in a positive way, the ongoing discussion on festival stakeholder power has identified issues of the misuse of power, particularly in relation to certain community groups, local or host communities. This chapter aims to contribute to the discussion of power on a broader socio-cultural level and explores a further challenge that comes with the misuse of power – intentionally or unintentionally – by looking at the event host community's sense of powerlessness and alienation.

Community alienation

In festival and event studies, it has been argued that the enthusiasm of the host community is a crucial element for the success of a festival (Gursoy et al., 2004); this suggests that if the host community have little interest in the festival it may fail to be a success, particularly in the long run. As an important part of sustaining a healthy community, festivals can help create a sense of community, which involves the image, spirit, character, pride, relationships and networking of a community (Derrett, 2003). If an event manager is able to take all of these factors into consideration, then a sense of community can be achieved. Furthermore, a sense of community can be created when there is a shared vision, a clear sense of purpose and all individuals' ideas and contributions towards solving problems, community issues and celebrations are valued (Derrett, 2003). This suggests that event organisers should ensure the host community are aware of and agree with the event objectives, welcoming any ideas of improving event related issues as well as community issues.

Although some communities simply value the "feel-good" factor of hosting an event, most communities expect a more involved role, allowing them to have a shared vision as well as a clear sense of purpose, and resulting in them feeling more valued (Derrett, 2003). Involving the host community with the event will, however, depend upon the cooperation of the event managers, the extent to which they empower the host community, include them in the decision-making process and co-create the festival experience with them (Derrett, 2003; Clarke & Jepson, 2011; Rogers & Anastasiadou, 2011; Jepson & Clarke, 2016). If managers fail to fulfil the needs of the host community, this could create disastrous results, jeopardise the future of the event and alienate the community in the long term (Gursoy et al., 2004).

Community alienation is a factor that has contributed towards the failure of festivals for many years (Rogers & Anastasiadou, 2011), suggesting that festival organisers are failing to recognise the importance of involving the host community. The concept of alienation has received a lot of attention in the wider sociological literature, where "[a]lienation is seen as a sign of personal dissatisfaction with certain structural elements of society" (Lystad, 1972: 90). Individuals' being dissatisfied with this situation express their feelings of powerlessness, meaninglessness, normlessness, social isolation, and self-estrangement (Seeman, 1959; Lystad, 1972). For the purpose of this chapter, the sense of powerlessness and meaninglessness will be discussed further.

Seeman (1959) regards powerlessness as a result of alienation when an individual expects that their own behaviour does not have an impact on the outcome they seek. In a similar sense, this can be described as power being exercised by somebody 'over' the individual in one way or another. The individual then "suffers from alienation in the form of 'powerlessness' when she is conscious of the gap between what she would like to do and what she feels capable of doing" (Kalekin-Fishman, 1996: 97). Closely related to powerlessness is the issue of meaninglessness, which can also be caused by alienation. Meaninglessness refers more specifically to the perceived ability to predict outcomes rather than the sensed ability to control outcomes (Seeman, 1959). In a festival context, therefore, community alienation may involve an isolated experience from the host community due to the (perceived) negative impacts of the event. Gursoy et al. (2004) argue that if nothing is done to minimize the negative impacts of an event, this may damage the image and cohesiveness of the local community, and their local pride. Negative impacts that come with large, high profile events, including overcrowding, traffic congestion, increased crime, bad press, damage or injury to participants, can contribute towards community alienation (Bowdin et al., 2006). The host community may become concerned that the event will turn into a "tourist trap" diminishing the authenticity of the event (Gursoy et al., 2004), and hence rendering it meaningless. This suggests that some festival organisers are not considering the host community, with the motives behind many festivals being to maximise financial achievement; solely benefitting the festival organisers (Rogers & Anastasiadou, 2011).

Physical impacts, however, are not the only causes of community alienation. Many event managers have rushed to mould their events to meet the demands of other – in many cases, more powerful – event stakeholders (Yeoman et al., 2004), suggesting that the needs of the host community are being forgotten. Ignoring the conceptual development and design of their event, said to be the heart and soul of a successful event, can cause host communities to feel alienated (Yeoman et al., 2004). Originally, festivals and events were a celebration of ceremony and ritual; a way of recognising the culture of a community (Yeoman et al., 2004), advocating that event organisers need to remain true to the cultural roots of an event. Jepson et al. (2013) also stated that in order for the host community to participate in a festival, the festival must demonstrate solid, cultural foundations.

Gelder and Robinson (2009) found that Glastonbury Festival developed its own culture, which was influenced by its original hippie ethics. This suggests that the Glastonbury Festival organisers have considered the cultural roots of the community – ensuring that this follows through into the event itself; thus decreasing the risk of community alienation by giving the festival a specific meaning. However, Flinn and Frew (2014) found that Glastonbury Festival has in recent years become a co-created consumption experience where the true sense of its anti-commercial countercultural roots has become lost in the mass-produced fantasy experience.

As previously mentioned, when festivals increase in size, it may be required to hire professionals to take over the event (Gursoy et al., 2004). Professional organisers may be less likely to involve and cooperate with the host community as not only do they feel no attachment towards the local area; they also have a greater institutional background within the event industry (Gursoy et al., 2004). This can lead to professionals imposing their power and ideas upon the community where the event is then executed in a way that does not satisfy the needs of the host community. The host community in turn will feel a sense of powerlessness and meaninglessness through being alienated.

Methods

Glastonbury Festival was chosen as a single case study for this research project with the aim of gaining an in-depth understanding of a contemporary phenomenon through gathering rich data and seeing the case from the perspective of those involved (Charmaz, 2006; Eisenhardt, 1989; Gillham, 2000; Stake, 1995; Yin, 2009). Glastonbury Festival is "the largest greenfield music and performing arts festival in the world and a template for all the festivals that have come after it" (Glastonbury Festival, 2016). The festival was founded by Michael Eavis in 1970, and its attendance has since then grown from 1,500 to 135,000 in 2015 (Glastonbury Festival, 2016). Since 2002, the professionally run event company Festival Republic has been managing the logistics and security of the festival. What was once a small family run festival has now become "a huge tented city" where, although British Laws still apply, the rules of society are "a bit different, a little bit freer" (Glastonbury Festival, 2016). Glastonbury has successfully supported Greenpeace, Oxfam and Water Aid for a number of years, and raising money for these charities continues to be one of the main objectives of the festival.

The first author conducted semi-structured interviews in Glastonbury and Pilton between January and March 2014 with six members of the community and three members of the community who were also festival volunteers.

This allowed an in-depth exploration of their perceptions of Glastonbury Festival, its impact upon the host community and other stakeholders. A snowball sampling technique was deemed appropriate for this study, as the desired population was hard to make contact with. The interviews followed a one-to-one, face-to-face approach, and lasted between 45–60 minutes. Questions asked were very broad and allowed for further probing – e.g., what are your first memories of Glastonbury Festival? What are your opinions on the festival overall? Do you think it has enhanced the community? If so, how and why? How would you describe your relationship with the event organisers?

All interviews were recorded and later transcribed verbatim and coded manually by both authors. The first author thereby acted as an insider, who has lived in the Pilton area and experienced the festival on a number of occasions, while the second author provided a different perspective as a critical outsider (Lofland & Lofland, 2006) who has never attended Glastonbury Festival. A Critical Management approach was applied throughout the analysis of the data, whereby it is acknowledged that managers or other experts usually are in charge of making decisions due to their training and level of professionalism; however, proponents of Critical Management further argue that this traditional view has a range of limitations. A Critical Management approach is therefore based on the premise that

> current management practices [are portrayed] as institutionalized, yet fundamentally precarious, outcomes of (continuing) struggles between those who have mobilized resources to impose these practices and others who to date have lacked the resources to mount an effective challenge and thereby establish an alternative.
>
> (Adler et al., 2007: 9)

This chapter aims to explore these perspectives and generate new insightful knowledge by looking at "alternative views 'from below'" (Adler et al., 2007: 30). From a Critical Management perspective it is therefore important to acknowledge and discuss power relations, conflicts of interest, disagreements and inconsistencies, features that are oftentimes hidden but nonetheless relevant to today's work organisations and environment (Fournier & Grey, 2000).

Findings and discussion

Through a constant comparison and discussion method between the two authors, it was found that the host community felt alienated due to a lack of shared vision between event organisers, the host community and volunteers. Without this shared vision, the local pride and excitement around the festival became meaningless, and the host community felt a sense of powerlessness, as they did not know how to navigate the political minefield around Glastonbury Festival where power was exercised over them. Each theme will be discussed in more detail next.

Lack of a shared vision

One crucial factor in ensuring the success of an event is for event organisers to have a cohesive relationship with the host community, which can only be ensued by having a shared vision as well as a clear sense of purpose; this makes the host community feel more valued, particularly when they are able to contribute towards problem solving and community issues (Derrett, 2003; Gursoy et al., 2004). This suggests that a more cohesive relationship between the event organisers and host community is required to generate community pride. The question, therefore, arose, whether Glastonbury Festival organisers, volunteers and the host community share a common vision for the festival. Glastonbury Festival does not have an official vision or mission statement, but rather a set of objectives originally put together by Michael Eavis in 1992 when he formally registered the company, which to a certain extent still apply today (Glastonbury Festival, 2016). The main objective is to make the festival more sustainable through working together with Greenpeace, Oxfam and Water Aid (Glastonbury Festival, 2016). Table 3.1 outlines the main aim from the perspective of the festival organizers, volunteers and the host community based on the official Glastonbury Festival objectives, as well as identified through interview statements. It summarises some of the benefits different stakeholder groups hope to gain from the festival.

The interview statements earlier illustrate that there was no clearly identified vision or mission for Glastonbury Festival as perceived by event volunteers and the host community. There is some consensus as to the charity work the festival does and the local projects which aim to give back to the community (2, 4, and 5), but these only to a certain extent match the originally stated festival objectives (1 and 2). Lack of a shared vision can thus be identified as one factor alienating the host community. Without a common sense of purpose, the overall aim of the festival becomes meaningless for this group of stakeholders, who perceive their ability to predict outcomes very differently to how to control these outcomes.

At the same time, amongst the host community, the lack of shared vision was perceived as an opportunity for event organisers to exercise power "over" them. Participants believed they should be involved in any decisions made, however they did not seem powerful enough to do so.

> It does make you feel like they [event organisers] are the most powerful as they have all the money and it's just one person's opinions against thousands of others.
>
> (Interview 2)

> I'm sure they wouldn't appreciate someone like me attempting to suggest how they run their festival.
>
> (Interview 3)

Table 3.1 Stakeholder objectives of Glastonbury Festival

Stakeholder	Stakeholder Objective	Supporting Interview Statements
Event Organisers	(1) Encouragement and stimulation of youth culture from around the world in all forms (Glastonbury Festival, 2016). (2) Allowing improvements to be made onsite as well as distributing large amounts of money towards Greenpeace, Oxfam, Water Aid and other humanitarian causes (Glastonbury Festival, 2016).	(1) "Well, I suppose I'm a bit of a hippy at heart so I suppose, I think it has lost some of the hippy parts. There are still hippy parts – which are very hippyish – but I mean it's very commercialised now. It's very much about money. Which I think is a shame. I think that's what it has lost" (Interview 7). (2) "It's generating money for charity. And it's not chucked in your face like Children in Need or Comic Relief or Sport Relief " (Interview 8).
Event Volunteers	(3) Safety and security at the festival (4) Money raised for charity and other local projects	(3) "I think any of the negative things you get, that's what you get at every festival really and because of how well it's organised, with security and the local police, it's sort of handled quite well" (Interview 6). (4) "It's great as it brings lots of money to the local area. It raises lots of money for charities as well, such as WaterAid and Greenpeace" (Interview 1).
Host Community	(5) Benefits provided to the local community such as local projects.	(5) "My son's school, parents do stewarding at the Festival and they get given a cheque . . . for about 20,000 pounds for the PTA. And I mean most PTA's in most schools couldn't even dream of having that amount of money in their bank account . . . lots of things are paid for by the Festival" (Interview 7).

Source: Authors, 2017

> I think being a local I should have a bit more input.
>
> (Interview 8)

> I think probably, in the first place, when Michael (Eavis) was actually running it . . . it was a completely different set up and things were done on a handshake. He would come and talk to people and people would talk to him. But you can't get anywhere near him anymore. It's just not possible.
>
> (Interview 7)

Particularly the last statement suggests that the Glastonbury Festival organisers today fail to work with the host community. This could to a certain extent be due to the festival growing to such a large size that professional organisers had to be hired in resulting in a change in power relations between organisers and host community. Interview participant 7 went on to explain, "The festival isn't run by Michael Eavis [founder of Glastonbury Festival] anymore, at all really. He is just a figurehead. And the people who do actually run it are very different." Participants, therefore, felt as though the power relations between event organisers and host community have changed, suggesting that if managers fail to fulfil the needs of the host community this could lead to community alienation and jeopardise the future of the event (Gursoy et al., 2004).

Considering many participants felt they should have some input in the decisions made, it was interesting to find that none of the participants saw themselves as contributing towards the Glastonbury Festival experience. It was acknowledged that the organisers "involved" some of them in the experience by providing free tickets to "compensate them" (Interview 1) and as a "thank-you for putting up with all this" (Interview 2). However, this is dependent upon them falling within the local ticketing catchment area, and it is not the main objective of the festival. Allocating free tickets to the host community can only to a certain extent create positive feelings towards the event, but it is a clear expression of the exercise of power "over" the host community. It does not contribute to a shared meaning of what the festival is about and is hence not something the host community can believe in and support.

Local pride rendered meaningless

All participants were asked what their opinions of Glastonbury Festival were, with many participants giving statements that closely linked to local pride (see the examples that follow), which is made apparent by the outpouring of emotion felt towards an event:

> Best thing to do in the summer. I literally love it . . . I have only been once. But I absolutely love it.
>
> (Interview 1)

> I love it, I absolutely love it. I think it's amazing . . . I think we are really lucky to have it so close to us.
>
> (Interview 3)

> I think the Festival is absolutely amazing . . . I can't imagine anything better.
>
> (Interview 8)

Contrasting to the previous statements, one participant stated that he felt "disillusioned" by the festival and disliked the "underbelly" of it all. However, the same participant continued to state that they "do feel proud of the festival but not particularly as a local resident. But as a British person maybe I do think it is a good thing" (Interview 7). This goes one step further than community pride; echoing Gelder and Robinson's (2009) statement that the local residents of Glastonbury Festival should be proud to host such a widely known event as Glastonbury Festival has become a British institution that people are proud of.

While local pride is an important element and positive social impact of a mega-event such as Glastonbury Festival, the question remains what the host community are in fact proud of. The interview statements earlier show some consensus in terms of the host community's and volunteers' passion and excitement for the festival, however, without a clear vision of what the festival is about, their sense of pride becomes meaningless. This meaninglessness may alienate the local community in the long run; make them feel isolated and powerless. It was expressed further in terms of not knowing how to navigate the political minefield that undermines Glastonbury Festival and creates an even stronger feeling of powerlessness amongst the host community, whereby the host community are conscious of the gap between what they would like to achieve and what they feel capable (or not capable) of achieving (Kalekin-Fishman, 1996).

Navigating the political minefield

Various interview participants touched on the issue of allocation of free tickets to the host community, stating that there was "politics about who's got tickets and who hasn't got tickets and how they got their tickets and who they know and who they don't know" (Interview 7). This suggests that although festival organisers look to create a cohesive community, the politics behind who is allocated free tickets and where the catchment area should be may cause controversy and dispute between members of the host community. The festival organisers use their power "over" the community and create a sense of powerlessness amongst the host community, who do not know how to contribute to the festival in a constructive way. This further suggests that the host community will obey the event organisers so as not to jeopardise their chances of receiving free tickets and other benefits. It is echoed in the following statement made by the same participant,

> Lots of things are paid for by the festival. Which makes for a really thriving community in lots of ways. . . . there is a feudal thing going on where you don't want to upset the master in case he doesn't give you any treats.
>
> (Interview 7)

When further asked whether they felt valued by the event organisers, one participant stated,

> No, not at all. I don't think they give a monkey's about me. I can't cause them any difficulty. For me personally, I don't own any land they might need. They give me a ticket but they could withdraw that at any point. There's nothing I can do about that. So no, I don't think they really care.
>
> (Interview 3)

Derrett (2003) suggested that festivals can act as 'gatekeepers', encouraging some people in whilst keeping others out. Considering this particular participant does not own any land that the festival may require, the festival organisers would have no reason to interact with them, as they have nothing that would help to benefit the festival; thus the member of the host community may develop feelings of isolation, lack of belonging and even alienation in the long run.

Lastly, several participants perceived the festival to be a "political minefield," which strongly suggests that the festival affects the cohesiveness among the host community. Without a cohesive community, however, members of the host community will be unable to develop a substantial network of friends, allies and collaborators within the event environment (Getz, 2012). This can lead to conflict, the misuse of power by certain stakeholder groups, while at the same time create a sense of powerlessness and alienation for the host community. One participant summarised this issue by saying the overall perception of the participants involved is that

> It's such a political minefield that I personally prefer living here when it's not festival time . . . (but) a lot of people, including myself to an extent, will just roll and say "well alright then, you do what you want because I want to go to the Festival."
>
> (Interview 7)

In this sense, the host community feels powerless because they expect that no matter what they do or want to achieve, their own behaviour will not have an impact on the outcome they seek. They are conscious of the gap between wanting to go to the festival, and hence having to obey the rules, yet at the same time not being able to change anything or to contribute to the festival in a constructive and meaningful way. Their perceived ability to predict outcomes differs from the sensed ability to control these outcomes and hence contributes to a feeling of powerlessness and alienation (Seeman, 1959; Kalekin-Fishman, 1996).

Recommendations and conclusion

A Critical Management approach was applied to this case study to explore and investigate community perspectives, which in our society are often forced into a subordinate role due to "dominant mechanisms for allocating resources" (Adler et al., 2007: 7).

The aim of this chapter was not to highlight the personal failures of Glastonbury Festival organisers or their poor management, but rather to explore broader issues of community alienation within a complex system of stakeholder power relations, which Glastonbury Festival organisers – perhaps unconsciously – serve and reproduce.

Although the majority of interview participants in this study felt they should have some involvement with the decisions regarding Glastonbury Festival, it was discovered that they were not included in any decision-making processes. This may place risks upon the success of the festival such as damaging the community image, damaging the cohesiveness of the local community and hence community alienation (Gursoy et al., 2004). And even though event organisers allocate free tickets for Glastonbury Festival, this is very much dependent on whether one falls within the allocated catchment area. Furthermore, despite being allocated free tickets, participants felt as though they did not contribute towards the event experience, mainly because they had no involvement in any decision-making processes and did not share a common vision for the festival with other stakeholders. This rendered the local pride generated through the festival meaningless and led to a sense of powerlessness amongst the host community.

Meaninglessness and powerlessness have been identified as elements constituting community alienation, where in the case of Glastonbury Festival the lack of a shared vision allowed festival organisers to exercise power "over" the community. Drawing on the community event and festival literature (see, for example, Derrett, 2003; Clarke & Jepson, 2011; Stadler, 2013), in order to avoid further community alienation and jeopardise the future of the festival, festival organisers should in the first instance focus on creating and communicating a shared vision with all stakeholders. A shared meaning of what the purpose and objective of the festival is can reshape power relations between stakeholder groups and empower the host community. Local pride within the Glastonbury area is currently high and well established, yet without including the host community in the festival planning process and in important decisions made, there is a danger of turning community pride into community alienation in the long run. It is hence crucial to give the host community a voice and to co-create the festival experience with them, rather than merely provide free tickets for the festival in an attempt to 'engage' the community.

In line with the Critical Management approach suggested in this chapter, a final recommendation for event organisers is to engage in more reflexive management practices and to critically rethink any decisions made. According to Fournier and Grey (2000: 18), within any organisation, "things may not be as they appear." A proud host community from the outside might in fact feel powerless and alienated by the festival – issues that can be dealt with more effectively, if event organisers start to reflect on and change their own management practices.

References

Adler, P. S., Forbes, L. C., & Willmott, H. (2007). Critical management studies. *The Academy of Management Annals, 1*(1), 119–179.

Batty, R. J. (2016). Understanding Stakeholder Status and Legitimate Power Exertion within Community Sport Events: A Case Study of the Christchurch (New Zealand) City to Surf. In *Managing and Developing Communities, Festivals and Events* (pp. 103–119). London: Palgrave Macmillan.

Bowdin, G., O'Toole, W., Allen, J., Harris, R., & McDonnell, I. (2006). *Events Management*. New York and London: Routledge.

Charmaz, K. (2006). *Constructing Grounded Theory: A Practical Guide through Qualitative Research*. London: Sage Publications Ltd.

Church, A., & Coles, T. (2006). *Tourism, Power and Space*. New York and London: Routledge.

Clarke, A., & Jepson, A. (2011). Power and hegemony within a community festival. *International Journal of Event and Festival Management, 2*(1), 7–19.

Clegg, S. (1998). Foucault, Power and Organizations. In A. McKinlay & K. Starkey (Eds.), *Foucault, Management and Organization Theory – from Panopticon to Technologies of Self* (pp. 29–48). London, Thousand Oaks, New Delhi: Sage Publications Ltd.

Derrett, R. (2003). Making sense of how festivals demonstrate a community's sense of place. *Event Management, 8*(1), 49–58.

Eisenhardt, K. M. (1989). Building theories from case study research. *Academy of Management Review, 14*(4), 532–550.

Flinn, J., & Frew, M. (2014). Glastonbury: Managing the mystification of festivity. *Leisure Studies, 33*(4), 418–433.

Foucault, M. (1978). *The History of Sexuality* (R. Hurley, Trans.). New York: Pantheon.

Fournier, V., & Grey, C. (2000). At the critical moment: Conditions and prospects for critical management studies. *Human Relations, 53*(1), 7–32.

Gelder, G., & Robinson, P. (2009). A critical comparative study of visitor motivations for attending music festivals: A case study of Glastonbury and V festival. *Event Management, 13*(3), 181–196.

Getz, D. (2012). Event studies: Discourses and future directions. *Event Management, 16*(2), 171–187.

Gillham, B. (2000). *Case Study Research Methods*. New York: Bloomsbury Publishing.

Glastonbury Festival (2016). www.glastonburyfestivals.co.uk/ [accessed 02/11/2016].

Gramsci, A. (1971). *Selections from the Prison Notebooks of Antonio Gramsci* (G. Nowell-Smith & Q. Hoare, Eds.). London: International Publishers.

Gursoy, D., Kim, K., & Uysal, M. (2004). Perceived impacts of festivals and special events by organizers: An extension and validation. *Tourism Management, 25*(2), 171–181.

Jepson, A., & Clarke, A. (2016). An Introduction to Planning and Managing Communities, Festivals and Events. In A. Jepson & A. Clarke (Eds.) *Managing and Developing Communities, Festivals and Events* (pp. 3–15). London: Palgrave Macmillan.

Jepson, A., Clarke, A., & Ragsdell, G. (2013). Applying the motivation-opportunity-ability (MOA) model to reveal factors that influence inclusive engagement within local community festivals: The case of UtcaZene 2012. *International Journal of Event and Festival Management, 4*(3), 186–205.

Kalekin-Fishman, D. (1996). Tracing the growth of alienation: Enculturation, socialization, and schooling in a democracy. *Contributions in Sociology, 116*, 95–106.

Lofland, J., & Lofland, L. H. (2006). *Analyzing Social Settings*. Belmont, CA: Wadsworth Publishing Company.

Lystad, M. H. (1972). Social alienation: A review of current literature. *Sociological Quarterly, 13*(1), 90–113.

Macleod, D. V., & Carrier, J. G. (Eds.). (2010). *Tourism, Power and Culture: Anthropological Insights* (Vol. 19). Bristol, UK: Channel View Publications.

Reid, S. (2011). Event stakeholder management: Developing sustainable rural event practices. *International Journal of Event and Festival Management, 2*(1), 20–36.

Rogers, P., & Anastasiadou, C. (2011). Community involvement in festivals: Exploring ways of increasing local participation. *Event Management, 15*(4), 387–399.

Seeman, M. (1959). On the meaning of alienation. *American Sociological Review, 24*(6), 783–791.

Stadler, R. (2013). Power relations and the production of new knowledge within a Queensland Music Festival community cultural development project. *Annals of Leisure Research, 16*(1), 87–102.

Stake, R. E. (1995). *The Art of Case Study Research*. Thousand Oaks, CA: Sage Publications Ltd.

Weber, M. (1978). The distribution of power within the political community: Class, status, party. *Economy and Society, 2*, 926–940.

Yeoman, I., Robertson, M., Ali-Knight, J., Drummond, S., & McMahon-Beattie, U. (2004). In *Festival and Event Management: An International Arts and Cultural Perspective* (pp. 65–69). Elsevier, London.

Yin, R. K. (2009). *Case Study Research: Design and Methods* (4th ed.). Los Angeles et al.: Sage Publications Ltd.

4 Event evolution and the planning process

The case of the Finnish housing fair

Karine Dupre

Introduction

Finland is a young nation, for it became independent only in 1917. However, the country has a rich cultural past, noticeably in terms of territorial and political dominations, which profoundly affected its national culture. Being for centuries mostly a rural country, it falls under the Russian rule that Finland, as a Grand Duchy of Russia, saw the rise of the Finnish national movement with the first real Golden Age for arts and culture (Valkonen and Valkonen, 1994). The first Finnish song and dance festivals were developed during this period and many more events have been created since then. Today, Finland offers a wide variety of tourism attractions that take advantage of the country's cultural heritage and the territory's great natural assets; 86% of the country is forest area and 10% covered by water (FTS 2020, 2011). For example, the country hosts the yearly world championships in contemporary events such as wife-carrying, mobile phone-throwing or rubber boot-throwing, but it also, and more traditionally, offers theatre and opera festivals, music and film festivals and sport and city events. Finland has international event heritage having hosted the Olympic Games in 1952 and twice the European Capitals of Culture (Helsinki in 2000 and Turku in 2011).

Despite the international scope and appeal of some of these events, Finland's tourism sector remains relatively small and underdeveloped as an industry. For instance, in comparison to the European countries with more or less the same population as Finland (around five-and-a-half million in 2016, FP, 2016), Finland welcomes almost the same amount of international visitors as Norway (around four and a half million), but far less than Slovakia (six and a half million) or Denmark (ten million) (WTO, 2016). In the same way, the 81 officially registered festivals of the country gather constant audiences totalling more than 1.8 million people. Yet 45% of these festivals host less than 5,000 visitors. Another 45% of these festivals welcome between 5,000 and 50,000 visitors and only 7% accommodate for over a 100,000 (FF, 2016). In order of attendee numbers, they comprise the Kotka Maritime Festival (232,090 visitors), Helsinki Festival (211,688), Pori Jazz

Festival (140,000), Lakeside Blues Festival (125,000), the Tango Festival in Seinäjoki and the World Village Festival (both around 105,000 visitors, FF, 2016). There is clearly room for growth in Finland's tourism industry, as both identified by scholars and the government (Rahman, 2014; FTS, 2011; Vuoristo, 2002).

However, at domestic level, there is one national event that almost every single year has accommodated more than 110,000 visitors steadily for the last five decades: this is the Finnish annual Housing Fair (Suomen Asuntomessut). Which immediately raises the question as to what factors have led to the longevity and success of this event, especially if one considers that the event is not marketed outside of Finland. One could suggest that this is because it is intrinsically connected to community and urban development. The purpose of this chapter is to critically discuss how this major community event is planned, constructed and what have been the factors influencing its success since its inception in 1966.

Background

The shift towards a more leisure-oriented society for most industrialised countries not only paralleled the growth of tourism industries but also the (re)discovery of cultures and heritage. Economical reconversion has led many cities to question anew their cultural identity, attractiveness, and image, as well as their local and international influence. As such, it often ends with the traditional practice of segregating tourism and culture from city (re)development. At different scales, but all with success, the conversion of the Ruhr Valley in Germany, of the city of Bilbao in Spain or of the High Line in New York City have proved the positive weight of culture and tourism within a collaborative tourism-planning scheme. Within this context, it can be argued that tourism affects more significantly the conception, the fabrication, the practice and the everyday life experience of permanent residents or tourists visiting contemporary cities (Gravari-Barbas, 2013). Behind its material functions, tourism with its intangible dimensions obviously challenges the sense of place and its identity (Derrett, 2003), the relationship between supply and demand, and the inhabitants' concerns such as social inequalities and the sense of belonging (Tosun, 2002; Pearce et al., 1996; King et al., 1993)

Today, engaged in the fierce economic and cultural competition of a globalised world, numerous cities have chosen their tourism development as a major pull factor, not only to attract domestic and international visitors but also to retain or/and gain more permanent or semi-permanent inhabitants. In this context, to have 'something attractive' –whether that be tangible or intangible – has been used as significant leverage for both local and tourism development. Events have been instrumental in doing so for the last 150 years (Syme et al., 1989; Chalkley and Essex, 1999; Carriere and Demaziere, 2002) with a variety of forms that prompted a refinement in event classification (see Ritchie, 1984; Hall, 1992; Getz, 2008). In his book *Events and Urban Regeneration*, Andrew Smith (2012) defines the urban regeneration projects according to their relation to events: event-led, that is a project related to staging an event, or event-themed, which is a project development in conjunction with an event. Arguably, this relationship can be broadly extended to urban projects in general. The growing interest on how events are linked to urban development and its planning processes shows the weight events have regarding quality of life (QOL) (see Jepson and Stadler, 2017). Yet further studies are still required to better understand why events fail, what the risk management factors and strategies are, or the value of the events (Getz, 2008). Event evolution studies have contributed by shedding light on these questions by specifically addressing long temporality analysis and by proposing life-cycle models. From the transfer of Levitt's (1965) contribution on the product life cycle or Butler's (1980) tourist area cycle, four or five main identified stages seem both universal and consistent. They consist of birth, growth, maturity, decline and/or revival. Although several scholars have discussed the model since (Quinn and Cameron, 1983) and might propose some slight variations (i.e. Beverland et al., 2001 added a first phase called conception) or factors that might influence the life-cycle model (Prideaux, 2000), these stages have rarely been fundamentally questioned.

In this chapter, the idea is not to produce a discursive essay, but rather an empirically based article with a case study that relies on a long lasting successful event as the main incentive for local urban development. By identifying the factors that are shaping this specific event's evolution and how the event has developed, it will help either to confirm the existing life-cycle model or, on the contrary, to evidence the need for new theoretical advances. Besides, more practically, in a highly competitive world, this knowledge can show additional value when developing strategies for event planning development, marketing and sustainability.

Methods

Methodologically, qualitative and quantitative approaches have been combined to reveal the main features of the event. The study included yearly site visits and spatial analyses since 1995, that were supplemented by several additional forms of documentation related to the project development including electronic media, newspaper articles, master plan, business case and local government internal documentation. This diverse selection of source material facilitated the contextualisation of the interviews that were conducted on site and elsewhere with some visitors and key stakeholders. Besides, the housing fair website was systematically browsed to retrieve quantitative data regarding attendance, characteristics of the visitors (age, gender, profession, interest focus), satisfaction, travelling distance to the event and event location features (place, year, surface, built area), which were extracted from the housing fair's yearly reports.

In 2016, Seinäjoki was the host city for the Finnish housing fair. After several years of planning, debates, changes of methods and stagnation, the city decided to apply to be the host of the housing fair, as a clear incentive to start developing the new precinct of Pruukinranta, which was a former natural area (mostly forest along the lake) in the southern west outskirts of Seinäjoki. The plan is now for it to become a new green district in relation to the Finnish ideal to live by the water (Kuusisto, 2009; Karvinent, 1997). In 2015, the housing fair was hosted by Vantaa, a city suburb of the country's capital Helsinki, addressing the contemporary questions of urban sprawl and densification. The chosen site, a former agricultural and forest land in the close vicinity of Helsinki airport, intends to become a new residential centre for 30,000 residents providing both modern features, transport access and closeness to nature. In 2011, the housing fair was located in Kokkola, a city plainly looking for post-industrial revitalisation and renewal. The chosen site was one of the city's former industrial areas.

For each of the cities involved, the yearly housing fair provided at least two great opportunities: to nationally advertise their latest residential development and – or mainly – to challenge this development through the incentives of the unusual requirements of the Housing Fair Finland Co-operative (the organisational body). This is in view of these considerations, that rather than being interested by the outputs and results of the housing fairs, it was decided to examine this Finnish housing fair, its contributors and processes, as a case study. After a brief presentation on what the Finnish housing fair is, its organisation will be examined prior to trying to understand why today it can be considered as a clever and innovative instrument to achieve long-term event sustainability, along with higher-quality urban developments.

Finnish housing fairs: an evolutionary trend

The Finnish housing fair is an annual event that promotes the quality of housing and living conditions in Finland by displaying innovative building products and buildings in a clearly defined location looking for sustainable retrofitting (e.g. a former industrial district to become residential such as Kokkola, 2011) or new sustainable urbanisation. In every case, relation to the natural environment and energy efficiency of the buildings will be scrutinised and accounted for. The fair is held in a different city across the country each year and usually attracts more than 110,000 visitors for a one-month period during the summer time. It is usually the opportunity for the host city to develop a full new precinct or to redevelop part of or the entirety of an older one. In any case, the operation is often considered as a representation of the current modernity both at the urban and architectural scale. Indeed, as announced in its objectives, the fair reflects the housing ideals and innovations of the year, as well as providing an overview of state-of-the-art developments in building design and construction. In the housing fair area, the audience can familiarise themselves with houses and gardens on the site and obtain information about housing, construction, gardens, landscaping, energy matters and interior decoration. Families usually move into the housing fair houses after the closing of the fair, which is maybe one of the most original and atypical features of this fair. Yet its organisation reveals some unusual settings.

First of all, the housing fairs are run by the Finnish Housing Fair Co-operative Organisation (FHFCO hereafter), which is a non-profit organisation, and any financial surplus is used to further the development of the organisation's activities and to promote further housing research. Second, the FHFCO was founded in 1966 by four people (two lawyers, a professor in public administration and a department chief) and included seven members. Mainly associations, public administrations and banks, they are the Finnish Housing Reform Association (Asuntoreformiyhdistys ry), the Finnish Housing Association (Suomen Asuntoliitto ry), the Finnish Fair Foundation (Suomen Messusäätiö), the Finnish Savings Banks Association (Suomen Säästöpankkiliitto ry), the Federation of Finnish Financial Services (Suomen Pankkiyhdistys ry), OP- Pohjola Group Central Cooperative (Osuuspankkien Keskusliitto ry) and Sampo Bank (Postisäästöpankki) (Asuntomessut, 2016). Members display an incredible longevity, for they are, as of today, exactly the same members but with one addition (the Association of Finnish Local and Regional Authorities), which emerged from changes in the Finnish municipal administration at the end of the 1990s. Seemingly the goals and values are remarkably steady after 50 years of activity.

Secondly since its foundation in 1966, with the first housing fair held in 1970, until the present day, it is 'always a joint project' and 'together in partnership' (Asuntomessut, 2016) with an individual theme that provides the guidelines for design and construction. Cooperation is the operating method, following the same principles described by Boyle (1989) regarding the Glasgow Action case study (private-public partnerships, implementation of an overall strategy led by the a private organisation and the combination of commercial goals with more altruistic objectives) and slowly adapting to new strategies such as network-based, as discussed by Stokes (2006) and as a developmental tool to stimulate creativity, enhance competitiveness and achieve visionary results (UNWTO, 2015). Yet the main difference resides in the fact the FHFCO is a non-profit organisation and does not pay taxes for its activities. Basically, the FHFCO is responsible for general public services, technical issues related to the fair and the marketing of the event. The host municipality is responsible for the target area's land use plan and the public utilities timetable, along with the fair's car parking. The developers and builders are responsible for the completion of their own projects, their financing and any promotional material for the fair. As such, there is multifaceted cooperation between the various related organisations, companies and the future residents of the area (Asuntomessut, 2016). Moreover, the functions of the contributors have not changed despite being something new for each city. Thus, this structural continuity has allowed an uninterrupted flow of reinvigorated energy due to the turnover of the fair's locations, as well as building up a data of knowledge from past experiences.

Thirdly, the short lead time of the project – between four and five years from the start of the planning to the completion of the fair area offers quite interesting guarantees to the host municipality. A new, appealing and well-publicised area is developed in a duration that usually is much shorter than in 'more classic' development. Since 1995, the average surface being developed or redeveloped is around 14 hectares with around 140 buildings erected which brings a built density close to ten (Asuntomessut, 2016). These numbers don't include all the infrastructures either created or retrofitted to access the housing fair area such as roads, bridges and public transport. Most of the time, the infrastructures are ready at the opening of the housing fair, but there is an additional one or two-year work for major new developments. In the same way, depending on the urban context of the housing fair and its potential remoteness, the level of built infrastructure might quite vary from one fair to the other, as well as its overall cost. Based on the fair final reports (Asuntomessut, 2016), there are two main types of investors (from the FHFCO and the local municipality) and there are five major expenditure items. The first four items are covered by the FHFCO. They concern the administrative running of the fair, marketing and information expenses, parking, transport and signage and the investment in the fairground and the buildings. Once again, each fair might see a different distribution of these costs. For example, for the 2009 fair (Valkeakoski), administrative expenses accounted for 684,387 euros (near 28% of the total cost); marketing and information expenses for 204,144 euros (slightly over 8% of the total); parking, transport and signage costed 1,017,769 euros (42%); and the investment in the fairground and the buildings was 547,562 euros (22% of the total cost). Analysis of the yearly reports show there usually is a 10% variation in one way or the other regarding the distribution of these major budget items. At last, the fifth item, invested by local government, relates to work such as street building, water management, landscaping and lighting. It can greatly vary from one fair to the other, either the expense matching more or less the investment from the FHFCO or tripling it. Revenues include mostly ticket sales, parking fees and the sale and rental income of constructed plots in the fair. Net profit has been on average about 100,000 euros, with one exceptional peak at 400,000 euros in 2002 (Hyvönen, 2004). It has also wider positive effects, as it brings external investment in the local area as well as income generated locally by the fair's visitors. It also improves employment and increases attractiveness of the area both as a residential, research and business destination. Every year, a Casa Humana scholarship of 45,000 euros is granted to support housing research involving regional universities (Asuntomessut, 2016). This is the reason why there is no shortage of location for new fairs, as it is considered as a very efficient trigger for local governments. But it also impacts the administration level since the FHFCO requires increased cooperation and therefore challenges operational models. This results in experimenting, testing and daring to contribute to the implementation of collaborative working relationships between several sectors of the city administration and other partners. More than one city host acknowledged the contribution of the FHFCO for some of their administrative changes of approach, and it has also been internationally recognised via the Vuores-Tampere housing fair of 2012 (Gaffron et al., 2005) for example. As such, not only governance is challenged but also economical features for private-public partnerships (PPP) might be a first for some host cities. This phenomenon aligns with the latest UNTWO report on PPP (2015), which evidenced the relevance of PPPs not only in the general development of tourism but also in bringing together skills and knowledge. In this Finnish case, the regional and local governments benefit from a shift from the traditional planning model that evolves from the involvement of mostly public sector stakeholders to a wide range of public and private sector stakeholders, communities and various types of organisations.

Lastly, the flexibility of the housing fair's locations and themes within the frame of very clear goals actually ensures there is a fight against a certain numbness or routine, whilst it offers the possibility to reflect upon the latest trends and current social issues. In terms of location, since its inception the housing fairs have indiscriminately taken place all over the country (Figure 4.1), usually in the ten most populated cities, but also in less dense areas that were looking to and intended for development. Some repetition of city locations are actually masking the fact that the fair took place in a brand new neighbourhood or in redeveloped areas of the town that might be quite eccentric.

Surprisingly, when analysing the fair attendance in regards to location, it is impossible to observe a geographic relationship pattern. One could have imagined that the most populated and urbanised areas would entertain more attendees, but this is not the case. This is explained by the extreme mobility of the visitors, who will not hesitate to drive long distances. A small comparative study on travel destinations between 2010 and 2016, based on the data provided by the housing fair's yearly reports, indicates that the average drive for the visitors is 240 kilometres, with 33% driving between 300 and 1000 kilometres to the fair. This is concomitant with Bohlin's (2000) analysis, which was determined using the distance-decay function, that travel declined with distance, as expected but well-established, recurring events had the greatest drawing power. If it is true that analysing attendance numbers (Figure 4.2) shows some clear drops below 110,000 visitors in 1976, 1981 and 1993, respectively, in Oulu (the sixth largest city of Finland), Helsinki (first) and Lahti (seventh), it does not reflect a problem in location but rather societal crisis and the recession periods of Finland. The same reason can be invoked for 1984 and 1989, when no fair was organised. In some extent, this is also true for 1971 and 1973 but after the first fair in 1970 and the second in 1972, there was also a need to fine-tune the event.

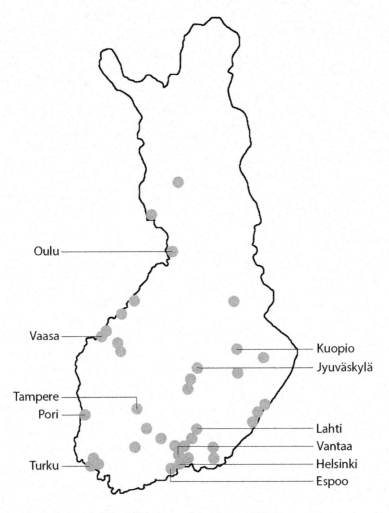

Figure 4.1 Locations of Finnish housing fairs since 1970
Source: Asuntomessut, 2016; adapted by the author, 2017

Looking at the fairs from their themes' this perspective also demonstrates their permeability to trends and social issues. For example, an overall chronological study on the themes developed by the housing fairs since 1991, shows evidence of the emergence of environmental concerns in the 1990s with sustainability becoming a recurrent and highlighted topic (see Figure 4.3). Lost in the translation from Finnish to English, topics with emphasis on recycled materials (1993 fair), free energy and energy efficiency (1990, 1981, 1977 fairs) also reflect the major recessions in Finland. But the themes developed after the 2000s also show a more comprehensive approach both in terms of environment and lifestyle as seen in the word cloud picture in Figure 4.4

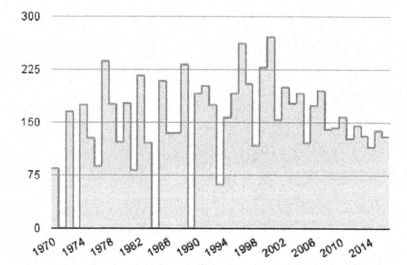

Figure 4.2 Yearly visitors (in thousands), according to housing fair attendance
Source: Asuntomessut, 2016; adapted by the author, 2017

1970 Tuusulan: Home sweet home
1991 Varkaus: New construction and renovation
1992 Mäntsälä: Sustainable development
1993 Lahti: Sustainable development, blocks of flats
1994 Pietarsaari: Small blocks of flats
1995 Joensuu: Accessibility
1996 Ylöjärvi: Modern apartments, and healthy living
1997 Raisio: Safe and healthy living environment, natural landscaping and lighting
1998 Rovaniemi: Winter construction, natural landscaping
1999 Lappeenranta: Good design, natural landscaping
2000 Tuusula: renewal of damaged landscapes and protection of underground water
2001 Kajaani: Sustainable ecology and examples of timber housing for all ages and elderly
2002 Kotka: Nature and sense of the place
2003 Laukaa: Child friendly design
2004 Heinola: The living lifecycle, shoreline building
2005 Oulu: Individual planning and northern light
2006 Espoo: Working and home, diversity
2007 Hämeenlinna: Good design, communities, nature and best ideas for home
2008 Vaasa: Homes for everyone and ecology
2009 Valkeakoski: Sweet living and energy efficiency
2010 Kuopio: Well-being and quality of life, low energy houses and own gardens
2011 Kokkola: Homes in all sizes and energy efficiency
2012 Tampere- Vuores: Eco-city
2013 Hyvinkää - Resident oriented approach and environmental responsibility
2014 Jyväskylä - Northern Gardens & City Lights
2015 Vantaa: Little everyday luxuries and green oases
2016 Seinajoki: Ostrobothnian will to craft

Figure 4.3 List of housing fair themes 1991–2016

Source: Asuntomessut, 2016; adapted by the author, 2017

44 *Karine Dupre*

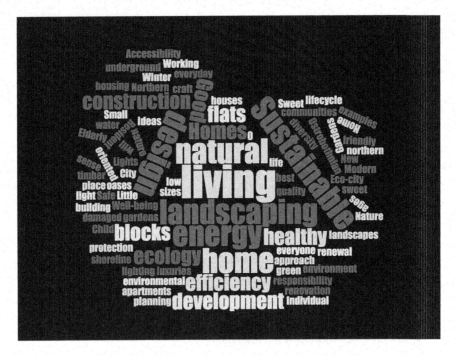

Figure 4.4 A wordle diagram to demonstrate the major themes of the Finnish housing fairs

Source: Asuntomessut, 2016; adapted by the author, 2017

(where the size of the words is proportional to their repetition), reflecting a concern on well-being common to many developed countries. However, we can observe throughout the decades, the recurrence of wording around nature and landscaping. One could interpret it as the legendary green approach of the Nordic countries, but beyond the cliché there is also deeper cultural attachment to the natural environment that transpires (Dupre, 2012).

Findings and conclusions

This case study has revealed three types of findings. The first is structural and reveals 'hard and soft bodies', as expressed in biology. 'Hard bodies' are basically the non-negotiable points, which include the status of the organisation (a cooperative, Asuntomessut, 2016), the goals (innovation and state of the art in residential buildings) and method (processes) to achieve the latter (cooperation between different contributors). Because of their nature, they actually induce and increase technical and administrative innovation, as well as putting forward the role and function – and competences – of the contributors, but not their personalities. It also favours inclusion of multiple stakeholders. On the other side, the 'soft bodies' contain the flexible parts, which are the fair's location, theme and even contributors to some extent. It ensures renewal of interest, a global-local (glocal) approach and a specific relation to the notion of project duration, which has incidences on how much and how long a community can involve itself.

Moreover, it is also important to underline that this structure has contributed to the longevity and success of the event. This is made clear when comparing the event's life cycle with the previously discussed life cycle (birth, growth, maturity, decline and/or revival). The first three phases are easily identified: 1966–1970 as the birth phase with the creation of the association and event planning, 1970–1985 as the growth phase with the temporal and spatial rhythm of the fairs being tested (either being produced every second year, every year or even in several places during a single year) and, lastly, from 1985 until the present day as the maturity phase. Yet the striking difference is that the latter phase has now lasted three decades without showing any signs of decline. Beverland et al. (2001) commented that when analysing the life-cycle model Prideaux (2000) asked, 'What planning action is required to facilitate the move from one stage to the next?' Throughout this Finnish housing fair case study, it is believed this is the result of a strong commitment towards strategy and event planning which ended up with the aforementioned structural approach rather than a focus on event tourism development and marketing tactics. The long-term sustainability is the result of a careful strategic and structural approach, reflecting very much on country national governance as well as a certain image of national identity.

The second finding relates to the notion of flexibility. The created system has the benefit of being adaptable to the specific needs of the housing fair but also those of the host city. Thus it is scalable and non-rigid. As such, it allows a variety of host locations, as well of topics, that can easily adapt to societal changes and audience' expectations. It seems obvious that in this case study, adaptation has been treated as a process, yet as Smith (2012) discussed, at this stage, there is little evidence that this adaptation strategy is really a catalyst for social change. A brief overlook at the visitor socio-economic categories over the last decade (2016–2006) demonstrates that women have been visiting the fair in larger volume continuously: 65% women and 35% men (Asuntomessut, 2016). Yet in Finland, women are still a minority in holding powerful positions and thus being agents' in decision making. Although the country is definitively at the forefront of gender equality, the *Women and Men in Finland 2016* report shows a large domination of men in city and municipal manager positions (18% against 82%), as well as a remaining 18% of gender pay gap (ST, 2016). Seemingly, a merger 2% of the visitors acknowledged working in the building industry, thus showing that even if the housing fair is really popular in the country, building professionals don't seem to be much concerned with it.

Lastly, the third finding refers to what we could call sideways outcomes, for it generates new competences that can be seen directly or indirectly among existing professionals and others. For example, the recent focus on energy efficiency developed not only new job profiles and skills in for example property management and project economy management but also changed the approach used by the building professionals regarding projects. Architects, urban planners or landscapers work with that focus in mind from the start of their designs. More broadly, this creates new ground for policy implementation and an overall ground for innovation and entrepreneurialism.

Over the two decades running 1996–2016, it was also investigated whether the Finnish housing fair was represented as a topic for articles in the main Finnish professional architectural magazine (*Finnish Architectural Review*). Although every year the journal presented some projects that were built during the fair, not a single article related to the housing fair directly. As such, it can be concluded that the event is not yet considered as a means of change by this category of professionals, although the topics might have some effects.

To conclude, many internationally recognised case studies exist that establish procedures for realising positive outcomes, but often fail to have the tactics employed known or understood beyond the immediate context of engagement. Many of them also lack insight into the processes that causes the shift of the research perspective to move from the 'product' to the origin of its production. This was specifically the focus of this paper with a particular scrutiny on the contributors and their relationships to the processes, as well as on the processes themselves. It now seems obvious that further research to understand more of the influence of these fairs on the public and professional knowledge and understanding of issues of housing and urban design, layout, management and use would be needed. Further research on event geography would also be interesting in an attempt to learn more about what impact of the housing fairs have to place making and as agents of territorialisation.

References

Asuntomessut (2016). www.asuntomessut.fi [Accessed 26/10/2016].

Beverland, M., Hoffman, D., and Rasmussen, M. (2001). The evolution of events in the Australasian wine sector. *Tourism Recreation Research*, 26 (2), pp. 35–44.

Bohlin, M. (2000). Traveling to events. In L. Mossberg (Ed.). *Evaluation of Events: Scandinavian Experiences*, Cognizant, New York, pp. 13–29.

Boyle, R. (1989). Partnership in practice: An assessment of public-private collaboration in urban regeneration-a case study of Glasgow action. *Local Government Studies*, 15 (2), pp. 17–28.

Butler, R. W. (1980). The concept of a tourist area cycle of evolution: Implications for management of resources. *Canadian Geographer/Le Géographe Canadien*, 24, pp. 5–12.

Carriere, J. and Demaziere, C. (2002). Urban planning and flagship development projects: Lessons from Expo 98, Lisbon. *Planning Practice and Research*, 17 (1), pp. 69–79.

Chalkley, B. and Essex, S. (1999). Urban development through hosting international events: A history of the rganiz games. *Planning Perspectives*, 14, pp. 369–394.
Derrett, R. (2003). Making sense of how festivals demonstrate a community's sense of place. *Event Management*, 8, pp. 49–58.
Dupre, K. (2012). Ville ou quartier durable en Finlande: entre modele et fantasme. In *Deshima 6*, UDS, Strasbourg, pp. 41–67.
Finland Festival (FF) (2016). www.festivals.fi/en/statistics/audience-figures-2012/#.WHhCF1e1I64 [Accessed 20/10/2016].
Finland Population (FP) (2016). www.worldometers.info/world-population/finland-population/ [Accessed 26/12/2016].
Finland's Tourism Strategy 2020 (FTS 2020) (2011). www.tem.fi/files/28018/Finlands_Tourism_Strategy_to_2020.pdf [Accessed 23/10/2016].
Gaffron, P., Huismans, G., and Skala, F. (2005). *Ecocity 'Urban Development towards Appropriate Structures for Sustainable Transport' (2002–2005)*, Facultas Verlags und Buchhandels AG, Vienna.
Getz, D. (2008). Event tourism: Definition, evolution, and research. *Tourism Management*, 29, pp. 403–428.Gravari-Barbas, M. (2013). Amenager la Ville Par la Culture et le Tourisme, coll. *Ville-aménagement, éditions Le Moniteur*, pp. 105–106.
Hall, C. (1992). *Hallmark Tourism Events: Impacts, Management and Planning*, Belhaven Press, London.
Hyvönen, V. (2004). *Asuntomessujen talous kestää yhden epäonnistuneen vuoden.* www.ts.fi/uutiset/talous/1073979855/Asuntomessujen+talous+kestaa+yhden+epaonnistuneen+vuoden [Accessed 2/05/2017].
Jepson, A. and Stadler, R. (2017). Conceptualising the impact of festival and event attendance upon family quality of life (QOL). *Event Management*, 21 (1), pp. 47–56.
Karvinent, M. (1997). Kaupungin ranta kulttuurisena rajana. In T. Haarni, M. Karvinen, H. Koskela, and S. Tani (Eds.). *Tila, paikka ja maisema. Tutkimusretkiä uuten maatieteeseen*, Vastapaino, Tampere, Finland, pp. 143–162.
King, B., Pizam, A., and Milman, A. (1993). Social impacts of tourism: Host perceptions. *Annals of Tourism Research*, 20, pp. 650–665.
Kokkola. (2011). www.asuntomessut.fi/sites/default/files/loppuraportti.pdf.
Kuusisto, E. (2009). *Land of Islands and Waters*, The Island Committee, Ministry of Employment and the Economy, Forssa.
Levitt, T. (1965). Exploit the product life cycle. *Harvard Business Review*, 11, pp. 81–94.
Pearce, P. L., Moscardo, G., and Ross, G. F. (1996). *Tourism Community Relationships*, Elsevier, Oxford.
Prideaux, B. (2000). The resort development spectrum-a new approach to modelling resort development. *Tourism Management*, 21, pp. 225–240.
Quinn, R. E. and Cameron, K. S. (1983). Organizational life cycles and shifting criteria of effectiveness: Some preliminary evidence. *Management Science*, 29 (1), pp. 33–51.
Rahman, H. (2014). *Tourism Development in Finland: Case Study-Tourism Development in Lapland and Its Socioeconomic Impacts*. Thesis. Kokkola: Centria University of Applied Sciences.
Ritchie, J. (1984). Assessing the impact of hallmark events: Conceptual and research issues. *Journal of Travel Research*, 23 (1), pp. 2–11.

Smith, A. (2012). *Events and Urban Regeneration*, Routledge, New York and London.
Statistics Finland (ST) (2016). *Women and Men in Finland 2016*, Tilastoskeskus. www.tilastokeskus.fi/ajk/julkistamiskalenteri/kuvailusivu_en.html?ID=16133 [Accessed 2/01/2017].
Stokes, R. (2006). Network-based strategy making for events tourism. *European Journal of Marketing*, 40 (5/6), pp. 682–695.
Syme, G. J., Shaw, B. J., Fenton, D. M., and Mueller, W. S. eds. (1989). *The Planning and Evaluation of Hallmark Events*, Avebury, Aldershot.
Tosun, C. (2002). Host perceptions of impacts. *Annals of Tourism Research*, 29 (1), pp. 231–253.
Valkonen, K. and Valkonen, M. (1994). *Festival Fever: Finland Festivals*, Otava Publishing Company, Finland.
Vantaa-Kivisto. http://vantaankivisto.fi/fi/kivistö-new-home-town-helsinki-metropolitan-area [Accessed 26/12/2016].
Vuoristo, K.-V. (2002). Regional and structural patterns of tourism in Finland. *Fennia*, 180 (1–2), pp. 251–259, Helsinki.
World Tourism Organization (UNWTO) (2015). *Affiliate Members Global Reports, Volume Eleven-Public-Private Partnerships: Tourism Development*, UNTWO, Madrid.
World Tourism Organization (UNWTO) (2016). *Yearbook of Tourism Statistics, Compendium of Tourism Statistics and Data Files: International Tourism, Number of Arrivals*. http://data.worldbank.org/indicator/ST.INT.ARVL?locations=FR [Accessed 26/12/2016].

5 The sporting and heritage festival of Landsmót in Iceland

Identity expressions and performances of nation, gender and rurality

Susanna Heldt Cassel

Introduction

Events and festivals, celebrating national identity or the uniqueness of the cultural and traditions of a specific region or place may be interpreted as arenas where identities of both people and places are staged and performed. Sports and cultural events, may enhance and play with identities, such as the co-construction of gender identities and national identities, as a part of the event or festival itself (Merkel, 2015). These co-constructions and expressions of identity discourses as part of events and festivals are not least reinforced with the impact of social media and the posting of images by many other actors than the organisers and managers of the event.

This study is guided by the fundamental principle that a national event, such as the sport and heritage festival of Landsmót, a national competition and show of the Icelandic horse, studied in this chapter is an arena for performing and expressing identity discourses of places, social groups and individuals. The starting point of this study is articulated nicely by Merkel (2015:5) who suggests, "The key characteristics of local, national, and international events and festivals alike is their contribution to formation and expression of identity discourses and narratives". The impact and significance of the festival may vary in scope from the personal to the national or international, but it is clear that it in different ways it creates collective and place identities, and enhances the social and cultural capital of the participants (Merkel, 2015).

The identities of people and places are often expressed within hegemonic and dominant discourses, such as traditional gender identities in specific social settings, but may also be expressed in more alternative ways through events and festivals, that offers a contestation of the traditional and dominant (see Chen, 2009; Gilmore, 2010 for examples). By studying the staging and visualisation of the key components and signifiers that together captures the cultural and social meaning of a festival, put on display by organisers, participants and spectators, the identity discourses that the festival construct, may be unpacked and analysed in a more critical way.

Tourism as a performance practice means that tourism activates and promotes certain social roles of hosts and guests (reflexively or un-reflexively) that are acted out in ways that may reproduce or challenge social norms and identities (Edensor, 2001). The tourism products are co-created by active guest participation and are scripted and regulated in specific ways. Staging of tourism experiences, such as a festival, involves displacement of cultural production and modification to fit the new demands of the specific context in which the cultural production is performed (Chhabra, Healy & Sills, 2003). The hosts or producers of the festival are performing the identities and places expected by the guests, including gender identities and thereby often reproduce stereotypical images of themselves as men and women and their places. Through the use of social media visitors are co-constructing and critically evaluating for themselves and others images of places and events as they post pictures and tag places and relate them to emotions, experiences and expressions of identity.

The biannual sport and heritage festival of Landsmót is perhaps the most prestigious competition of Icelandic horses in the world. Apart from being an arena for showing and competing with some of the best Icelandic horses of the world, the Landsmót attracts a lot of domestic Icelandic as well as international visitors. The event is a competition and a breeding show that goes on for a week in late June. In 2016, it took place between the 27 of June until the 2 of July. It is touring around in different places in Iceland, but also, and not least, a meeting place and a spectacle for entertainment and celebration of the Icelandic heritage and the relationship between (wo)man and horse (Helgadottir & Dasper, 2016).

This chapter critically analyses the way in which Landsmót functions as an arena for the construction and expression of national identities through communication of images on Instagram and through performances of participants and visitors together with the staging on site at the Landsmót event. Analysis is undertaken here into how the event is represented externally; what images that are connected to it through tagging in social media and how this may be interpreted using a framework of different performance practices of national identities and gender identities. The chapter explores the role of key signs, symbols, performances and landscapes used in constructing the event and how are identities of people and place expressed in relation to the event. Finally, it evaluates which attributes, knowledge and appearance are valued as important and necessary according to what is shown and how these are represented.

Methods

The data of this study consist of text and visual images of social media posts (the around 780 images on Instagram with the tag "Landsmót" and "Landsmót 2016", posted up until December 2016), as well as field observations made on site by the researcher at the event in Holar, Iceland, in June

2016. These observations were made during three days of visits at the event, by watching the competition and shows, by walking around while taking field notes and photographs at the site.

The images were after collection, sorted into thematic groups and analysed through content analysis and critical semiology. The use of content analysis as an instrument of analysis in tourism inquiry and research has been widespread, particularly in the last two decades (e.g. Mehmetoglu & Dann, 2003). The method has been used more often with textual content, but pictorial material can also be content-analysed. In cultural studies, imagery, including paintings, maps, videos and even landscapes, is often considered as a form of 'text' (Stepchenkova & Zhan, 2013). In this study, the content analysis has been used to structure and sort the material in categories and thematic groups, to quantify the motifs/objects but also to make sense of the contexts in which they are represented.

In this study the analysis has been particularly inspired by Rose (2001), who identifies semiology as a method for a critical approach to interpreting visual images. A framework usually used in semiotic analyses that has inspired this analysis is further to identify and deconstruct the popular representations in society that are used in the photographs (Jenkins, 2003). Key to visual semiotics is the idea that signs have layers of meanings. Denotation, which is the first layer in which something is described, is fairly easy to decode. Connotation, which is the second layer, refers to ideas which are structured to send particular messages, the ideological meanings, to the viewer of the text (Rose, 2001).

The observations on the site of the event and the field notes taken allowed for a somewhat broader perspective of the event and also gave a more nuanced and not always so picturesque representation of the event and the way in which it was structured and performed. The observations were made at the competition arena, as well as in the fair hall, in the cafeteria and in the surrounding area in Holar. The role of the observation was to get a deeper understanding of the event, a real-life experience, and these experiences also informed and became useful in conducting the analysis of the images from social media.

Festivals as markers and performances of national identity

Nations are not just geo-political entities but discursive constructs of identity and difference that include acts of inclusion and exclusion in an 'imagined community' (Anderson, 1983). Specific representations of what is typical for a nation is constructed in 'narratives of nation' including a set of stories, symbols and events that produce and reproduce meaning and delineates a nation from others (Hall, 1992).

Events and festivals may be conceptualised as communal social experiences that create; a sense of togetherness, social bonding and belonging in a space and time separate from the everyday as participants of different kind come together (Hannam & Halewood, 2006; Ziakas & Costa, 2010). An event or festival is however not only creating a sense of belonging for those who are 'insiders', and identify with the cultural expressions or activities of the event, but is at the same time also sites of exclusion for those who are not identifying with or belonging to the event (Clarke & Jepson, 2011).

Festivals and events are according to Ma and Lew (2012) possible to understand and describe by using a tourism contextual framework that distinguishes different types of festivals. This typology differentiates between festivals that are of contemporary vs of traditional origin and thereby conceptualised as more or less authentic and furthermore between festivals that are based on local identity versus uniqueness and related more or less to place-specific assets and symbolism.

National heritage festivals are one type of festivals described by Ma and Lew (2012) that is of traditional origin and perceived as authentic but not necessarily place specific in terms of the event venue. However, the degree to which a specific national event is rooted in place is not only about the importance of the location of the venue itself, but from a wider perspective also a matter of how the nation is symbolised through specific places and symbolic constructions of nation in the places where the events and festivals take place. This description of what is typical for a national heritage festival fits well with the way in which Landsmót is staged and performed, and this way of conceptualising the Landsmót event is useful for its interpretation in this chapter.

The geographical issues important for festivals and tourism discussed by Ma and Lew (2012) are local identity and uniqueness. Local identity is derived from a specific geographical location and its physical landscape, but also from history, heritage and culture of that place where the festival is an arena for the display and ritual performance of that local heritage. Tourists then come to see a site to experience the unique symbolism of the place and local identity. "Some tourist attractions, for example, develop such a high level of symbolic meaning that they become a sign of a national identity" (Ma and Lew, 2012:17)

Public rituals, such as those performed at events and festivals are important in the discursive production of belonging and 'we-ness', and the construction of difference between insiders and outsiders of national communities (Zuev & Virchov, 2014). Images and narratives of a specific place or country are expressed and reproduced through the performance at events and festivals. In the case of national festivals focused on sport heritage, such as Landsmót, the national symbolism is discursively constructed and expressed through images of landscapes, horses and participants in the festival arena.

Landsmót as a national event which carries symbolism and traditions closely connected to the national heritage of Iceland but is at the same time embedded in the landscape and specific place of the event. The event tours around Iceland, but has been taking place in the outskirts of the capital of Reykjavik quite a few times and in a few different rural places, where

Holar represents one of the most peripheral and remote locations in terms of populated centres. The national identity and symbolism performed at the horse sport event of Landsmót is largely related to the Icelandic countryside and rural identities as well as traditions of farming and horsemanship. The place-specific component is to a large extent represented by images containing landscape scenery where the rurality and the natural landscape of Iceland becomes the stage where the event takes place.

Sport can be heritage, concludes Ramshaw (2007) and points to several different ways in which sports are important components of national heritage and heritage tourism. As with all heritage, it involves ideas, values and narratives of what community and belonging means, including sometimes problematic expressions of rivalry, homophobia, sexism and even violence. Sporting events of different kind are arenas in which this heritage is celebrated and the identity discourses of the nation, region or team is manifested thorough the achievements of the competitors or athletes (Ramshaw, 2007).

One of the most powerful narratives of nation produced in sport events are where the country and nation is closely linked through performances of the sporting participants, the visitors and the event organisers. In a study by Hogan (2003) the discourses of national identity of opening events of the Olympic Games were analysed. The staging and performances of the ceremonies were found to be discursively produced and reinforcing specific versions of national identities closely related to gender, ethnicity and class. This was done through the performance of the parades, the choice of music, the flags and other national symbols and the way in which national heritage was displayed. The ceremonies at the events typically showcased the host nation's culture, history and achievement.

In this way, sporting events, just as cultural events and festivals related to arts, food or intangible heritage, they reinforce and reproduce notions of national identity in various ways. The ceremonies and performances surrounding the actual competitions are often closely related to the identities of the nation by celebrating the best athletes or competitors by a notion of the competitors as carriers of national pride and patriotic symbolism. Sporting events, such as national competitions on various sports are more or less related to national identity. The more typical or popular a specific sport is in a country or region, the more identity constructions of place and nation is incorporated in the staging and performance of the sporting event itself. One example of this is the way in which cross-country skiing, which is considered the national sport in Norway is representing Norway as a country of sporty, healthy red-cheeked people engaged in tough outdoor winter activities in the landscape. The national image of Norway is perceived to be one closely related to cross-country skiing, outdoor activities in mountainous winter landscapes (Borchgrevink & Knutson, 1997), and their national image is reproduced through international skiing competitions.

Rural gendered identities

The importance of place, such as the rural, in the construction of gender has been highlighted in geography, rural studies and tourism research since the 1990s (Cloke & Little, 1997; Pritchard & Morgan, 2000; Halfacree, 1995). Studies drawing on the notion of the rural as a social construction can be seen as a foundation for the development of understandings of the construction of associated identities. Gendering of men and women correlates with work and activities depicted as typical for the countryside, predominantly farming and forestry (Brandth, 1995; Brandth & Haugen, 2000; Little, 2002). This is similar to the ways in which masculinity and femininity are constructed in relation to nature and wilderness (Brandth, 1995; Saugeres, 2002). Nature, wilderness and agricultural landscapes are all symbolically constructed, where the male domination and physical taming of the wilderness/nature is implicit (Little, 2002). According to Woodward (2000), masculinity within the armed forces similarly focuses on physical strength to survive and express manhood in inhospitable landscapes and extreme weather conditions.

Rural societies and communities are thus highly gendered and rural spaces have traditionally been dominated by men and connected to masculine identities of agricultural production. As the countryside has been transformed from a landscape dominated by production (farming and forestry) towards a landscape of consumption and leisure, where the urban population may relax, enjoy nature and engage in sports the meaning and use of the farming landscape is challenged (Dashper, 2015; Cassel & Pettersson, 2015).

The origins of modern equestrian sports lie in the military and the different branches of the sport, such as dressage and show jumping developed from strongly masculine origins (Dashper, 2012). One outcome of the change in use of the horse from a work animal to a leisure animal has been the feminisation of horse riding and the horse industry (Hedenborg & Hedenborg White, 2012; Plymouth, 2012). Even if men are still in majority when it comes to the elite levels of the horse sports, the riders and equestrian competitors at lower levels and a vast majority if the leisure riders in Great Britain, as in the other European countries and the Western world are women. Horse riding has evolved to a predominantly female activity, and as such, it offers potentials for challenging traditional gender norms related to rurality and sports and leisure in the countryside. As her study in the equestrian world of the British countryside (Dashper, 2016) shows that women begin to challenge some of the gender norms and restrictions of rural communities as well as of sporting institutions, by the introduction of alternative rural femininities embracing physical strength, sporting capabilities and know-how in land management and horse farming. Riding and competing with Icelandic horses, as well as breeding and working on horse farms, are in Iceland work and tasks typically coded as masculine. The gender identities constructed in relation to riding and horses on Iceland are culturally and historically rooted in traditions of farming and rural life.

The branding and identity constructions of Iceland and the Icelandic horse

Iceland has experienced rapid growth in tourism in recent decades (Jóhannesson, Huijbens & Sharpley, 2010). According to Ferðamálastofa (2013) visitor numbers have more than doubled since 2002. In 2012, 673,000 visitors arrived on Iceland, and if this trend continues, the number will increase to approximately one million visitors in 2020. Therefore, tourism in the present day can be seen as one of the central pillars of Iceland's economy (Jóhannesson, Huijbens & Sharpley, 2010). One important sub-sector in the tourism industry is horse-based tourism due to the fact that in 2013 17.3% of foreign visitors went horseback-riding in the summer and 10.3% during the winter (Ferðamálastofa, 2013). Iceland is also one of the top destinations worldwide for horse-based tourism (Helgadóttir, 2006; Helgadóttir & Sigurðardóttir, 2008). The branding of Iceland has been framed around concepts of "pristine nature", "purity" and "wildness" (Ólafsdóttir & Runnström, 2011; Sæþórsdóttir, 2010), and part from tours to the natural scenery and famous sites of hot water springs, volcanoes and glaciers, tours of horse-back riding on Icelandic horses is a large tourism product and an important part of the Icelandic tourism brand. The branding of horse-based tourism in Iceland is mainly focused on the natural landscape and pristine nature in which the riding tours take place and in that way the horse-based tourism brand is closely related to the branding of nature tourism, and of the Icelandic nature and scenery in general (Husmann, 2014).

The Icelandic horse (Figure 5.1) is the only breed of horse in the country and no records exist of imported horses since around 1100. As Iceland is an island, this isolation can be maintained. This is done both for quarantine reasons and to ensure the purebred status of the Icelandic horse (Helgadottir & Dashper, 2016). Since Icelandic horses, by law, cannot be sent back to Iceland once they have been exported for competition or other purposes, the World Championships, which is the largest competition, is not known to have all the best horses. Many of them are instead kept in Iceland for breeding and shown at Landsmót.

This makes Landsmót a highly symbolic event, where the Icelandic horse is embodying the symbolism and nation specific features of the Icelandic horsemanship and equestrian culture, also an important part of the branding of Iceland. Thus, in the marketing discourse for the Icelandic horse, the official country of origin (Iceland) is central and conversely, the Icelandic horse is an icon used in destination marketing of the whole country. National branding of Iceland as a destination that is 'pure' and 'wild' is a key element in the construction of the Icelandic horse scene internationally (Helgadottir & Dashper, 2016).

Landsmót (Figure 5.2) is the site and scene where the Icelandic identity related to the Icelandic horse is expressed and performed and where inclusion/exclusion related to the community and identity of Icelandic horsemanship is taking place.

Figure 5.1 The Icelandic Horse
Source: Authors, 2017

Figure 5.2 Landsmót a national sport and heritage festival
Source: Authors, 2017

As an event with such a specific and specialised focus as the showing of and competing with Icelandic horses, it is not surprising, as Helgadottir and Dashper (2016) notes that the event functions as a marker of those who belong to the community and thus are 'insiders' of this Icelandic as well as international subworld. Apart from visiting the event, the subworld of the Icelandic horse friends is also characterised by a strong interest in Iceland and the traditions and cultural practices surrounding the Icelandic horse community. However, at the event of Landsmót, the insiders of the community are clearly separated and constructed as different from the outsiders at the event, who are called the "international friends" in the information material and at the opening ceremony. The Landsmót event is, according to the findings of Helgadottir and Dashper (2016), somewhat difficult to fully understand as an outsider, and there are several markers of difference between those who are insiders and have the full knowledge and those who are just spectators and outsiders, yet part of the event and the celebration of the Icelandic national identity and horse community. There is a strong connection between being an insider at the Landsmót event and the celebration of Icelandic nationalism.

Findings and discussion

Landsmót as a national sport and heritage festival carries symbolism and traditions closely connected to Iceland and the Icelandic, but it is at the same time embedded in the landscape and specific place where it takes place. Landsmót is touring around Iceland, but has been taking place in the outskirts of the capital of Reykjavik quite a few times and in a few different rural places, where Holar represents one of the most peripheral and remote locations in relation to populated centers. Even though the sporting competition is not international in the sense that several nations are competing against each other it is still of international importance within the Icelandic horse community and very prestigious.

The findings of the analysis of the observations that were made during the event and the image analysis of the 780 photographs uploaded on Instagram (with the tag Landsmót or Landsmót 2016 by October 2016) by organisers, participants and spectators show how the event Landsmót is highlighted as a national sporting competition and at the same time as a national heritage festival including the celebration of the Icelandic identity and culture. The themes derived from the material analyzed are: equestrian sports, national symbolism, heritage and tradition, scenic nature and landscape, gendered identities of horsemanship and rurality.

The first theme, equestrian sports, is represented in a large share of the images and is also one of the major themes structuring the content of the experience as a visitor at the event. It is by images of horses and riders in action that the event itself is promoted and visualised in marketing material and on official websites. Horses with riders at the riding arena dressed for competition with the typical clothing and gear are also a frequent attribute on posted images on Instagram. Almost half of the images of the sample (780) contained horses with riders in some form. The horses and riders participating in the competitions are depicted as strong, powerful and professional, with the riders dressed up for competition with an aura of control, strength and capability and horses in action with manes blowing and legs raised in powerful fast and/or carefully controlled gaits. The images were the riding equipages are photographed from a distance also captures some of the audience, the green lawns and landscape surrounding the arena and the presence of numerous Icelandic flags. The act of competing is depicted as prestigious and glorious and the performances of the riders and the way they are controlling their horses are highlighted by excitement and respect by the audience and the speakers at the competition.

Landsmót is constructed as a professional sporting event and at the same time as a heritage festival closely connected to national Icelandic identity and nationalism, where national flags, the language of communication at the event as primarily Icelandic, together with the images of riders and horses with the Icelandic landscape scenery as a background frames the expressions and performances of the event. The images connoting the Icelandic heritage and landscape is also together with the expectations from the organisers of knowledge about the Icelandic horse riding culture and traditions delineating the non-Icelandic from the Icelandic at the Landsmót.

The event itself is not particularly visitor friendly or international in terms of information in other languages than Icelandic or explanation of what the competition is about and the rules and procedures of the different branches and ways of counting points. This may be interpreted as unintentional, were the organisers do not really perceive of the event as an international tourist attraction and thereby did not plan for hosting visitors without special knowledge in the sport. This somewhat introvert and national focus of the event may also be interpreted as intentional where the organisers clearly understand that foreign visitors or first time visitors will not really understand what they see, but this in turn makes the competition and the event even more exclusive and mysterious. To be able to participate and take part in the different happenings in the event you need knowledge about Icelandic horse riding culture and the specific rules of the sport and that seems to create a sense of community and a clear insider/outsider relation between those who are participants and those who are spectators with limited previous experience. This is reinforced by signposts, information material and by how the event is staged. The interpretation of the event as a marker of belonging creating a notion of 'insider/outsider' has also been made previously by Helgadottir and Dashper (2016) who noted that the event is difficult to fully understand as an outsider visitor. The knowledge and traditions embedded in the notion of Icelandic horsemanship and the community of the Icelandic horse, include specific ways of dealing with horses, the symbolic and practical role of the horse in the rural communities and in the country as a whole, but also ways in which horse-people interact, dress and express the uniqueness of their identity (Helgadottir & Dashper, 2016).

The Icelandic is not only expressed in the competition arena, but is also visible and expressed in images of spectators and other participants in the ways they are dressed and the way the images of people are tagged and commented on related to Landsmót. An example of the expression of how the Icelandic is constructed and expressed in photographs are images of people dressed in heavy, warm and practical clothes such as rain gear, winter boots, hats, gloves and warm sweaters, not the least the Icelandic wool sweater was spotted on many male as well as female bodies. Comments like "the typical weather" or smiling faces in pouring rain, people slipping in muddy water and pictures of rows of tents and caravans in rain and heavy wind embedded in a vast mountainous landscape signals how the nature, landscape and the harsh weather conditions are adding to the national symbolism of the event and is an ingredient in the way of expressing the Icelandic identity as a rural identity and closeness to nature. Even in images showing sunny blue skies and green grass, it is evident that the landscape and nature itself is an important scene, adding to the overall experience.

The specific location of the event in 2016, Holar, is visualised on several images with the tag "2016". The landscape scenery with the high green mountains, small creeks and streams, with mountaintops covered in mist and the white church and small village with stone houses in white and brown in the center of the great valley forms the background and the stage for the expression of the national identity discourses at the event. The closeness to nature and the remote location of the small village of Holar frames the whole experience of attending the Landsmót, since it adds to the sense of being out in the wild nature, far from the urban world. The place of the venue itself is thus important as a specific geographical context or stage where the symbolic constructions of the nation is materialised (Ma & Lew, 2012).

The national identity and symbolism communicated in the virtual and real world, at the national sport and heritage festival of Landsmót is largely related to the Icelandic countryside and rural identities as well as traditions of farming and horsemanship. The place-specific component is to a large extent represented by images containing landscape scenery where the rurality and the natural landscape of Iceland is the stage where the event takes place. Images and observations bring about a notion of the Landsmót as part of a national heritage of Icelandic horse-back riding, combining nature and culture in a very practical and hands on way through endurance, strength and skills in how to live and spend time outdoors in cold, rainy and windy conditions together with and in close relation to horses. The images of the event highlight that it is aimed for tough and experienced people, for professionals, for Icelanders and horse-people, that are not hesitating to work hard and to be outdoors or even camp in cold and rainy weather.

The female and male identities expressed in the images of riders and breeders are closely related to rurality (rural masculinity and femininity) and the gender relations are depicted as quite equal, where both genders are depicted as in charge of the knowledge and resources necessary to be horse(wo)mans. This equality is further emphasised through the similar clothing and appearance among the participants, with focus on practical clothing for outdoors and the same dressing for competition. However, the top riders at the competition that got most attention from speaker and audience were predominantly male, and there is a tendency that the best horses were rode by men. This is also the case also in most other equestrian sports internationally, even though the equestrian sport in general is dominated in numbers by girls and women (Dashper, 2012). The images of riders are to a vast majority images of men, and the appearance of the riders and other participants at the Landsmót are dressed in ways that connote rurality. The femininities and masculinities constructed in the collection of the posted images are all closely related to the countryside and to farm life, when it comes to the participants, through clothing and through the activities related to horses such as breeding and the dealing with the horses at the arena. The female participants are depicted as strong, capable and confident, in action dealing with horses, with practical warm clothing such as overalls or rain gear, no makeup or typical (urban) feminine outfits or appearance, but rather expressing a rural femininity connected to the outdoors and thereby somewhat different from the stereotypical rural femininity of the farm women as care takers and home makers, performed in farm tourism in other Nordic contexts (e.g. Cassel & Pettersson, 2015). The expressions and performances of rural femininities at the Landsmót event is closer to the typical rural masculinities, where physical strength and the know-how of outdoor life and the domination of nature are important features (Woodward, 2000; Saugeres, 2002). This is in line with what Dashper (2016) has noted as a possible ongoing transforming of rural femininities in the countryside, through women's increased involvement in equestrian sports.

The rural femininities of the Icelandic horse women are expressed in images of Landsmót in two categories, as participants and as visitors. The participants are depicted as described earlier as strong and capable, very much with similar gender connotations as the masculine participants, yet not as glorious as the male top riders. The female visitors depicted are mostly young women in groups looking excited and interested, wearing Icelandic sweaters and practical clothing, some images also showing women in party mood at the camping site or at the arena, drinking beer and having a laugh with friends. By looking at the text attached to the tags it is easy to see that many of them are Icelandic, but quite a few of the women on the pictures are from other countries, mostly from North-Western Europe (Great Britain, Germany, Holland, Norway and Sweden). They are then most likely both insiders and outsiders, in terms of knowledge and previous experience, but all expressing femininities strongly related to rurality and signaling membership in the community of the Icelandic horse subworld, through clothing and appearance. The images of men on Instagram showed mostly men as riders in the competition, and a smaller part as visitors together with women or as part of family groups. There were no obvious images signaling that men in groups from other places and countries were visiting the festival in the same way as was obvious when analyzing the images of women. The masculinities that were expressed through the images were mainly connected to riding and the Icelandic equestrian sport, as well as visitors (mainly Icelandic) enjoying the opportunity to party and hang out with friends. In both cases, the dominant masculine identities are constructed in close relation to the notion of rurality.

The audience and spectators registered on site were both women and men in all ages, which is a bit different from for example show jumping or dressage competitions, where the audience is often heavily dominated by women. One possible explanation for this is the traditions and heritage of Icelandic horse-back riding stemming from practices of rural life and farming in Iceland and the contemporary importance of riding and keeping horses as a part of the rural communities (Helgadottir, 2006). The traditions of riding still seems to have strong connection to horsemanship and farming, closely related to masculine tasks and work (farmers), where riding is included as a natural part.

Conclusion

To finally conclude upon the analysis of the images of Landsmót, the overall impression is that the event is national and Icelandic in focus, and not really arranged as an international event, but with the symbolism of the nation as mysterious, exotic and attractive, but at the same time excluding and introvert. The relationship between the images of Landsmót and the tourism marketing of Iceland corresponds partly, were an important part of the nation brand is oriented towards nature and outdoor activities, challenging weather conditions, beautiful sceneries and the encounter with horses and strong and competent horse-people. This overall image of Landsmót clearly adds to the branding of Iceland as a tourist destination for; nature experiences, outdoors with particular focus on riding and encounters with horses. In the future, the suggestion is to promote the event more internationally and to also 'internationalise' the event by more information and the development of package tours for un-experiences visitors. Clearly, the close connection to the national heritage of riding and horse-keeping as part of a rural and typically Icelandic culture, the event may become even more important in the future as an event that attracts tourists seeking for an authentic Icelandic experience.

In terms of future research, there is a potential for refining and developing the methods and analysis of different types of user-generated content and how social media posts may be used to study the experiences of events and festivals, as well as the role of previously posted images for the expectations visitors have of the event. For future research on cultural and sport festivals as ways of promoting particular versions of national identity, there is an opening for studies that further explores how national identities are constructed and reproduced in official performances at festivals and how these may be reconstructed to become less stereotypical and more inclusive allowing for different versions of national identities to be expressed.

References

Anderson, B., (1983). *Imagined communities*. London: Verso.
Borchgrevink, C.P., & Knutson, B.J., (1997). Norway seen from abroad: Perceptions of Norway and Norwegian tourism. *Journal of Hospitality & Leisure Marketing*, 4(4), 25–46, http://dx.doi.org/10.1300/J150v04n04_02
Brandth, B., (1995). Rural masculinity in transition: Gender images in tractor advertisements. *Journal of Rural Studies*, 11(1), 123–133.
Brandth, B., & Haugen, M.S., (2000). From lumberjack to business manager: Masculinity in the Norwegian forestry press. *Journal of Rural Studies*, 16(2), 343–355.
Cassel, S.H., & Pettersson, K., (2015). Performing gender and rurality in Swedish farm tourism. *Scandinavian Journal of Hospitality and Tourism*, 15(1), 138–151.
Chen, K.K., (2009). *Enabling creative chaos: The organization of behind the Burning Man event*. Chicago: University of Chicago Press.
Chhabra, D., Healy, R., & Sills, E., (2003). Staged authenticity and heritage tourism. *Annals of Tourism Research*, 30, 712–719. DOI: 10.1016/S0160-7383(03)00044-6
Clarke, A., & Jepson, A., (2011). Power and hegemony within a community festival. *International Journal of Event and Festival Management*, 2(1), 7–19. DOI: 10.1108/17582951111116588
Cloke, P., & Little, J. (eds.), (1997). *Contested countryside cultures: Otherness, Marginalisation and rurality*. London: Routledge.
Dashper, K., (2012). Together, yet still not equal? Sex integration in equestrian sport. *Asia-Pacific Journal of Health, Sport and Physical Education*, 3(3), 213–225.
Dashper, K., (2015). Rural Tourism: Opportunities and Challenges. In: Dasper, K. (Ed.), *Rural tourism: An international perspective*. Newcastle: Cambridge Scholars (pp. 1–20).
Dashper, K., (2016). Strong, active women: (Re)doing rural femininity through equestrian sport and leisure. *Ethnography*, 17(3), 350–368. DOI: 100.1177/1466138115609379
Edensor, T., (2001). Performing tourism, staging tourism: (Re)producing tourist space and practice. *Tourist Studies*, 1, 59–82. DOI: 10.1177/146879760100100104
Ferðamálastofa, (2013). *Tourism in Iceland in Figures, April 2013*. Retrieved on January 3, 2014 from: www.ferdamalastofa.is/static/files/ferdamalastofa/talnaefni/tourism-in-iceland-in-figures-april-2013.pdf
Gilmore, L., (2010). *Theater in a crowded fire: Ritual and spirituality at Burning Man*. Berkley and Los Angeles, CA: University of California Press.
Halfacree, K., (1995). Talking about rurality – social representations of the rural as expressed by residents of 6 English parishes. *Journal of Rural Studies*, 11(1), 1–20.
Hall, C.M., (1992). *Hallmark tourist events: Impacts, management and planning*. London: Belhaven.

Hannam, K., & Halewood, C., (2006). European rgani themed festivals: An expression of identity. *Journal of Heritage Tourism*, 1(1), 17–31. DOI: 10.1080/17438730608668463

Hedenborg, S., & Hedenborg White, M., (2012). Changes and variations in patterns of gender relations in equestrian sports during the second half of the twentieth century. *Sport in Society*, 15(3), 302–319.

Helgadóttir, G., (2006). The culture of horsemanship and horse based tourism in Iceland. *Current Issues in Tourism*, 9(6), 535–548. DOI: 10.2167/cit297.0

Helgadóttir, G., & Dashper, K., (2016). Dear international guests and friends of the Icelandic horse: Experience, meaning and belonging at a niche sporting event. *Scandinavian Journal of Hospitality and Tourism*, 16(4), 422–441. DOI: 10/80/15022250.2015.1112303

Helgadóttir, G., & Sigurðardóttir, I., (2008). Horse-based tourism: Community, quality and disinterest in economic value. *Scandinavian Journal of Hospitality and Tourism*, 8(2), 105–121. DOI: 10.1080/15022250802088149

Hogan, J., (2003). Staging the nation: Gendered and ethnicized discourses of national identity in rganiz opening ceremonies. *Journal of Sport and Social Issues*, 27(2), 87–99. DOI: 10.1177/0193732502250710

Husmann, A., (2014). *Brand identity in horse based tourism: A case study if Iceland.* Degree Project in Tourism Studies, DiVA, Dalarna University, Sweden.

Jenkins, O., (2003). Photography and travel brochures: The circle of representation. *Tourism Geographies*, 5(3), 305–328.

Jóhannesson, G.T., Huijbens, E.H., & Sharpley, R., (2010). Icelandic tourism: Past directions – future challenges. *Tourism Geographies*, 12(2), 278–301. DOI: 10.1080/14616680903493670

Little, J., (2002). Rural geography: Rural gender identity and the performance of masculinity and femininity in the countryside. *Progress in Human Geography*, 26(5), 665–670.

Ma, L., & Lew, A.A., (2012). Historical and geographical context in festival tourism development. *Journal of Heritage Tourism*, 7(1), 13–31. DOI: 10.1080/1743873X.2011.611595

Mehmetoglu, M., & Dann, G., (2003). Atlas/ti and content/semiotic analysis in tourism research. *Tourism Analysis*, 8(1), 1–13.

Merkel, U., (2015). *Identity discourses and communities in international events, festivals and spectacles.* Lesiure Studies in a Global Era Series. Basingstoke: Palgrave MacMillan.

Ólafsdóttir, R., & Runnström, M.C., (2011). How wild is Iceland? Wilderness quality with respect to nature-based tourism. *Tourism Geographies*, 13(2), 280–298. DOI: 10.1080/14616688.2010.531043

Plymouth, B., (2012). Gender in equestrian sport: An issue of difference and equality. *Sport in Society*, 15(3), 335–348.

Pritchard, A., & Morgan, N.J., (2000). Privileging the male gaze: Gendered tourism landscapes. *Annals of Tourism Research*, 27, 884–905.

Ramshaw, G., (2007). Conclusion: The Future of the Sporting Past. In: Gammon, S. and Ramshaw, G., (Eds.), *Heritage, sport and tourism: Sporting pasts – tourist futures.* London: Routledge (pp. 248–260).

Rose, G., (2001). *Visual methodologies: An introduction to the interpretation of visual materials.* London: Sage Publications Ltd.

Sæþórsdóttir, A.D., (2010). Planning nature tourism in Iceland based on tourist attitudes. *Tourism Geographies*, 12(1), 25–52. DOI: 10.1080/14616680903493639

Saugeres, S., (2002). The cultural representation of the farming landscape: Masculinity, power and nature. *Journal of Rural Studies*, 18, 373–384. DOI: 1016/S0743-0167(02)00010-4

Stepchenkova, S., & Zhan, F., (2013). Visual destination images of Peru: Comparative content analysis of DMO and user-generated photography. *Tourism Management*, 36, 590–601.

Woodward, R., (2000). Warrior heroes and little green men: Soldiers, military training, and the construction of rural masculinities. *Rural Sociology*, 65(4), 640–657.

Ziakas, V., & Costa, C.A., (2010). "Between theatre and sport" in a rural event: Evolving unity and community development from the inside-out. *Journal of Sport and Tourism*, 15(1), 7–26. DOI: 10.1080/14775081003770892

Zuev, D., & Virchov, F., (2014). Performing national identity: The many logics of producing national belongings in public rituals and events. *Nations and Nationalism*, 20(2), 191–199. DOI: 10.1111/nana.12063

6 Personal networks in festival, event and creative communities

Perceptions, connections and collaborations

David Jarman

Introduction

The effective planning, delivery and evaluation of local community festivals and events is dependent on the means by which each contributor is afforded opportunities, and support, to play a meaningful role (Foley et al., 2012: 89–101). Recent years have also seen the establishment of the professional strategic event creator (Bostok, 2014), a parallel development to the modern pursuit of memorable and meaningful event experiences (Wilks, 2009). Those who seek to produce and consume events and festivals are often united through shared motivations and characteristics, yet observers must remember that 'we're all individuals' (Chapman et al., 1979). This chapter focuses on the individuals involved in creative communities, as seen in their networked context: the fundamental question driving this chapter is a need to examine personal relationships, with a view to better understanding communities and their events.

'Ego network' based research provides a means by which we might describe and examine the social environments within which festival and event creators operate, as introduced and applied within this chapter. Ego network analysis is a form of social network analysis (SNA), a broader method of enquiry that has seen increased attention and application in recent years (Borgatti et al., 2013; Christakis & Fowler, 2010; Prell, 2012; Scott, 2013). What makes ego network analysis stand out from other forms of SNA is its attention on specific individuals (egos) and the people they themselves identify as their connections (alters), whereby the nature of those connections is defined by the themes of the research (Crossley et al., 2015: 18–19). As Prell suggests, ego networks are 'defined as they are perceived and reported by respondents . . . each respondent is seen as the centre of his or her own network' (Prell, 2012: 118). From this vantage point, the observer can draw inferences relating to social capital, power and other key determinants of social influence.

Data collection for ego network research is based upon engagement with egos themselves, with the resulting network data a reflection of the ego's perceptions of their alters. As with most SNA, this is a combination of connections and attributes (Scott, 2013: 2–4): valued relationships between people (or the lack thereof), and those people's relevant characteristics. The basis on which those connections are revealed depends on what the research is trying to discover: professional connections, sources of advice and shared projects have been identified as relevant considerations when studying creative 'ecosystems' (Warwick Commission on the Future of Cultural Value, 2015). The ego's views of their alters' attributes are also key, revealing something about the sorts of people they are associating with, and resources that the ego does or does not have access to as a result. It follows that research of this kind opens up means by which social capital can be examined (Crossley et al., 2015: 25–43), as will be discussed next. If an individual's perceptions of the social world around them influence the ways they interact with it, then the more those perceptions are understood the better as such interactions can be predicted, planned for, resourced and supported.

Over the following pages, this chapter explores a variety of themes, concepts and case studies, to justify the relevance of ego network analysis in pursuing a better understanding of the social environments in which festival, event and creative practitioners operate. Two case studies are explored, presenting research into egos at the conspicuous heart of networked communities in a Scottish city. Awareness of the importance of creative communities has grown in Scotland in recent years, as seen in the publication of research (Cunningham, 2015; Desire Lines, 2015), the prominence of networking organisations (Creative Dundee; Creative Edinburgh) and the support for new co-working spaces (The Whisky Bond). Such publications and organisations highlight the contributions of both creative people and the institutions (both digital and physical) that support their work: reflections on both individuals and networks. The primary research outlined next draws from these communities, focusing on two people who hold high profile professional positions within their networked communities. Their experiences will illustrate this chapter's introduction to ego network analysis as a foundation for exploring communities, festivals and events and future research in this area.

A stakeholder focused inheritance: the primacy of perception

Much of the existing academic literature on festivals and events reveals a tacit awareness of ego to alter connections, without using the terminology of SNA. The dominant language is that of 'stakeholders', with the data collected in such research often taken from the perspective of key individuals (Getz et al., 2007; Getz & Andersson, 2010; Izzo et al., 2012). Having often been identified according to their formal position within an institutional hierarchy, respondents are then charged with representing their organisation, rather than themselves. This is despite a broadly understood and frequently articulated awareness among events academics, and their students, of the short-term nature of much work in this industry (Bowdin et al., 2011: 323–364). While both commercial and community events are often able to sustain longer-term and permanent positions, the reality for many is a more itinerant existence, without long-standing ties to a particular organisation. In this interpretation, employees and volunteers move from role to role, accumulating experiences and connections as they go (Jarman, 2016). Unless and until stakeholder-based analysis of festivals and events is able to accommodate a finer grained level of data, the unit of analysis will too often remain blurred, clumping people together into seemingly homogenous stakeholder groupings and organisations.

The underlying value and worth of a 'stakeholder centric approach' to festival and events management becomes more apparent when it helps to shape the way industry practitioners undertake their work (Bostok, 2014). Focusing on the needs and desires of one's stakeholders lies at the heart of widely accepted definitions of strategic management (Johnson et al., 2008: 3), and there is growing pressure on the broader creative industries to conform to such an approach (Higgins, 2012). This trend can imply a contractual basis to inter-stakeholder relationships, bound up with an instrumentalist approach to public policy in the arts and culture (Belfiore, 2012). However, in a sign of its pervasive success in shaping the discussion, the vocabulary of stakeholders is also used by those advocating a collaborative and socially sustainable approach to the management of festivals and events, in order to benefit the less empowered within their communities (Bostok, 2014: 23–24; Foley et al., 2012: 163–169). Bostok goes on to reinforce 'the locality as a focus' for this stakeholder centric approach to festival and event management, for it encourages practitioners to 'create value for the greatest number of stakeholders' (Bostok, 2014: 34). The relevance of perceived relationships, relative empowerment and locality are all directly applicable to the current research.

Events analysis framed within a stakeholder paradigm has thus drawn attention to a range of pertinent themes, often emphasising the role of research subjects themselves and their comprehension of the world around them. To these examples may now be added work from a 'critical event studies' standpoint, such as participatory research that emphasises the co-creation of data collection and analysis with participants themselves (Finkel & Sang, 2016). From the same volume, autoethnographic (Dashper, 2016) and ethnographic (Pavoni & Citroni, 2016) methods have been examined as potential approaches for events analysts, each in turn emphasising the importance of individuals' and events' relationships to their social environment. Contemporary events researchers are therefore the inheritors of literature that prioritises the subject of analysis in a social setting, emphasising the subject's own interpretations. Such lines of enquiry will be examined further in this chapter, drawing on the egos' own perspectives of their social and professional worlds.

This chapter, and the methods it uses, are cognisant of interpretivism's limitations and its merits, prioritising the experiences and perceptions of its subjects, and benefiting from relationships built up between them and the researcher (Dupuis, 1999: 58). Dupuis goes on to state (in a first-person account) that interpretivist researchers must set out the context and process of their work in detail (ibid), which this chapter seeks to achieve next. Before looking to such topics, discussion will first turn to instances where SNA has already been used to pursue a closer understanding of festival and event communities.

Festivals, events and social network analysis

A recent review of the literature reveals that research into festivals and events has made some use of SNA methods, to the benefit of both practitioners and host communities (Jarman et al., 2014). Work has even been done to apply SNA techniques to networks of researchers in the broader tourism field (Tribe, 2010). SNA's focus on relational data can bring fresh insights to event management issues, from the personal scale of human resources management (Jarman, 2016), to the multi-actor workings of inter-organisational relationships (Mackellar, 2006; Stokes, 2006; Ziakas & Costa, 2010). SNA has also been brought to bear on larger scale and more conceptual topics, including festivals, events and local development (Izzo et al., 2012; Jones, 2005), and the tourism policy making process (Pforr, 2006). Finally, work that places events within a dynamic 'network society' contributes to a body of literature that sees their potential as contemporary forces for progressive social change (Richards, 2015a; Richards, 2015b). SNA offers fresh perspectives and shifts in emphasis across a range of research themes: it prompts us to ask different questions, and it provides the means by which to seek answers.

The underlying conundrum at the heart of this chapter concerns the experiences of individuals within the networked environments in which they operate, and SNA excels where personal relationships are concerned. It is possible to infer and reveal much from the twin considerations of connection (the presence or absence of the ties that bind us together, as nodes in a network graph) and contagion (representing 'what, if anything, flows across the ties' between those nodes) (Christakis & Fowler, 2010: 16). SNA of festival, event and creative communities provides a means to better understand the individual relationships that they facilitate. There is also an opportunity, perhaps a requirement, for detailed research of this type to inform tangible attempts to boost network building efforts: the Leith Creative report calls for 'regular forums for connectivity', from which many of their other recommendations might be met (Cunningham, 2015). Much of this is instinctively known and understood by the members of creative and cultural communities, and it is incumbent on researchers to inform the ensuing discussion.

The wide range of situations in which SNA may be usefully applied to academic research has seen its use increase in recent years, accompanied by greater popular awareness of social networks in general (Christakis & Fowler, 2010: 252–286; Scott, 2013: 1–2). The advent of social media platforms and online collective activity has helped fuel this trend (Boyd & Ellison, 2008), although it is instructive to note the similarities and distinctions between a person's offline and virtual communities (Shirky, 2009). In either environment, SNA can tell us much about the density of a community (how well connected are its members overall), it can identify sub-groups such as clusters and cliques (areas of higher network density), and it can reveal something of the relationship between a community's core and its periphery (Borgatti et al., 2013: 181–206; Prell, 2012: 166–174; Scott, 2013: 83–98). Such analysis is typically pursued via 'whole network' research, where information is sought from or about all members of a population (Baggio et al., 2010). In this manner, whole networks are distinct from the more concentrated ego network approach, yet the former can still be revealing about individuals (Crossley et al., 2015: 8–16). From a whole network starting point, each individual's centrality within a network can be established against a range of criteria, likewise their membership of sub-groups, positions of influence and brokerage and the extent to which their position in a network reflects where they sit in a formalised hierarchy (Borgatti et al., 2013: 163–180; Prell, 2012: 95–117). SNA, therefore, provides means by which questions and responses can be offered to better understand the effective functioning of communities.

Ego network analysis in creative communities: opportunity, anonymity and methodology

The primary difference between a whole network and an ego network is the latter's focus on a single person: it is 'the network of contacts (alters) that form around a particular node (ego)' (Crossley et al., 2015: 18). Any number of motivations may lie behind the choice of ego, such as the identification of their prominence (or obscurity) in a piece of whole network research. Moreover, the nature of the whole network analysis tends to allow for the extraction of ego network information, facilitated through the judicious removal of extraneous data (ibid). As has been noted, the egos that feature in the case studies that follow have been selected because of their publicly visible and relatively high status positions within their local creative communities. The value of focusing on such individuals reflects a key finding from Edinburgh's 2001 Festivals Strategy, that many 'senior staff have worked for more than one festival or Edinburgh cultural organisation', but that 'this sense of collaboration is not co-ordinated systematically' (Graham Devlin Associates, 2001). The balance between individual experiences and collective strength was thus recognised by both policy and industry several years ago, but it is still not fully understood. Ego network analysis therefore offers a unique methodology in pursuit of this goal, to learn more about the ways an ego relates to their alters and, hence, to their wider community.

Methods

Data collection for SNA, including personal networks, is a relatively open field that can accommodate a variety of data types and forms (Christakis & Fowler, 2010; Jarman et al., 2014). It is subject to the usual methodological considerations of validity, reliability and adherence to the key themes of the research in question (Bryman & Bell, 2011: 157–161). With social relationships central to SNA, data capture might focus on social media connections, email and phone records, historical communication through archived letters, or common membership of groups and societies: SNA offers itself wherever 'people do not live in isolation, but in society' (Ormerod, 2012: 7). Attendance at the same events is another established foundation for SNA work, as found in examples of 'two-mode' network analysis (Crossley et al., 2015: 16–17). This approach typically combines two sets of data (the people and the events): individuals' connections to each other are represented by co-attendance at events; while the events are also tied where they share attendees (Prell, 2012: 16–18). Overall, Scott identifies three styles of research that are pertinent to SNA: documentary (evidenced through texts), ethnographic (via observations) and survey research (through questionnaires and interviews), as discussed next (Scott, 2013: 4–5).

Prell emphasises anonymity as among the most important ethical considerations of social research, with particular relevance to SNA (Prell, 2012: 79–81). She reflects upon the 'ownership' of a social relationship, whereby one person's perceptions of connections are being relied upon to account for something that by definition they are not solely responsible for (Prell, 2012: 80). Researchers must be cognisant of the potential for their work to impact on egos' and alters' well-being, professional standing, prospects and privacy, discussing the matter within their institution as appropriate (Bryman & Bell, 2011: 128–136). In the current research, both egos were aware of the other's participation, though only one ego and the researcher were present in each interview. As such the identity of any alters identified is known only to the researcher and the respective ego. At an early stage of the data analysis, names and other identifiers were replaced by the researcher's coding. As a corollary to this discussion, during early preparation discussions one ego highlighted the potential value of this work to their own professional interests, which include justifying their network building activities to potential funders (Fox et al., 2014: 8). Prell would likely agree that discussions around anonymity are influenced by context, which in itself is a major contributor to both the value and validity placed on any piece of social science research.

Individual interviews thus provided the foundation for the case studies that follow using specific ego network methods that rely upon the egos' perceptions of their professional relationships. These personal views and experiences are vital, almost regardless of any contradictory or complementary evidence that might be available through other means (Edwards, 2010: 7–8). That being said, mixed methods in general offer much to SNA (Crossley, 2010: 1) and preparatory desk research using a range of data has informed the primary data collection. The resulting interviews contained four distinct stages: name generator questions, position and resource generators, name interpreters and name interrelaters. When combined, they provide both the relational and attribute data on which SNA is based.

The following consideration of these methods draws from Borgatti et al. (Borgatti et al., 2013: 263–270) and Crossley et al. (Crossley et al., 2015: 44–57). These texts set out key considerations, which are considered here alongside existing research from the fields of events, festivals and tourism.

Name generators

In order to build up a picture of an ego's perceptions of their social network, a list of relevant names is required from the ego 'that we can then systematically ask the respondent about' (Borgatti et al., 2013: 263). Both key texts highlight the need to focus on specific types of connections when helping the ego to generate such a list, in line with the aims of the research. Such connections could be based on roles and relationships (such as friendships, or co-working), interactions (including meetings and mediated communication), exchanges (for example, those who provide tangible support), geography (highlighting those with a local interest) or affective ties (maybe those the ego feels particularly close to) (Borgatti et al., 2013: 263; Crossley et al., 2015: 50–52). Using multiple approaches in the same research will tend to result in overlaps between the lists of names that are generated, but it also stands a better chance of uncovering deeper complexities within the ego's perceived network, its density, tie strengths and other factors (Crossley et al., 2015: 51).

Work on the 'Tribes, Territories and Networks' of tourism academics makes use of both interviews and email correspondence to elicit relational data from its respondents, identifying overlapping, 'blurring and interconnectedness' between networks (Tribe, 2010). It is conceivable that the relatively independent nature of academics might be instructive when looking at those in the creative industries, with each environment encouraging collaborations of varying durations that help to shape an individual's perception of their social world. This work may be time consuming, demand a great deal of the interviewees, and be subject to important limitations. For example there are legitimate risks that some egos will report vast networks that require some containment, such as placing a time limit on the recency of the connections discussed, or a maximum number of alters in each category (Crossley et al., 2015: 51). Alters identified in this manner are rarely asked for consent, which raises interesting ethical considerations. Nonetheless, both in general and with reference to the current two case studies, name generator questions are vital elements in the task of representing real world networks through this form of SNA.

Position and resource generators

Rather than always asking alters to name specific individuals, position and resource generator questions tend to focus on types of people, the resources they have at their disposal, and the ego's access to them (Borgatti et al., 2013: 264). This is an exercise in empirically operationalising and representing social capital (Crossley et al., 2015: 45). Both of these texts emphasise the specificity of relevant 'positions' and 'resources' which are highly applicable to this research. For example, those working in creative communities are likely to benefit more from social connections to directors of relevant public agencies (and their funding programmes) than they might to consultants in a local hospital. Research has also shown that access to one form of resource indicates a higher probability of having access to other resources (Crossley et al., 2015: 48). Reflections on existing work in related areas are therefore vital to the task of defining relevant positions and resources to the task at hand. Festival and event stakeholder analyses are valuable here, for while they tend to look at the connections between organisations (rather than individual people), they often do so from a perspective of access to power and resources (Getz & Andersson, 2008). This latter paper, for example, draws on a range of conceptual frameworks to examine industry relationships: stakeholder theory, the political market square, new institutionalism and festivalisation are all reflected upon (Getz & Andersson, 2008: 8–10). In order to operate effectively in their creative communities, the two case study egos need access to valuable people and resources; therefore, it stands to reason that to others in the community they are themselves performing this role.

Name interpreters

The process of generating a set of alters results in a list of names that the ego and researcher can flesh out with greater detail, revealing the ego's perceptions of their alters' characteristics through a series of 'name interpreter' questions (Borgatti et al., 2013: 267; Crossley et al., 2015: 54–55). The answers provide the attribute data which can be very revealing in SNA. A key question to ask is whether the ego is most closely connected to others who are perceived to be of a common background, career stage, family situation, age, education, sexuality, race, gender or social class. SNA is an important sociological tool for those seeking to understand 'homophily', whereby we are often attracted to those like us ('selection'), and in turn, we can influence each other ('diffusion') (Christakis & Fowler, 2010: 16; Prell et al., 2010: 36). It follows on that attraction and influence can be mutually reinforcing, with implications for cultural and social capital: an ego may benefit from the close company of likeminded alters, yet this is not necessarily ideal for the receipt and dissemination of innovative ideas should they fail to penetrate a tight social circle (Crossley et al., 2015: 26–30). Knowing something about the individuals represented in a social network diagram allows for analysis of homophily within a festival network, and in addition, it allows further analysis to take place and reflect change over time through subsequent data collection (Jarman, 2016). It is this attribute data that transforms SNA from a mathematical puzzle into something with human characteristics.

Name interrelaters

Just as ego network research asks something of the alters' attributes (according to the ego's knowledge of them), it also calls on the ego to outline their understanding of ties between those alters (Borgatti et al., 2013: 268; Crossley et al., 2015: 52–54). The ego is asked to reveal their perceptions of the connections between their connections. If desired, the strength of such connections may also be captured: a researcher might ask if two alters would acknowledge each other if they met on the street, if they are believed to be close friends or if they have worked together. Depending on the nature of the research it isn't always necessary for the ego to be accurate in their judgements, for it can be their perceptions that matter most (Borgatti et al., 2013: 268). As we navigate our communities we rely upon our understanding of the social world around us, and SNA gives us means by which we might capture those instincts and put them to the test. This element of data capture recognises and emphasises the networked environment in which egos operate – a point highlighted in Baggio and Cooper's characterisation of tourism destinations as networks of organisations (Baggio & Cooper, 2010: 1758). Without capturing the relationships between alters, an ego network diagram would be a star, with all points tied to the centre and only limited structural analysis possible. However, once we add the interrelationships, some of SNA's most valuable analysis tools become available.

The four stages outlined earlier demonstrate the potential complexity of any ego network analysis focused on those working within explicitly 'creative' communities. They also suggest the means by which such a research approach may capture an individual's perceptions of their community and networks. This is explored further in the following two case studies.

Case studies: justification and data collection

In order to help justify the place of ego network analysis in this book, and the choice of case study egos to this chapter in particular, it is helpful to refer back to the overarching themes of the current volume. The workings of local communities and their events, through networks and processes of management, are explored in a number of the neighbouring chapters. Themes of sustainability, diversity and power are also present, in tune with existing work from the editors (Clarke & Jepson, 2011; Jepson & Clarke, 2014; Jepson & Clarke, 2016). The methods chosen for the current research offer an accessible means of exploring all of these topics from the unique perspectives of individual people. The two people examined here are known to be socially prominent and culturally important in their respective (overlapping) networks. This section anonymously introduces each case study in turn, alongside the sorts of organisations and projects they are most closely associated with. It then outlines preparatory information that was collected ahead of the data gathering interviews, as well as the resulting questions that formed the basis of those conversations. Initial visualisations of each ego's network are then provided.

Case study A: freelance creative producer and head of a creative industries networking organisation in Scotland

Ego A's professional life is focused on creating, building and sustaining networks within cultural communities. The organisation they lead prides itself on being among the largest networks of its kind in the city, supporting its members and promoting both the impact and value of their endeavours. The organisation's work is primarily carried out through running events, mentoring members, and hosting online showcases of their work. Ego A has also contributed to research and policy on creative communities.

Case study B: freelance festival and events producer, director of community arts festival and researcher into local creative communities

In their most prominent role, Ego B's position as director of a community orientated creative arts festival sees them coordinating an annual cycle of events and workshops, as well as the main festival itself. This person also advises and contributes to research and organisations that identify and better support those involved with the creative industries.

Round one interviews: name, position and resource generator questions

In the first round of interviews, both egos were asked to name their 'most important professional connections' when prompted by a range of criteria, thus drawing up a single list of alters around which the subsequent SNA could be carried out. No restrictions were placed on the number of contacts mentioned by an ego, except that they were asked to concentrate on activity carried out over the previous two years (Crossley et al., 2015: 51). From a researcher's perspective, it is important to recognise the considerable investments in time that can be required of egos during such data gathering, which would have been compounded had multiple sets of alters been pursued against different criteria. The decision to focus on a single list of names reduces some of this burden of duplication, and in the chosen context better reflects the fluid nature of employment and activity in the festival, events and creative industries (Graham Devlin Associates, 2001). It was, therefore, anticipated that some alters would be relevant across multiple criteria. In order to draw up a list of alters for each ego the interview focused upon three types of questions: (i) name generators based on projects that the ego had been involved in, (ii) name generators based on the ego's engagement with relevant stakeholder groups and (iii) position and resource generator questions highlighting access to alters of significance according to relevant criteria.

i The 'name generator (project-based)' questions took the form of, 'Who have been your most important professional connections for support and collaboration across your projects, over the past two years?' A list of potentially relevant projects was drawn up by the researcher in advance to prompt the egos, drawn from desk research into their principle organisations' websites and their LinkedIn profiles. These lists were systematically worked through in the interviews, with the ego identifying people accordingly and the researcher typing their names concurrently.

ii For the 'name generator (stakeholder-based)' questions, each ego was asked, 'Who have been your most important professional connections for support and collaboration in the follow categories, over the past two years?' Alters not identified from the first set of project-based questions had a chance to become apparent here, potentially identifying weaker ties (Crossley et al., 2015: 35–36). This question was based upon stakeholder categories identified in 2007 as being important in the production of festivals (Getz et al., 2007): co-producers, facilitators, suppliers and venues, audiences and the impacted, regulators and allies and contributors.

iii The 'position and resource generator' questions focused on the egos' access to people in positions of influence or status, reflecting both indirect and direct access to relevant resources. It is often appropriate to consider these two separately (Crossley et al., 2015: 45–49), though in this research they have been conflated through the form of the question, 'Who have been your most important professional contacts (if any) over the past two years when accessing people in the following positions or with access to the following resources?' As such, this research has gathered data about named alters, via the positions and resources they might provide access to. Mainstream academic events management literature has again inspired the positions and resources investigated, primarily embodied by those in influential positions within key stakeholder groups (Richards & Palmer, 2010: 152–168). These being funding opportunities and other support from the public sector, both at national and local levels; festival and event producers and artists; creative community organisers; funding opportunities and other support from commercial organisations; influential figures in the mainstream and social media; and members of the public able to reflect the views of relevant host communities.

As one might imagine with this initial round of data collection it generated a considerable list of alters' names for each ego, raising the prospect of 'respondent fatigue' which the researcher sought to manage ahead of the second round of interviews (Borgatti et al., 2013: 268). Following the lead of two studies into 'personal networks' (Marin & Hampton, 2007; McCarty et al., 2007), simple random sampling was employed on each list of alters. As noted, ego network research builds on an ego's perceptions of their alters' attributes and ego's perceptions of alter-alter connections. A list of 50 alters would require the ego to consider a daunting 1,225 undirected ties. The chosen sampling technique limits this burden and is referred to as the 'multiple generator, random interpreter', or MGRI (Marin & Hampton, 2007: 181–182). This approach retains the validity benefits of asking multiple name generator questions, which can facilitate a broader picture of an ego's network and a greater chance of uncovering their weaker ties, then takes a random sample from the ensuing list of names (McCarty et al., 2007: 309–310). Both papers comment on the relative effectiveness of this sampling technique in comparison to potential others, noting that 'the MGRI maximizes content validity, reduces respondent burden, and provides a reliable spectrum of network measures' (Marin & Hampton, 2007: 188). Comparative analysis suggests that from an initial list of 45 'free-listed alters' just ten randomly selected alters can produced 'similar structural estimates for several measures' (McCarty et al., 2007: 309). For the purposes of the current research, each ego's initial list of alters was randomly sampled using the Random Sequence Generator at random.org to produce a list of 25 alters for the second round of interviews.

Round two interviews: name interpreters and interrelaters

In a second round of interviews, carried out a few days after the initial lists of alters were drawn up, each ego was asked to comment on the randomly selected set of 25 alters produced from those lists: as before, the egos' perceptions are key.

During the 'name interpreter' phase of data collection, the egos provided information about their own attributes and characteristics, and those of their alters. With attribute data to hand, and mindful of limitations ensuing from the sampling process, it is possible to consider aspects of diversity in an ego's network and thus the presence or otherwise of 'homophily' (Christakis & Fowler, 2010: 95–134). As noted, this concept 'refers to the social situation of actors preferring to have social relationships with others who are similar to themselves' (Prell, 2012: 129). Guidance on which attributes to capture has come from the SNA literature (Prell, 2012: 129–131; Borgatti et al., 2013: 267; Crossley et al., 2015: 54–55) and from characteristics identified in recent analysis of a creative community in Scotland (Cunningham, 2015). The request to each ego was, 'To the best of your knowledge, please provide the following information about yourself and each of the people in the sampled list of your professional connections'. The attribute categories were gender, age, place of work (in geographic relation to the ego's own location), primary field of activity, employment status and employment role (including as an independent creative, or in a leadership position). These data were anonymised against the codes assigned to those alters in the sampled lists of alters.

The final stage of data collection elicited the ego's perceptions of professional connections between their alters, known as 'name interrelaters'. It is this part of the research that allows for further structural information about the network to be captured and analysed (Crossley et al., 2015: 82–83). To capture these data, each ego was presented with a large paper matrix of the sampled alters and asked, 'To the best of your knowledge, which people from the sampled list have collaborated professionally in the past two years?' (Borgatti et al., 2013: 267–269). The egos were asked to consider this question from the point of view of each alter in turn, providing an opportunity for collaborations to be identified from either perspective: a positive response either way was sufficient to count as a connection, and the resulting ties are therefore undirected (McCarty et al., 2007: 305). From the paper matrix, the researcher entered the alter-alter ties into spreadsheet software, against the same anonymised codes used for the name interpreter attribute data.

Following this exhaustive process, case study Ego A's original list of collaborators included 109 alters, reduced to 25 through MGRI random sampling. A total of 53 ties were identified between the sampled alters. The resulting network can be presented in a 'wheel sociogram' (Figure 6.1).

Ego B's original list contained 82 alters, again sampled down to 25 for analysis. A total of 18 ties were identified between the alters, as presented in Figure 6.2.

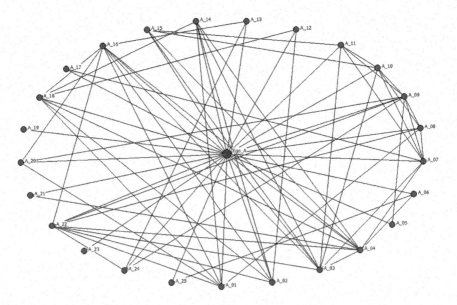

Figure 6.1 Network wheel sociogram for 'ego A'
Source: Author, 2017

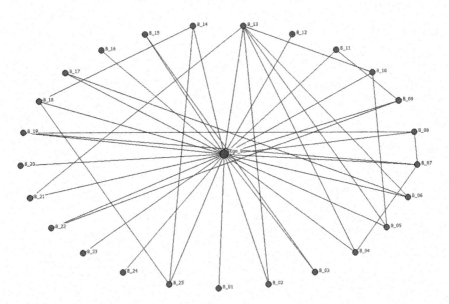

Figure 6.2 Network wheel sociogram for 'ego B'
Source: Author, 2017

Case studies: data analysis of ego network data

Analysis of the data was carried out using E-NET, a software package designed for ego network analysis (Borgatti, 2006). The structure of this section follows the themes of an accompanying introductory article (Halgin & Borgatti, 2012), in line with other sources (Borgatti et al., 2013: 270–276; Crossley et al., 2015: 76–104). Initial discussion focuses on compositional elements of the two networks, followed by structural considerations.

'Alter central tendency' and 'alter dispersion' measures provide us with a straightforward sense of the proportion of an ego's alters that are perceived to fall into one category or another (Crossley et al., 2015: 79–80). The two case studies reported the following in terms of alters' gender, age and work location, presented as percentages (Table 6.1).

It is apparent that Ego A has a somewhat more balanced network in terms of gender and age, but also one that is more heavily concentrated geographically. In contrast, Ego B's connections are notably female, in their '30s and active across a wider geographical area that extends beyond Ego B's base city. It would appear from these data that the two egos might have forged their networks on differing criteria: one based on location, the other on demographics. E-NET allows for further measures along these lines, investigating for heterogeneity using Blau's index and Agresti's IQV (Halgin & Borgatti, 2012: 42–44). Both measures reflect greater diversity where the resulting scores are closer to 1, and for these two case studies, such results are indeed observed.

Further insight is gained when data about the respondents themselves are also considered, identified as 'ego-alter similarity' (Borgatti et al., 2013: 273–274; Crossley et al., 2015: 80–82). This is an attempt to identify and describe occurrences of homophily, and by contrast heterophily, against different criteria. Both of the cited texts draw on the 'EI index' here, attributing it to Krackhardt and Stern (Krackhardt & Stern, 1988). The EI index produces results from −1 (where ego only has ties with alters in the same category as them: perfect homophily) to +1 (where ego's ties are all in different categories: perfect heterophily). This is derived from 'EI = E − I/E + I': E (external) is the number of ties ego has to alters in a different category to them, and I (internal) is the number of ties to alters in the same category as ego. Some notable results

Table 6.1 Alter attributes

	Gender: Female	Gender: Male	Age: 20–29	Age: 30–39	Age: 40–49	Age: 50–59	Work: Local area	Work: Wider city	Work: Outside the city
Ego A	52	48	16	40	32	12	64	28	8
Ego B	64	36	8	48	28	16	8	44	48

Source: Author, 2017

for Ego A include an EI for age of 0.2, rising to 0.8 for work location (reflecting heterophily). For Ego B, gender returned an EI of –0.3 (reflecting a degree of homophily), while both age and work location were relatively neutral at 0.0 and +0.1, respectively. Without access to further information, such as longitudinal data, it is not possible to distinguish between the processes of selection and diffusion that might have led to these results, although it is likely that the category of gender is governed more by the former, for example. It is known that Ego A has a more stable location in which to work that could influence the people they connect with: their primary organisation has an office in an area that contains multiple individuals and organisations with shared professional interests to Ego A. Even though their activities are citywide, with few connections identified outside the city they are primarily associating professionally with those perceived as being based in the local area. Ego B, by contrast, works across multiple projects in a more independent manner, and is less tied to a particular city for professional purposes. These network analyses, from an MGRI-inspired sample of the original lists of alters, appear to reflect the lived experiences of these two egos.

During the first round of interviews, both egos expressed an interest in noting the strength of their tie to each alter, against criteria that each ego felt to be personally appropriate. This was therefore partly a heuristic device to help the egos classify and clarify their connections. These data were captured, with a score of 1 for the closest connections and 3 for the weakest. E-NET provides a means of visualising this through sociograms: Figures 6.3 and 6.4 show the egos' networks with the ego-alter tie lengths adjusted to reflect the strength of tie.

The same data are also presented in Table 6.2, as percentages of the 25 alter random samples.

E-NET allows for the filtering of alters, although this can result in some very small sample sizes. It is however notable that when Ego A's alters are filtered for 'local' work location only 12.5% of the remaining 16 people fell into the strongest tie category, down from the 20% noted in Table 6.2 Of the seven people classed by Ego A as working outside the city, three (42.9%) were among their closest ties. This is evidence to suggest that Ego A has managed to build and maintain strong professional connections to key individuals that persist despite geographical separation, while building effective professional relationships with those working closer to home. Whether there is a potentially damaging vacuum between the two (those working in the wider city that Ego A has a professional interest in supporting) is a topic worth considering for further research.

As these reflections move towards structural approaches to data analysis, the perceived alter-alter ties captured in the second interviews become more important. These were identified on the basis of professional collaborations that the two egos were aware of. Figures 6.5 And 6.6 Help to illustrate this, employing E-NET's 'spring embedding' algorithm to reposition the nodes on the two sociogram graphs.

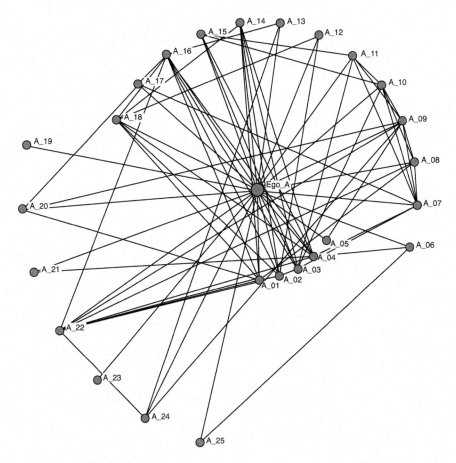

Figure 6.3 Ego A's network with the ego-alter tie lengths adjusted to reflect the strength of tie

Source: Author, 2017

These figures help demonstrate the increased complexity of Ego A's network, with its 53 alter-alter ties compared to Ego B's 18. Ego B's graph also contains six 'isolates' who are not connected to another alter, whereas Ego A has only one. Taking into account the limitations associated with the MGRI sampling, while also recognising that each ego is operating without full knowledge of their alters' professional activities, there is evidence here that Ego A feels they are operating in a denser social network. There can be advantages to this in the festival, event and creative industries communities, such as the development of trust and efficiency through more frequent or meaningful collaborations within a tighter knit group of people. Yet there are potential disadvantages to a too-tight network that risks cutting itself off

82 David Jarman

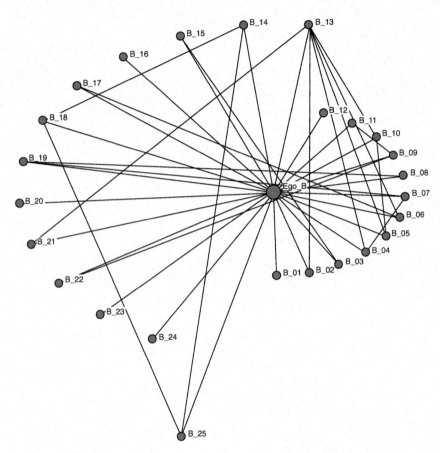

Figure 6.4 Ego B's network with the ego-alter tie lengths adjusted to reflect the strength of tie

Source: Author, 2017

Table 6.2 Perceived tie strengths

	Tie strength: 1	Tie strength: 2	Tie strength: 3
Ego A	20	52	28
Ego B	48	48	4

Source: Author, 2017

from the wider population, leaving it less capable of absorbing new information, ideas, resources and, perhaps, people. With what is known of these two egos from earlier paragraphs, there is perhaps a good fit between the apparent density of their networks and their professional interests.

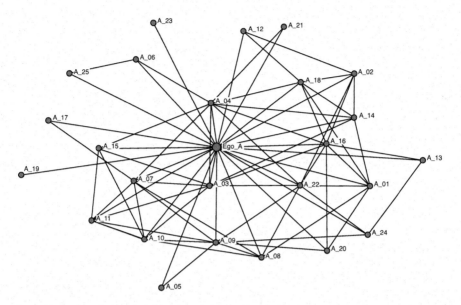

Figure 6.5 Employing E-NET's 'spring embedding' algorithm to reposition the nodes on the sociogram graph (ego A)

Source: Author, 2017

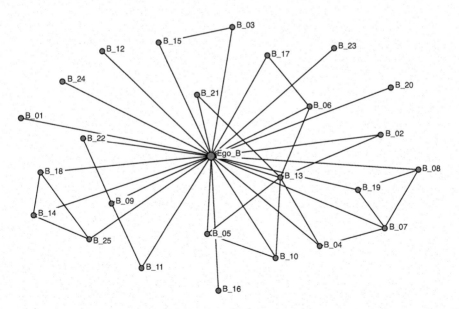

Figure 6.6 Employing E-NET's 'spring embedding' algorithm to reposition the nodes on the sociogram graph (ego B)

Source: Author, 2017

Table 6.3 Structural holes data

	Degree	Density	Effective size	Efficiency	Constraint
Ego A	25	0.088	20.76	0.830	0.126
Ego B	25	0.030	23.56	0.942	0.096

Source: Author, 2017

Consideration of 'structural holes' facilitates analysis of personal networks to the extent that the ego provides an important connection between two alters and thus potentially between different components of their network (Burt, 1992). It follows that ties to unconnected alters may provide an ego with opportunities to act as a broker between them, conferring on the ego network power that they might be able to use to the advantage of both them and (if they wish it so) their alters. It follows that consideration of structural holes is a valuable contribution to the identification and analysis of social capital (Prell, 2012: 46–47; Borgatti et al., 2013: 274–276; Crossley et al., 2015: 25–43). E-NET provides a variety of measures for structural holes, as applied in Table 6.3, with all ties assumed to be the same weight.

Here degree confirms that each network is based on 25 alters surrounding the ego. Density relates to the number of perceived ties divided by the total possible number of ties, and here has been calculated without the inclusion of ego's own ties. A lower figure, as seen for Ego B, suggests fewer opportunities for the alters to connect without Ego B's involvement: this could confer greater brokerage potential, and fewer constraints on the ego's behaviour because inconsistencies when dealing with different people are less likely to become apparent (Borgatti et al., 2013: 274). Effective size is a measure of ego's degree (in these cases 25) minus the average degree of the alters, whereby a higher figure (as seen for Ego B) reflects a greater level of disconnection between alters. This calculation is an attempt to account for the redundancy of some ties, where multiple alters might duplicate each other in providing the ego with access to resources: the ego's network is effectively smaller when this occurs (Crossley et al., 2015: 83–85). In the following section, efficiency takes effective size and divides it by degree, suggesting that a more 'efficient' network for the ego is one in which they are maintaining ties with unconnected alters who can give them access to greater resources, which is apparent in the higher score for Ego B. These data also suggest that Ego B is less constrained by their alters, whereby constraint is a measure of the alternatives open to alters to bypass the ego in their dealings (Crossley et al., 2015: 85). An ego who perceives fewer connections between their alters is one that is less constrained by those alters, more free to operate in a brokerage role and to perceive a greater level of social capital (Borgatti et al., 2013: 275–276).

Discussion and conclusions

Chris Rojek dismisses the 'people power' that is supposedly in evidence when high profile events are pressed into service to rectify some social, economic or political injustice (Rojek, 2013: 184). Likewise, in the conclusion to their paper on events and stakeholder power, Tiew et al. state their believe that 'control of critical resources is more important than network centrality in generating power for the stakeholders in an event organization' (Tiew et al., 2015: 539). To this end it's not who you know that counts, but what you've got and how effectively you can deploy it. Yet to overlook the importance of social connections is to abandon consideration of the primary context in which individuals operate. The festival, event and creative industries are networked communities, and they are only truly intelligible when a broad sense of overview and perspective is matched to the specific perspectives of those who navigate their pathways and connections. Evidence presented in this chapter demonstrates how a snapshot in time of an individual's network can reveal something of their working practices, the relative breadth and variety of people they work with, and the extent to which perceived connections between those people (or the lack thereof) might influence how the individual acts around them. It may often be true that resources can be critical, but as shown earlier, a person's social capital can be judged according to both their direct and indirect access to such assets; here it is relationships that matter.

The importance of perceptions in the process of documenting, analysing and understanding networked communities is central to the work described earlier. Data from the two case study egos is likely to be incomplete, for they should not be expected to know of every connection and collaboration between their alters. These data are also likely to be empirically wrong in parts, or at least open to interpretation, such that not every alter would classify the nature or scope of their work in the same way that has been reported by the respondent. How each ego sees their place among the 25 alters analysed here, and the remaining names on their initial list, and indeed everyone else they interact with, influences how they engage with their community. The desire, or perhaps compulsion, to invest in long-term relationships offers an individual stability, support and security. Meanwhile a more transactional relationship might present a complex yet intuitively understood opportunity for personal or collective gain, and it is instructive to note that five different forms of broker role can be considered in this regard (Prell, 2012: 125–128). Those pursuing a lower density, higher efficiency network had better have the skills at hand to maintain this pattern of relationships, or at least they should perceive this to be the case.

This chapter opened with a plea that stakeholder level analysis of festivals and events be complemented by more detailed, more nuanced forms of research, that better suit the people and the communities that host, support and manage them. It closes with a realisation that ego network analysis is only part of the answer, to which might be added other forms of SNA, qualitative evidence from the perspectives of both egos and alters, and a better understanding of the data that communities generate about themselves all day every day, including online. Where it is in the gift of researchers to help individuals and communities know themselves and what they are capable, that could be the most powerful relationship of all.

References

Baggio, R. & Cooper, C., 2010, Knowledge transfer in a tourism destination: The effects of a network structure, *The Service Industries Journal*, 30(10), pp. 1757–71.

Baggio, R., Scott, N. & Cooper, C., 2010, Network science, *Annals of Tourism Research*, 37(3), pp. 802–27.

Belfiore, E., 2012, "Defensive instrumentalism" and the legacy of New Labour's cultural policies, *Cultural Trends*, 21(2), pp. 103–11.

Borgatti, S.P., 2006, *E-Network Software for Ego-Network Analysis*, Analytic Technologies, Lexington, KY.

Borgatti, S.P., Everett, M.G. & Johnson, J.C., 2013, *Analyzing Social Networks*, Sage Publications Ltd., London.

Bostok, J., 2014, Stakeholder Centric Approach, in L. Sharples, P. Crowther, D. May & C. Orefice (eds.), *Strategic Event Creation*, Goodfellow Publishers Limited, Oxford, pp. 21–42.

Bowdin, G.A.J., Allen, J., O'Toole, W., Harris, R. & McDonnell, I., 2011, *Events Management*, 3rd ed. Butterworth-Heinemann, Oxford.

Boyd, d.m. & Ellison, N.B., 2008, Social network sites: Definition, history, and scholarship, *Journal of Computer-Mediated Communication*, 13, pp. 210–30.

Bryman, A. & Bell, E., 2011, *Business Research Methods*, Oxford University Press, Cambridge; New York.

Burt, R.S., 1992, Structural Holes, in J. Calhoun, J. Gerteis, J. Moody, S. Pfaff & I. Virk (eds.), *Contemporary Sociological Theory*, 3rd ed., Oxford, Transaction Publishers, pp. 204–19.

Chapman, G., Cleese, J., Gilliam, T., Idle, E., Jones, T. & Palin, M., 1979, *Monty Python's Life of Brian*, HandMade Films, UK.

Christakis, N.A. & Fowler, J.H., 2010, *Connected: The Amazing Power of Social Networks and How They Shape Our Lives*, HarperPress, London.

Clarke, A., & Jepson, A.S., 2011, Power, Hegemony, and relationships in the festival planning and construction process, *International Journal of Festival and Event Management*, 2(1), pp. 7–19.

Creative Dundee, About Us, *Creative Dundee*. Retrieved November 27, 2016, from http://creativedundee.com/about/

Creative Edinburgh, About, *Creative Edinburgh*. Retrieved October 9, 2016, from www.creative-edinburgh.com/about

Crossley, N., 2010, The social world of the network: Combining qualitative and quantitative elements in social network analysis, *Sociologica*, 4(1), pp. 1–34.

Crossley, N., Bellotti, E., Edwards, G., Everett, M.G., Koskinen, J. & Tranmer, M., 2015, *Social Network Analysis for Ego-Nets*, Sage Publications Ltd., London.

Cunningham, M., 2015, *Leith Creative: Understanding Leith's Cultural Resources and Creative Industries*, Leith Creative, Leith.

Dashper, K., 2016, Researching from the Inside: Autoethnography and Critical Event Studies, in I.R. Lamond & L. Platt (eds.), *Critical Event Studies: Approaches to Research*, Palgrave Macmillan, London, pp. 213–29.

Desire Lines, 2015, *Desire Lines: A Call to Action from Edinburgh's Cultural Community*, Desire Lines, Edinburgh.

Dupuis, S.L., 1999, Naked truths: Towards a reflexive methodology in leisure research, *Leisure Sciences*, 21(1), pp. 43–64.

Edwards, G., 2010, Mixed-method approaches to social network analysis, *ESRC National Centre for Research Methods Review Paper*.

Finkel, R. & Sang, K., 2016, Participatory Research: Case Study of a Community Event, in I.R. Lamond & L. Platt (eds.), *Critical Event Studies: Approaches to Research*, Palgrave Macmillan, London, pp. 195–211.

Foley, M., McGillivray, D. & McPherson, G., 2012, *Event Policy: From Theory to Strategy*, Routledge, London.

Fox, D., Gouthro, M.B., Morakabati, Y. & Brackstone, J., 2014, *Doing Events Research: From Theory to Practice*, Routledge, Abingdon.

Getz, D. & Andersson, T.D., 2008, Sustainable festivals: On becoming an institution, *Event Management*, 12(1), pp. 1–17.

Getz, D. & Andersson, T.D., 2010, Festival stakeholders: Exploring relationships and dependency through a four-country comparison, *Journal of Hospitality & Tourism Research*, 31(4), pp. 531–556.

Getz, D., Andersson, T.D. & Larson, M., 2007, Festival stakeholder roles: Concepts and case studies, *Event Management*, 10(2–3), pp. 103–22.

Graham Devlin Associates, 2001, *Festivals and the City: The Edinburgh Festivals Strategy*, City of Edinburgh Council, Edinburgh.

Halgin, D.S. & Borgatti, S.P., 2012, An introduction to personal network analysis and Tie Churn statistics using E-NET, *Connections*, 32(1), pp. 37–48.

Higgins, C., 2012, Rift deepens between Scottish artists and Creative Scotland, as despairing open letter is published, *The Guardian*. Retrieved June 22, 2016, from www.theguardian.com/culture/charlottehigginsblog/2012/oct/09/open-letter-creative-scotland

Izzo, F., Bonetti, E. & Masiello, B., 2012, Strong ties within cultural organization event networks and local development in a tale of three festivals, *Event Management*, 16(3), pp. 223–44.

Jarman, D. 2016, The Strength of Festival Ties: Social Network Analysis and the 2014 Edinburgh International Science Festival, in I. Lamond & L. Platt (eds.), *Critical Event Studies: Approaches to Research*, Palgrave Macmillan, London, pp. 277–308.

Jarman, D., Theodoraki, E., Hall, H. & Ali-Knight, J., 2014, Social network analysis and festival cities: An exploration of concepts, literature and methods, *International Journal of Event and Festival Management*, 5(3), pp. 311–22.

Jepson, A. & Clarke, A. 2014, Future of Power and Decision Making in Community Festivals and Events, in U. McMahon-Beattie, I. Yeoman, M. Robertson, E. Backer & K. Smith (eds.), *The Future of Events and Festivals*, Routledge, Abingdon, Oxford, pp. 67–83.

Jepson, A. & Clarke, A. 2016, An Introduction to Planning and Managing Communities, Festivals and Events, in A. Jepson & A. Clarke (eds.), *Managing and Developing Communities, Festivals and Events*, Palgrave Macmillan, London, pp. 3–15.

Johnson, G., Scholes, K. & Whittington, R., 2008, *Exploring Corporate Strategy*, 8th ed. Pearson Education Limited, Harlow.

Jones, C., 2005, Major events, networks and regional development, *Regional Studies*, 39(2), pp. 185–95.

Krackhardt, D. & Stern, R.N., 1988, Informal networks and organizational crises: An experimental simulation, *Social Psychology Quarterly*, 51, pp. 123–40.

Mackellar, J., 2006, Conventions, festivals, and tourism: Exploring the network that binds, *Journal of Convention & Event Tourism*, 8(2), pp. 45–56.

Marin, A. & Hampton, K.N., 2007, Simplifying the personal network name generator alternatives to traditional multiple and single name generators, *Field Methods*, 19(2), pp. 163–93.

McCarty, C., Killworth, P.D. & Rennell, J., 2007, Impact of methods for reducing respondent burden on personal network structural measures, *Social Networks*, 29(2), pp. 300–15.

Ormerod, P., 2012, *Positive Linking: How Networks Can Revolutionise the World*, Faber and Faber, London.

Pavoni, A. & Citroni, S. 2016, An Ethnographic Approach to the Taking Place of the Event, in I.R. Lamond & L. Platt (eds.), *Critical Event Studies: Approaches to Research*, Palgrave Macmillan, London, pp. 231–51.

Pforr, C., 2006, Tourism policy in the making: An Australian network study, *Annals of Tourism Research*, 33(1), pp. 87–108.

Prell, C., 2012, *Social Network Analysis: History, Theory & Methodology*, Sage Publications Ltd., London.

Prell, C., Reed, M., Racin, L. & Hubacek, K., 2010, Competing structure, competing views: The role of formal and informal social structures in shaping stakeholder perceptions, *Ecology and Society*, 15(4), pp. 34–52.

Richards, G., 2015a, Events in the network society: The role of pulsar and iterative events, *Event Management*, 19, pp. 553–66.

Richards, G., 2015b, Festivals in the Network Society, in C. Newbold, C. Maughan, J. Jordan & F. Bianchini (eds.), *Focus on Festivals: Contemporary European Case Studies and Perspectives*, Goodfellow Publishers, Oxford, pp. 245–54.

Richards, G. & Palmer, R., 2010, *Eventful Cities: Cultural Management and Urban Revitalisation*, Butterworth-Heinemann, Oxford.

Rojek, C., 2013, *Event Power: How Global Events Manage and Manipulate*, Sage Publications Ltd., London.

Scott, J., 2013, *Social Network Analysis*, 3rd ed. Sage Publications Ltd., London.

Shirky, C., 2009, *Here Comes Everybody: How Change Happens When People Come Together*, Penguin, London.

Stokes, R., 2006, Network-based strategy making for events tourism, *European Journal of Marketing*, 40(5/6), pp. 682–95.

Tiew, F., Holmes, K. & De Bussy, N., 2015, Tourism events and the nature of stakeholder power, *Event Management*, 19, pp. 525–41.

Tribe, J., 2010, Tribes, territories and networks in the tourism academy, *Annals of Tourism Research*, 37(1), pp. 7–33.

Warwick Commission on the Future of Cultural Value, 2015, *Enriching Britain: Culture, Creativity and Growth*, University of Warwick, Coventry.

The Whisky Bond, About, *The Whisky Bond*. Retrieved November 27, 2016, from www.thewhiskybond.co.uk/about/

Wilks, L., 2009, *Initiations, interactions, cognoscenti: Social and cultural capital in the music festival experience*, Open University (unpublished PhD thesis).

Ziakas, V. & Costa, C.A., 2010, Explicating inter-organizational linkages of a host community's events network, *International Journal of Event and Festival Management*, 1(2), pp. 132–47.

7 Innovation in rural festivals
Are festival managers disempowered?

*Grzegorz Kwiatkowski and
Anne-Mette Hjalager*

Introduction

Rural festivals are numerous and remarkably diverse happenings. Ranging from harvest festivals to cultural celebrations and sports events, festivals have become a significant source of enjoyment, inspiration and business opportunities for the rural communities' members and visitors alike (Andersson, Getz & Mykletun, 2013; Gibson, Connell, Waitt & Walmsley, 2011; Jepson & Clarke, 2014). The dynamic development of the festivals' market in rural areas contributes to their attractiveness and resilience (Derrett, 2003; Jamieson, 2014; Kostopoulou, Kourkouridis & Xanthopoulou-Tsitsoni, 2015; Reid, 2011). If it is unique, authentic and fascinating enough, festival supply may create its own additional demand. However, if continued in a repetitive and non-innovative way, the festival market may also become overcrowded, leading to a fiercer competition.

The worldwide popularity and the economic importance of festivals have led to a wealth of research on the topic in recent years (Getz & Page, 2015; Wilson, Arshed, Shaw & Pret, 2016). However, most business related research on festivals is focused primarily on economic impacts on communities (e.g. direct economic impact, tax revenues, increased employment) (Kwiatkowski, 2016; Kwiatkowski, Diedering & Oklevik, 2017), whereas there is limited understanding of many other facets of the business-festival landscape including innovation, managerial and entrepreneurial aspects (Getz, 2010; Buch, Milne & Dickson, 2011; George, Roberts & Pacella, 2015; Hjalager, 2009; Hjalager & Kwiatkowski, 2017).

Rural festivals must evolve constantly in order to grow and contribute to the host community welfare. This process requires an empowerment of managers of single festivals, teams of managers as a group, and the sector as a whole. In this context, empowerment is defined as a participatory and trust-creating process that can accelerate business development both in scale and in scope (Andersson & Getz, 2009).

This study draws upon empirical evidence from 315 rural festivals hosted in Denmark, and collected through a survey among festival managers. Taking into account that festival management in Denmark is largely a bottom-up process occurring in a multi-actor environment (Hjalager & Kwiatkowski, 2017) the main question driving this contribution is to what extent festival management is empowered or disempowered in its endeavours to innovate the festivals. The study maps the organizational landscape of the Danish rural festivals and examines the local and external collaborative structures.

The presentation of the study in this chapter is structured as follows: Firstly, a literature review on empowering organizers in rural festivals for the benefit of innovation is presented. Secondly, the data collection and methodology is described. Thirdly, the results are summarized. Finally, conclusions are drawn and practical and policy-related implications are discussed.

Empowering organizer innovation in rural festivals

This study acknowledges the many different aspects of emerging festival research. First, attention is paid to an organizational angle of the festival literature, in which a number of studies have emphasized the importance of understanding how festivals are organized and stakeholder roles identified (Getz, Andersson & Larson, 2007; Larson, 2002; Reid, 2011). Second, this study also pays attention to the managerial literature which considers festivals as any other business activities where the exercise of coordinating authority may be of decisive importance for the festivals' successful operation and innovative development (Håkansson & Snehota, 2006). In connection therewith, the empowerment concept is of great relevance to explore in closer detail.

Several studies illustrate that a festivals' organization is a complex task which involves the coordination among multi-level layers of festivals functioning (Crespi-Vallbona & Richards, 2007; Getz, Andersson & Larson, 2007; Karlsen & Stenbacka Nordström, 2009; Reid, 2011). The festival's organization involves the management of entrepreneurial endeavours at a singular festivals level, but also connectivity with local resources and advantages stemming from building portfolios of events.

Drawing on a comprehensive study of the festival stakeholders' role, among others in rural areas, Getz, Andersson and Larson (2007) conclude that festivals are collaborative endeavours, and they defined the festival's organizer "as a dependent co-producer of a festival within a network of organizations and other stakeholder groups" (Getz, Andersson & Larson, 2007: 104). Accordingly, the organizer of the festival holds a position of authority to include and exclude other stakeholders in the festival production (Getz, Andersson & Larson, 2007; Clarke & Jepson, 2011). Therefore, as indicated by Getz, Andersson and Larson (2007: 106), "the organizer is the main gatekeeper exercising boundary control, and thereby controlling and coordinating cooperative activities and product development of the festival".

However, although the festival's organizer holds a position of power, other actors possess critical resources for the festival organization. Consequently, the organizer's power to decide, change and act independently is the subject of some dependency. Larson (2002) indicates, however, that not all festivals' stakeholders have the same position in the festival production, and categorize them as "replaceable" and "nonreplicable" stakeholders. Furthermore, among the first category, Larson (2002) identifies stakeholders which are exchangeable, as for example food and beverages providers and those, which substitution might be difficult and time consuming, for example sponsors. Undoubtedly, a nonreplicable festival's stakeholder, and thus somewhat privileged in the festival production, is a municipality. This is because, as indicated by Getz, Andersson and Larson (2007: 106) due to its "authority to decide if, when, and, to a certain degree, how the festival is to be organized".

As Getz, Andersson and Larson (2007: 121) point out,

> The festival organizations must strive to become institutions in their resource environments. This goes beyond the common strategies employed to obtain resources and reduce resource dependency. Institutionalization involves becoming so important to the community that the festival or the organization cannot be abandoned even in extreme cases of financial failure. It involves the creation of a unique support network so committed and powerful that the network itself takes ownership.

Under certain conditions, it is a question to what extent the festival organizers actually have the possibility to execute this sort of institutionalization, influence and decisive power. As showed by Clarke and Jepson (2011) festival directors might gain power and hegemony over the stakeholders involved in the festival from a number of techniques – e.g. restricting knowledge, using sites of power, and reducing the right to gain resistance to said power, the civilizing process. It is of critical importance to ensure that festivals are not matters of effortless stability and unquestioned continuity. Some festivals depend on discontinuity in the sense that they have to come up with novel offers in the program every year (Carlsen, Andersson, Ali-Knight, Jaeger & Taylor, 2010; Larson, 2009, 2011). Some stakeholders might want to change or adapt their role, or withdraw their participation entirely. Particularly in the most successful festivals, new stakeholders might want to join and strive to become part of the trend. Furthermore, Getz, Andersson and Larson (2007) and Karlsen and Stenbacka Nordström (2009) as well as Batty (2016) find that stakeholders frequently assume multiple roles. Hence, there is a plea for conflicts of interests and opportunity for synergy effects within stakeholder relationships. Especially, the role of the festival's host municipality is ambiguous, since it simultaneously serves as a regulator, partner and a co-producer of the festival (Getz, Andersson & Larson, 2007; Karlsen & Stenbacka Nordström, 2009; Batty, 2016). This, in turn, complicates the organizers' role as the gatekeeper, manager and power broker.

Accordingly, the reviewed literature illustrates that the collaborative structures of festivals are both complex and critical for their operation and management. The field of studies, which investigates different aspects of festivals' relations to their stakeholders, is emergent, and has hitherto been concerned with identifying different kinds of stakeholders "their roles and interactions, management of festival stakeholders, and their influence on festival strategy and survival" (Andersson & Getz, 2009: 8). Studies have been undertaken to classify different categories of stakeholders (Getz, Andersson & Larson, 2007; Larson, 2002; Reid, 2011), to look into stakeholder management strategies (Andersson & Getz, 2008), the way in which stakeholders influence the festival's organization (Spiropoulos, Gargalianos & Sotiriadou, 2006), different roles which stakeholders play when it comes to the sustainability and institutionalization of festivals (Andersson & Getz, 2009), as well as local inclusion in the festival construction process (Clarke & Jepson, 2011).

Donaldson and Preston (1995) highlight that festivals compete for resources and only the most efficient survive. In the same vain, Getz and Larson (2007) point out that managers must become skilled at managing stakeholders' relationship that can generate support and resources for the festival. Other sources support this point of view, yet struggle to accept that the world of festivals rarely adopts to business-like practices (Karlsen & Stenbacka Nordström, 2009).

The use of the empowerment concept serves to enhance the understanding of the festival organization and to address the managerial paradoxes mentioned earlier. "Power" and "influence" are issues raised in connection with particularly large and commercially orientated events (Parent, 2008; Frawley, 2015), a centralized phenomenon. In contrast, empowerment is a concept often used in terms of the mobilization of resources and enacting changes – for example, in (rural) communities reflecting the entire constellation of stakeholders (Anderson, Tyler & McCallion, 2005), heightening self-determination, improving intentionality and critical reflection on behaviour and encouraging effective behaviour are thought to maximize goal. However, more radically, empowerment means providing support for constructive self-help in ways that will be sustainable and viable in the longer term. This approach involves the creation of frameworks for equity and open decision making in the community. Accordingly, empowerment is advocated both for its efficacy and for the humanistic and democratic values it is associated with. The empowerment agenda is therefore widely recognized and accepted as a road to development (Craig & Mayo, 1995). In the process of upgrading and improving physical environments, providing people with the opportunity and the right to voice their opinions as well as to negotiate the fulfilment of their requests is considered essential. Access to relevant, unbiased information is very important. Notably, and crucially, locals are considered "experts" in their own area and capable of contributing new perspectives and ideas (Herbert-Cheshire, 2000). Institutions and agencies that grow from the bottom-up and that are composed of highly committed citizens can produce a rapid improvement in such areas. Self-esteem is thought to spread much like a *"virus"* under optimal circumstances, allowing capacity building to continue with voluntary effort. Positive processes that succeed without notable external assistance are often the ultimate outcome of community empowerment (Clark, Southern & Beer, 2007; Edwards, 1998).

In a spatial context, three dimensions of empowerment can be identified. In practice, these dimensions are not entirely separable. First, there is *self-empowerment* through an individual action, based on a self-directed interest of, in this case, festivals' entrepreneurs and their ability to transform ideas into innovation and profit.

A second category of empowerment pertains to "community relations", which involve a strong emphasis on the participation of many actors in the festival organization, with equal power, in more loosely coupled decision-making processes. Empowerment in community relations normally necessitates the establishment of structures that facilitate collaboration. When these structures are successfully created, power is not a zero-sum game, in which one organization's or individual's power diminishes that of another organization or individual (Rowlands, 1995). Instead, multiple structures and networks in a community are able to create a bridge between the interests of individuals and groups of different categories of organizations and inhabitants. These structures are sustained by charismatic individuals with specific competencies and profiles.

The third level of empowerment is "bridging structures" that formally distribute power and influence spatial boundaries. In other words, outsiders may hold significant influence on community empowerment and ensure knowledge transfers of critical importance for festival innovation processes.

The literature surrounding empowerment in events and festival management mainly addresses how disadvantaged groups may get a possibility to expose values and to gain recognition (Marschall, 2006; Odahl-Ruan, McConnell, Shattell & Kozlowski, 2015; Richards, 2016). Within the empowerment terminology, there are not many, if any, contributions which address the complex relationships between the rural festivals' stakeholders in charge of organizational matters. The different levels of the empowerment in rural festivals need further inquiry and analyses – an endeavour that this chapter commences.

Methods and data analysis

This study has strong empirical foundations in a uniquely large dataset, one of the first of its kind, covering 315 festivals hosted in the Danish countryside. Rural areas are defined according to the governmental definitions and include mainly parishes outside the eight biggest cities and these cities' rural hinterlands. The identification of the festivals took place by the media analysis, particularly Internet resources, and through contacts to a large variety of tourist and business organizations, authorities and interest groups. Altogether, 521 festivals were found, of which 60.5% agreed to take part in the online survey. To approach the leading person within the festival organization and to motivate him/her to response, all festivals were contacted by telephone prior to forwarding a structured questionnaire.

Data were collected in spring 2015 by means of an online survey with the intention that it was answered by the key individuals related to each of the festivals (e.g. acting leader, director organizer or funder). The survey collected data regarding (1) the festival's theme, history, occurrence and duration; (2) the objectives of the festival; (3) the festival's organizational and cooperative structure; and (4) the importance of the festival for the local community and various stakeholders. The questionnaire consisted mainly of close-ended questions with a single or multiple choice answers. The responses were measured using a five-point Likert-type scale, in which a lower score indicated stronger agreement (i.e. 1 = strongly agree; 5 = strongly disagree). The data exploration was based on all the usable observations available for a given question, which ranged between 209 and 315 observations. The study included also 14 qualitative case studies, details from these are also used in this article to support analysis.

The methodological part of the study involves calculation of the summary statistics, the Pearson's correlation test and calculations of the "connectivity index", which measures the "attachment" of particular types of festivals (e.g. according their theme, and the responsible organization) to local and external stakeholders. It has been calculated as a weighted average of the number of organizations involved multiplied by the number of hits in particular category and divided by the total number of the involved organizations.

The Danish rural festival scene

Over the past decades, Danish rural festivals' landscape has gained momentum. There has been a numerical and thematic proliferation of festivals followed by an increase in the audience size consisted of locals, day visitors and tourists. About 42% of the 315 rural examined festivals related to music (multi-purpose answers allowed), 20% to sports, 15% are markets types of festivals, 14% organized experiences in food, 14% contain arts and crafts as their dominant ingredients, and 51% served one or more special interests, for example within the fields of history, hobbies, religious and spiritual topics, etc. Many festivals have a significant and long history, and they have emerged from the agricultural heritage, but, nevertheless, succeeded in innovating their offers to become also appealing to new groups of customers. Indeed, recent years have witnessed a growing interest in organizing festivals with special interest, of which some remain rather small and conventional. On the other hand, the rural areas could become a platform for truly sophisticated or high cultural festivals such as opera festivals or open policy summits. Accordingly, the Danish festival landscape is found to be vital and for most of it thriving. The study shows, though, that the survival of some of the examined festivals is short, and evidence from both the survey and in-depth interviews indicate that all rural festivals need to pay a careful attention to continuity and the renewal.

Partnerships and stakeholder involvement in the festival organizations

The chapter is concerned with the organizational and managerial aspects of festival staging. The analysis is focused on individuals and groups of people, and the practice of their organization in the context of complex festivals organization and management. A principal finding from the conducted study is that rural festivals are, to a great extent, "home-grown". They are founded on and depend on active and socially cohesive local community organizations such as leisure clubs, agricultural associations, business collaborative units, tourism promotional originations, museums, churches, municipalities and local action groups. This study provides evidence that the existence of festivals in the rural areas would not be possible without the healthy ecosystem of local organizations which mobilize dedicated actors and commit manpower for both managerial and operational tasks. The organizations gain from the participation in terms of both identity, meaning and collaborative "glue", but also in terms of an allocation of funds for community work. There are only a few purely commercial and non-home-grown festivals among the 315 festivals examined in this study. Table 7.1 presents a breakdown of the number of organizations who are collaborating with the main organization responsible for delivering the festival.

Table 7.1 features the number of organizations involved in the festival as collaborating partners apart from the main responsible organization. As it can be seen, about one-third of the examined festivals is self-contained, whereas the remaining part benefits from collaboration with up to two local organizations (i.e. out of some 315 examined festivals 204 (64.5%) benefit from collaboration with local organizations, whereas 54 festivals (17.1%) do so from non-local organizations). Among the festivals collaborating with local organizations (n = 204), the majority cooperates with one (29.9%) or two organizations (21.1%). In the case of 40.2% festivals, a dedicated festival organization has been established to organize a festival. The recruitment of new stakeholders to a festival organization typically takes place by asking individuals known in the community for their networks and ability to make things happen. Those individuals tap into other local organizations, as can be observed in Table 7.2. Sports organizations often play a critical role for collaboration, partly because they have a (historically) important role in Danish rural communities and because of the possibility to recruit volunteers among members of the sports organizations.

A similar situation occurs in terms of the 54 festivals profiting from non-local organizations, where every second festival indicates one non-local

Table 7.1 Number of organizations involved in the festival as collaborating partners apart from the main responsible organization

Number of collaborating partners	Local organizations Total	%	Non-local organizations Total	%
0	111	35.2	261	82.9
1	61	19.4	26	8.3
2	43	13.7	12	3.8
3	22	7.0	11	3.5
4	27	8.6	0	0
5	14	4.4	1	0.3
6+	37	11.7	4	1.3
Total			315	

Source: Author, 2017

Table 7.2 The Pearson correlation between the number of involved organizations and several distinctive characteristics of the examined festivals

	Number of locally involved organizations	Number of non-locally involved organizations
Number of visitors 2014	172**	012
Number of volunteers 2014	217**	220**
Age of the festival	029	063
Number of days	008	034
Growth of festival 2010–2014 participants	0.029	0.015
Growth in exhibitors	24%	61%

Note: Number of observations: 209–315

Source: Author, 2017

organization as a collaborating partner. This result clearly illustrates that to a large extent, festivals are free-standing, and the formal partnerships are limited to a few organizations embedded locally. As such, it can be concluded that the formal non-local collaborative outreach of the Danish rural festivals is meagre. In the following, the Pearson correlation was computed to assess the relationship between the number of involved organizations in the festivals' organization and several characteristics of the examined festivals listed in Table 7.2.

The results show that there is a positive correlation between the number of volunteers engaged with the festival and the number of involved organizations, no matter of their origin (i.e. both local and non-local). Furthermore, the results show positive correlation between the number of non-locally involved organizations and attendees' figures, meaning that the larger festival is, the more significant the collaborative outreach is established. Interestingly, neither the length of the festival, nor its growth in recent years reveals a significant relationship with the number of involved organizations. Therefore, the results could indicate that larger festivals in the Danish countryside need to mobilize additional resources in order to exist. The mobilization of such resources occurs through local networks and it is rather independent from festivals' length or age. Involvement and collaborations takes place through the volunteers, rather than by means of the formal organizations. Moreover, the results demonstrate a crucial role of volunteers for larger festivals organizations and collaboration forming. The most self-contained festivals are the festivals with lower number of attendees.

Rural festivals are dynamic, and thus, it is of relevance to analyse whether more recently formed festivals forge more local and external alliances than the earlier-founded ones. As it can been seen in Table 7.2 the age of festivals is not an indicator of the partnership formation, but the connectivity index presented in Table 7.3 provides a hint to the importance of the thematic coverage. The niche festivals are by far the most networked, both locally and externally. A tractor-pulling festival represents an example from the study, where actors in local retailing are particularly active as well as sports organizations. For the benefit of marketing beyond the local area, the festival management envisaged the importance of orchestrating external activities with charity organizations and a radio station. Also, the art and craft festivals are well connected. For example, the organizational structures behind the Knitting Festival are eager in activating numerous local institutions and

Table 7.3 Connectivity index (by up to three main variables in the festival)

Festival's type	Partnership	Number of festivals	Connectivity index
Music	Local	133	2.24
	External		0.26
Sport	Local	101	1.67
	External		0.30
Art Craft	Local	67	2.75
	External		0.58
Market	Local	44	1.66
	External		0.20
Niche	Local	104	5.02
	External		1.11

Note: Number of observations: 237–315

Source: Author, 2017

associations, including the school, the senior organizations, the municipality, the museum and the tourist board. Externally formed contacts and partnerships are organized by knitting specialty groups in Denmark and abroad.

This information underlines the importance of the empowerment through alliances with local organizations. It is less frequent to establish partnerships with external actors, a step that would lead to an invitation of influence from strangers to the organization, no matter the benefits that collaboration could provide.

Purpose of organization and partnership creation

The results presented earlier suggest that festival organizers prefer to centralize power and influence, and thus responsibility, with the main organizational body. This might be considered as a pragmatic approach, as weakening of a centralized impact on the festival creation can lead to unwanted situations. The responsible manager of the Apple Festival claims, for example, that the negotiations with the municipality and the police authorities require an accumulated competence, and the centralization of this task works most effectively. There is also a need for "firm" operation at the event venue, where exhibitors set up tents in a way that all exhibitors have access to the flow of the audience, and that sanitary conditions become properly handled.

The low number of the established partnerships, particularly in relation to external partners, may also reflect a lack of networks. Asked about this, the manager of the Viking Market in Orø claims to have a rich external network, but chooses to mobilize resources through local structures and partnerships. The locals should not get the impression that the festival is governed by "arrogant introducers" from the metropolitan area. Table 7.4 shows our analysis in the form of a Pearson correlation between festival purpose and the number of organizations involved in the festival.

Table 7.4 features the results of the Pearson correlation between the purpose of the festival and the number of involved organizations. The results show a significant and positive relationship between the number of locally involved organizations and a series of festivals' objectives (i.e. (a) to promote and market the local area where the festival takes place, (b) to create more social cohesion in the local area, (c) to attract tourists to the area, (d) to keep old traditions and culture alive, to enhance creativity and resourcefulness and (f) to establish contacts between stockholders from and outside the local area).

This result suggests that the larger number of involved organizations positively influences realization of festivals primary objectives. An explanation of this situation might be the festival managers' belief that the larger number of stakeholders might create a synergy effect among individuals and groups of stakeholders.

Table 7.4 The Pearson correlation between the purpose of the festival and the number of involved organizations

	Number of locally involved organizations	Number of non-locally involved organizations
To promote interest in the activities and topics directly associated with the festival	0.042	0.076
To entertain	0.064	0.071
To promote and market the local area where the festival takes place	0.197**	0.018**
To create more social cohesion in the local area	0.264**	0.020
To attract tourists to the area	0.157**	0.030
To keep old traditions and culture alive	0.148*	0.082
To enhance creativity and resourcefulness	0.166**	0.115
To establish contacts between stockholders from and outside the local area	0.217**	0.054
To strengthen member engagement in associations.	0.055	0.009
To utilize and expose a specific local resources and specific characteristics	0.101	0.115
To create economic wealth for the festival organizers	0.001	0.012
To fundraise for associations and voluntary organizations	0.139*	0.039

Note: Number of observations: 237–315

Source: Author, 2017

Empowerment of the festival organizers

The aforementioned evidence illustrates that the rural festivals have, in terms of organization, a distinct local dependency. The empowerment of organizing actors is connected to the local environment, whereas the formal participation of external partners is rare. This is further illustrated in Table 7.5, which examines the associations between the established collaborations and the assessed local impacts. In line with the aforementioned findings, the local connectivity tends to be an explanatory factor that positively influence the number of locally involved organizations, with no significant effects revealed for the external partnerships. The seasonality aspect shows, however, a significant and positive correlation with the number of the external relationships, which might indicate that expanding the season requires stronger external relationships.

Table 7.5 A Pearson correlation between the festivals' assessed impacts and the number of involved organizations

	Number of locally involved organizations	Number of non-locally involved organizations
The media has influenced that the area has become better known	0.198**	0.093
The festival started as a mainly local attraction. but grow to attract also people from outside	0.131*	0.001
The festival has contributed to the viability of local associations	0.205**	0.012
The festival has contributed to the renewal of the identity of the local area among people from outside the area	0.192**	0.074
The locals have come to know each other better	−238**	0.043
Participating organizations have built competences that are useful in other contexts	0.224**	0.057
There have been conflicts with locals who do not like the alert	0.124*	0.027
The festival has created new networks with the outside world	0.199**	0.017
The festival is a good argument to move to the area	0.158*	0.107
The festival attracts a larger number of tourists	0.174**	0.073
The festival means more visits from the larger cities in the region	0.158*	0.058
The festival expands the tourist season	0.108	0.138*

Note: Number of observations: 237–315
Likert scale inversed

Source: Author, 2017

Findings and conclusion

This chapter has sought to create further understanding as to whether festival organizers are disempowered in introducing new directions to a festivals development and innovation. Particular focus was paid to the local and external collaborative structures within the Danish rural festival scene.

The results provide further evidence that the Danish rural festival market is vital and positively contributes to rural resilience. Moreover, the study demonstrates that the examined festivals are tightly integrated with the local organizations of different size and genres. In fact, the examined festivals frequently rely on services provided by local partners, including enterprises, organizations and individuals. However, in terms of the formal setup, here understood as the number of partners involved in the festival organization, the rural festivals are surprisingly more poorly integrated. The most striking finding stemming from this study is that the formal cooperation with partners from outside the local area is fairly negligible, which indicates that local partners are chosen, whenever possible, in a situation of formal partnerships' necessity.

There are several reasons for the limited outgoing attitude among festival managers, of which a central might pertain to the fact that dedicated festival organization's boards engage people active also in other organizations. In this respect, the festival organizations embed people and "fence" them into board logic. This can be regarded as way to empower the person or persons in charge, giving them a (necessary) freedom of operation and discretion in decision making. The qualitative part of the study provided examples of festival managers who bring the power to a board and exercise a significant influence on festivals functioning, in an attempt to, for example, eliminate the escalation of controversies associated with local events. Interviews also illustrate that a yearlong festival-commitment from one person is based on a personal compassion, charisma and the ability to motivate followers. In other words, a strong engagement of one person might be better for a smooth operation and sponsorship acquisitions than a "blurred" responsibility of too many individuals.

Festivals are arenas for self-empowerment. The study demonstrates that the organizing bodies and the responsible persons have, over time, acquired competences and practical skills that can be useful outside festival organizations. This includes, for example, the handling of emerging problems with associated partners and authorities that often have different priorities and goals, multitasking and are working under pressure (Lead time). The management of a festival for a longer period of time may, for some of the active partners, lead to other jobs and commitments, also in different sectors. Therefore, skills related to exercising authority towards exhibitors and visitors are rather universal managerial competences of high value in many businesses and jobs.

The community empowerment as a result of "festivalization" comes up strongly in this study. The communities here are empowered by successful festivals which cause numerous side effects, embracing both the tangible (e.g. direct economic impact, employment effects, tax revenues) and the intangible (e.g. civic pride, community integration, feel-good factor) effects to host destinations that together might be a potentially rich source of local well-being. The effect is widened when more partners are involved. This comes from the sharing of responsibility, and the commitment. Sharing in this sense, might mean that an individual manager or a team of managers find themselves in situations where more has to be negotiated and less can be decided top down. This is concurrent with the international literature on the festivals organizations, which further highlights the importance of bottom-up and inclusive planning processes (Clarke & Jepson, 2011).

However, the choice of collaborative partners in the local area seems to be carefully considered and the result shows that the stakeholders' resources and capacity are of great importance. Sports organizations are popular partners, possibly due to their high volume of volunteer manpower in disposal. Public authorities also have a high position, possibly due to financial resources and ability to make things happen. Contrary, the formal partnerships with actors outside the community are fairly weak. Festival organizers choose not to widen the field of authority and power beyond the community to any great extent, and *bridging structures* seem to be very rare. This may be of positive importance for the ability to control the festival from within. It might also be discussed whether the lack of formal bridging arrangements can hamper the innovative potential of the rural festivals. In favour of this argument might be the fact that the newest categories of rural festivals are also better linked with external partners, which in turn suggests, that mutual knowledge can contribute to the continuous development of the festivals' organization, contents and marketing.

This study has provided an initial insight into the realities of stakeholder relationships in rural festivals. The evidence presented here suggests that managers are not disempowered, and what they do and how they organize their alliances aims to stabilize the foundations of their own managerial groups' influence, and they are largely successful with this endeavour.

A closer inspection of the emerging types of festivals there is a reason to question the consolidating forces for the long-term sustaining of the rural festivals. The art and crafts and the niche festivals demonstrate the needs to be much more open and inclusive than more conventional types of festivals.

Innovative rural festivals must involve themselves with others and build bridges to the urban environments. The study portrayed LittTalk, which is indeed an example of the tendency. The festival is a small literature festival, but its attempts to communicate with the rest of the country make them festival attendants in new ways, mimicking the format and style of the more famous TedTalks.

As an avenue for future research, it would be worthwhile analysing more in-depth a single or a small number of rural festivals in order to carefully trace out the mechanisms of local and external partnerships forming, and thus provide more evidence on the "power-influence" paradox. Furthermore, it is equally important for future studies to broaden analyses about other stakeholders' – for example, the authorities – standpoints on collaboration with festival organizers.

References

Anderson, D., Tyler, P. and McCallion, T. (2005). Developing the rural dimension of business-support policy. *Environment and Planning C, 23*, pp. 519–536.

Andersson, T. D. and Getz, D. (2008). Stakeholder management strategies of festivals. *Journal of Convention & Event Tourism, 9*, pp. 199–220.

Andersson, T. D. and Getz, D. (2009). Tourism as a mixed industry: Differences between private, public and not-for-profit festivals. *Tourism Management, 30*(6), pp. 847–856.

Andersson, T. D., Getz, D. and Mykletun, R. J. (2013). Sustainable festival populations: An application of organizational ecology. *Tourism Analysis*, 18(6), pp. 621–634.

Batty, R. (2016). Understanding stakeholder status and legitimate power exertion within community sport events: A case study of the Christchurch (New Zealand) city to Surf. In A. Jepson and A. Clarke (Eds.), *Managing and Developing Communities, Festivals and Events* (pp. 103–119). London, England: Palgrave Macmillan.

Buch, T., Milne, S. and Dickson, G. (2011). Multiple stakeholder perspectives on cultural events: Auckland's Pasifika festival. *Journal of Hospitality Marketing & Management*, 20(3–4), pp. 311–328.

Carlsen, J., Andersson, T. D., Ali-Knight, J., Jaeger, K. and Taylor, R. (2010). Festival management innovation and failure. *International Journal of Event and Festival Management*, 1(2), pp. 120–131.

Clark, D., Southern, R. and Beer, J. (2007). Rural governance, community empowerment and the new institutionalism: A case study of the Isle of Wight. *Journal of Rural Studies*, 23(2), pp. 254–266.

Clarke, A. and Jepson, A. S. (2011). Power, Hegemony, and relationships in the festival planning and construction process. *International Journal of Festival and Event Management*, 2(1), pp. 7–19.

Craig, G. and Mayo, M. (1995). *Community Empowerment: A Reader in Participation and Development*. London: Zed Books.

Crespi-Vallbona, M. and Richards, G. (2007). The meaning of cultural festivals: Stakeholder perspectives in Catalunya. *Journal of Cultural Policy*, 13(1), pp. 103–122.

Derrett, R. (2003). Festivals, events and the destination. In I. Yeoman, M. Robertson, J. Ali-Knight, S. Drummond and U. McMahon-Beattie (Eds.), *Festival and Event Management: An International Arts and Culture Perspective* (pp. 32–50). Oxford: Butterworth Architecture.

Edwards, B. (1998). Charting the discourse of community action: Perspectives from practice in rural Wales. *Journal of Rural Studies*, 14(1), pp. 63–77.

Frawley, A (2015) Happiness research: A review of critiques. *Sociology Compass* 9(1), 62–77.

George, D., Roberts, R. and Pacella, J. (2015). "Whose festival?" Examining questions of participation, access and ownership in rural festivals. In A. Jepson and A. Clarke (Eds.), *Exploring Community Festivals and Events* (pp. 79–91). London: Routledge.

Getz, D., Andersson, T., & Larson, M. (2007). Managing festival stakeholders: Concepts and case studies. *Event Management*, 10, 103–122.

Getz, D. (2010). The nature and scope of festival studies. *International Journal of Event Management Research*, 5(1), pp. 1–47.

Getz, D., Andersson, T. D. and Larson, M. (2007). Festival stakeholder roles: Concepts and case studies. *Event Management*, 10(2–3), pp. 103–122.

Getz, D. and Page, S. J. (2015). Progress and prospects for event tourism research. *Tourism Management*, 52, pp. 593–631.

Gibson, C., Connell, J., Waitt, G. and Walmsley, J. (2011). The extent and significance of festival. In C. Gibson and J. Connell (Eds.), *Festival Places: Revitalising Rural Australia* (pp. 3–43). Bristol, UK: Channel View Publications.

Håkansson, H. and Snehota, I. (2006). No business is an island: The network concept of business strategy. *Scandinavian Journal of Management*, 22(3), pp. 256–270.

Herbert-Cheshire, L. (2000). Contemporary strategies for rural community development in Australia: A governmentality perspective. *Journal of Rural Studies*, 16(2), pp. 203–215.

Hjalager, A. M. (2009). Cultural tourism innovation systems – the Roskilde festival. *Scandinavian Journal of Hospitality and Tourism*, 9(2–3), pp. 266–287. doi: 10.1080/15022250903034406

Hjalager, A. M. and Kwiatkowski, G. (In Press). Entrepreneurial implications, prospects and dilemmas in rural festivals. *Journal of Rural Studies*. http://dx.doi.org/10.1016/j.jrurstud.2017.02.019

Jamieson, N. (2014). Sport tourism events as community builders – how social capital helps the "Locals" Cope. *Journal of Convention & Event Tourism*, 15(1), pp. 57–68.

Jepson, A. and Clarke, A. (2014). Defining and exploring community festivals and events. In A. Jepson and A. Clarke (Eds.), *Exploring Community Festivals and Events* (pp. 1–13). London and New York: Routledge.

Karlsen, S. and Stenbacka Nordström, C. (2009). Festivals in the Barents Region: Exploring festival-stakeholder cooperation, scandinavian. *Journal of Hospitality and Tourism*, 9(2–3), pp. 130–145. doi: 10.1080/15022250903157447

Kostopoulou, S., Kourkouridis, D. and Xanthopoulou-Tsitsoni, V. (2015). Rural tourism development and cross-border cooperation: Networking local products festivals. *Journal of Tourism Research*, 10, pp. 77–94.

Kwiatkowski, G. (2016). Composition of event attendees: A comparison of three small-scale sporting events. *International Journal of Sport Finance*, 11(2), pp. 163–180.

Kwiatkowski, G., Diedering, M. and Oklevik, O. (2017). Profile, patterns of spending and economic impact of event visitors: Evidence from Warnemünder Woche in Germany. *Scandinavian Journal of Hospitality and Tourism*, pp. 1–16. doi: 10.1080/15022250.2017.1282886

Larson, M. (2002). A political approach to relationship marketing: Case study of the Storsjöyran festival. *International Journal of Tourism Research*, 4(2), pp. 119–143.

Larson, M. (2009). Festival innovation: Complex and dynamic network interaction. *Scandinavian Journal of Hospitality and Tourism*, 9(2–3), pp. 288–307.

Larson, M. (2011). Innovation and creativity in festival organizations. *Journal of Hospitality Marketing & Management*, 20(3–4), pp. 287–310.

Marschall, S. (2006). Creating the "rainbow nation": The national women's art festival in Durban, South Africa. In: Picard, D., & Robinson, M. (Eds.) *Festivals, Tourism and Social Change: Remaking Worlds* (pp. 152–171). Clevedon: Channel View.

Odahl-Ruan, C., McConnell, E., Shattell, M. and Kozlowski, C. (2015). Empowering women through alternative settings: Michigan Womyn's music festival. *Global Journal of Community Psychology Practice*, 6(1), pp. 1–12.

Reid, S. (2011). Event stakeholder management: Developing sustainable rural event practices. *International Journal of Event and Festival Management*, 2(1), pp. 20–36. doi: 10.1108/17582951111116597

Richards, S. J. (2016). The space of the film festival. In *The Queer Film Festival* (pp. 217–237). New York: Palgrave Macmillan.

Rowlands, J. (1995). Empowerment examined. *Development in Practice*, 5(2), pp. 101–107.
Spiropoulos, S., Garagalianos, D. and Sotiriadou, K. (2006). The 20th Greek festival of Sydney: A stakeholder analysis. *Event Management*, 9(4), pp. 169–183.
Wilson, J., Arshed, N., Shaw, E. and Pret, T. (2016). Expanding the domain of festival research: A review and research agenda. *International Journal of Management Reviews*, 19(2), pp. 195–213.

8 The effects of supply chain management (SCM) activities and their impact upon festival management and the customer experience

W. Gerard Ryan and Stephen Kelly

Introduction

As the number of festivals and the need to provide more satisfying customer experiences continue to grow, the challenges faced by festival managers have become more complicated than ever. The demand to reduce costs and maintain quality, while dealing with the increasingly complex health and safety, sustainability, regulatory and technological landscape means that festival organisers are becoming progressively more reliant on their inter-organisational/delivery partners to sustain and improve their ongoing operational activity. These developments in festival delivery reflect how the competitive environment has changed. There has been a shift from organisations acting more in isolation, competing through strong brands and marketing budgets to competitive practices that actively involve all the organisations who provide goods and services in a particular supply chain (Christopher 2016). Supply Chain Management (SCM) provides a new dimension to the earlier models of competition, as collective co-operation can lead to the provision of superior value to customers. This chapter will offer insights into how the effective and efficient management of SCM carries additional benefits to festival delivery.

All of the organisations in a festival supply chain need to externally enhance information sharing and internally reduce differences between departments (Elrod et al. 2013; Aloini et al. 2015). This should be achieved not only from how festival managers maximise their own resources, but also in respect to how they manage the supply chain they are engaged in. Therefore, the competitive advantage achieved through effective and efficient SCM can only be achieved when the supply chain is clearly understood and managed well.

Although there has been substantial research on the relationship between event organisers, clients and suppliers in the events industry (Ritchie 1984; Allen et al. 2008; Emery 2010), this has tended to focus on stakeholder management (Ritchie 1984; Reid and Arcodia 2002; Arcodia and Reid 2005; Getz 2007; Chen 2011) in which a single or small number of direct suppliers are considered, or on specific supply related issues within logistics (Bowdin et al. 2011; Getz 2012; Shone and Parry 2013). A SCM perspective is prevalent in a number of different industry areas (Croom 2000), but the use of this more holistic perspective that this chapter advocates is thought to be very limited in festival management.

This chapter provides novel insights by investigating the application of SCM concepts and theories in a festival management context and asks whether it is possible to derive any insights for practice and theory that might improve the overall festival experience for festival attendees and suppliers alike. Taking a SCM perspective on the challenges and issues that festival organisers face, this chapter uses a focussed case study to make two contributions to the festival and event studies literature. First, the study illustrates the complexity and multiplicity of supply chains in the festival industry and highlights the reliance on trust, customer visibility and communication within the overall supply chain. Second, the chapter applies two models (theories) from the mainstream SCM literature – namely, the Bullwhip Effect and the Kraljic's Purchasing Portfolio Model to reveal the complex interactions between individual organisations in the supply chain. The main concept behind the Bullwhip Effect is the increasing swings in purchasing in response to shifts in customer demand as one moves further upstream in the supply chain (Lee et al. 2004; Okada et al. 2017) while the purpose of Kraljic's Purchasing Portfolio Model is to help purchasers maximise supply, security and reduce costs by making the most of their purchasing power and adopting purchasing practices that fit the goods and services they are buying (Padhi et al. 2012; Grefrath et al. 2017).

These models can illustrate the different pressure zones that can be created by poorly managed information flows; resulting in the adoption of inappropriate decision making. The main benefit to practice created when each organisation considers the other organisations involved in the festival supply chain is that operational activity is more effective and efficient. By adopting these approaches, this chapter argues that improved outcomes can be achieved that benefit everyone within the festival supply chain including; the audience's satisfaction, superior health and safety conditions, improved communication both up and down the supply chain and improved visibility of all those involved.

Overview of SCM in festival management

There have been a number of different areas that have contributed to the current research on SCM – e.g., purchasing, logistics, marketing, organisational behaviour, strategic management and economic development (Croom 2000). To provide some context to the conceptual perspective, a supply chain is the journey of goods and services, from a raw product to the end user (in this case the festival audience). Figure 8.1 provides an example of a supply chain taken from a 'traditional' SCM setting in the manufacturing sector.

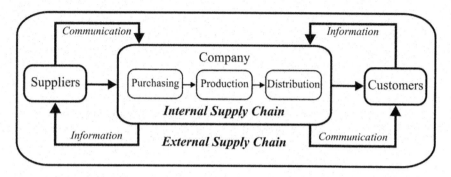

Figure 8.1 Simple diagram of activities and firms in a supply chain
Source: Bratić 2011

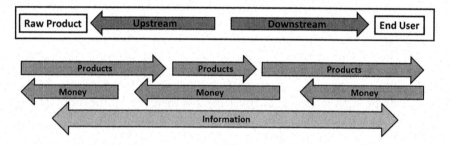

Figure 8.2 Multi-directional flow within a supply chain
Source: Ryan and Kelly 2017

Of course, the representation of any supply chain will look different from each organisation's perspective, since management of each organisation is likely to see its own organisation as the focal organisation and consequently will view its supply chain position and structure differently (Lambert and Pohlen 2001).

SCM is maintained through flows of money, information and products or services that move multi-directionally within the supply chain. These can move either upstream (towards the supply base) or downstream (towards the customer/end user). Generally, money flows upstream as it is introduced into the supply chain by the end user (by paying for tickets) while products or services flow downstream and back towards the customer to satisfy their requirements (e.g. the experience, live performance) as shown in Figure 8.2.

Monczka and Morgan (1997) suggest integrated SCM concerns moving from the external customer and then managing all the processes that are needed to provide the customer with value (or perceived value) in a horizontal way. In other words, information flows up and down the supply chain in the form of order information, new product information and demand, etc. (Slack 2009). Indeed, one of the key areas for co-ordinating amongst supply chain members is the management of information flows (Lee et al. 2004). There are exceptions to this as products in the process can be returned, money is often refunded and goods can be recycled. More sophisticated versions introduce concepts of value and trust (Christopher 1992; Ying and Xiaolin 2008; Oosterhuis et al. 2012) that is created between organisations within the supply chain.

Much of the work on SCM has its roots in manufacturing and production, with a more recent turn towards service industries and therefore it is not surprising that the SCM perspective is relatively underdeveloped in the festival and events field. Much of the literature that exists today focuses more on sustainability (Case 2013), supplies (Goldblatt 2008; Rutherford-Silvers 2012), suppliers (Ferdinand and Kitchin 2012; Rogers 2013; Daniels 2014), but not actual overall supply chain activities. The key characteristics of a festival supply chain show that a collection of diverse companies and individuals need to connect with each other to provide goods or services to a festival to ensure a satisfactory experience for the end user. Considering the importance of SCM in the delivery of all events, it is surprising to note its virtual non-existence in events education today (Ryan 2016). Festivals by nature are a coming together of numerous suppliers and therefore festival managers are becoming increasingly reliant on the performance of their suppliers within the supply chain. The study of SCM and events management is therefore all the more important. It is against this backdrop that a number of challenges to the festival supply chain exist and to which this chapter aims to address.

Festival suppliers are faced with an increasing pressure to reduce outgoing costs in an environment that is over-reliant on one source of income (Presenza and Iocca 2012). The demand for more cost-effective festivals and events has become important either because of increased national and international competition (Calvin 2012), increasing expenditures and requirement for more specialised technology (Robertson 2015) or the increase in complex legislation and regulation such as health and safety standards and environmental legislation (Arnott and Freire 2010; Lee et al. 2010; Markwell and Tomsen 2010; Tandon et al. 2012).

Basu et al. (2013) suggest the key challenges associated with events develop around the management of risk, resources, operations planning and stakeholder engagement. In light of these impacts and the actual nature of how a festival is brought together, it is now very unusual for festival organisers to perform all aspects of productive activity themselves (i.e. be fully vertically integrated).

The difficulties that festival managers experience when sourcing and dealing with suppliers has been discussed fairly widely (Reid and Arcodia 2002; Tum et al. 2006; Fields and Stansbie 2007; Yeoman et al. 2007; Bowdin et al. 2011; Shone and Parry 2013). These include the need to obtain cost-effective goods and services balanced against quality of product, the hire, make or buy decisions such as in-house or outsourcing production or service supply and services that go towards avoiding tensions between participant stakeholder groups. When tensions are experienced between participant stakeholders and poor management of suppliers, the knock-on effect can lead to a number of complications which impact on the event itself. This can include event cancellation, programme reduction or quality problems (Getz 2012, p. 277). This chapter considers these issues and seeks to understand if a study of the wider supply chain can provide any insights into how these problems occur.

Methods

This chapter uses a single in-depth case study, which involved interviews with multiple individuals and organisations in a festival supply chain. The relatively limited amount of research into SCM in festival and events management meant that empirical research was necessary if models and frameworks were to be proposed that can be used further (Burgess et al. 2006). Although this chapter is exploratory in its empirical research setting, it is testing theory from outside the traditional scope of events and festival literature, through the application of SCM principles. More quantitative methods of data collection and analysis would not be suitable since they offer little in terms of explanatory depth, which was needed for the research objectives of exploring festival supply chains and deploying SCM concepts, theories and models in this specific setting. Generalisability is often cited as a criticism of qualitative research and although such research is very specific to this context and a specific set of relationships between specific individuals, it does "provide sufficient information that can then be used by the reader to determine whether the findings are applicable to the new situation" (Lincoln and Guba 1985, p. 125). Although the context of the setting may not be replicated in other scenarios (as different organisations and individuals will be involved) it should be noted that the intent is to generalise to theory (Gioia et al. 2013) through showing the usefulness of the analytical framework and therefore being analytically rather than statistically generalisable (Yin 2002, p. 32).

To ensure research quality, we have made use of specific guidelines identified by Riege (2003), which have been widely accepted to demonstrate the rigour undertaken in qualitative research. Specifically, dependability concerns were addressed by careful data management through recording interviews wherever possible. There were several chance meetings where data was obtained that could not be recorded. However, field and verbal notes were taken as soon as possible afterwards. Similarly, having two research interviewers involved at certain stages increased this area of quality consideration. Furthermore, triangulation plays a key role in this area of research quality and therefore multiple perspectives from different interviewees were considered as well as the use of organisational artefacts to support findings.

The case of this chapter is a collection of organisations that, at this particular time and in this particular context, have buyer-supplier relationships with each other in the pursuit of providing services to festivals as part of a broader festival supply chain. The primary research included one-to-one interviews with senior individuals from three different organisations within a festival supply chain. These included the following:

- The national account manager (NAM) for Organisation A that is an international high-end Public Address (PA) system manufacturer
- Four directors (1, 2, 3, and 4) from Organisation B who are an international UK-based PA supplier to festivals and the music industry
- The festival director of a multi-international UK-based music festival (Organisation C) that attracts an audience in excess of 250,000 each year to its UK outdoor festivals

The interviews themselves took the form of semi-structured interviews that were based around a number of fundamental questions that covered purchasing activities, relationships with customers and suppliers, sourcing products and sales, the methods involved in these activities and the issues involved within the methods used. The semi-structured nature of the interviews allowed for open discussions that established how each organisation functioned within the festival supply chain and also what purchasing practices were used in line with the requirements from their customers and their customer's customers.

As the supply chains of organisations are often not openly revealed and therefore knowledge of them cannot be fully established prior to close organisational contact, snowball sampling (Babbie 2001) was used to obtain contact details and also introductions to other organisations in the focal supply chain. This ensures that matched pairs of organisations in the supply chain are included in the data collection, as they will be discussing the same goods/services that ultimately will be provided to the same set of customers.

Findings and discussion

This section is divided into two main parts and which reflect the objectives of this chapter. Firstly, we developed a view of the festival supply chain by identifying the different organisations within the supply chain study. This informed the need for the analysis in the second section which zooms in on specific interactions between organisations within a supply chain and considers the theory of the Bullwhip Effect and Kraljic's Purchasing Portfolio Model to provide a more structured discussion of the ramifications of these issues. A schematic of a supply chain was developed based on the data collected and supported by relevant organisational documentation. To illustrate the inherent complexity, a layered approach was developed that opens up the supply chain in much more detail and highlights the main area of focus. Figure 8.3 provides a view of a supply chain for a large festival and details the typical flow of information, money and products.

By focusing on a single supply chain (as per the circled area in Figure 8.3), the public address; a supply area, the complexity and relevant factors of

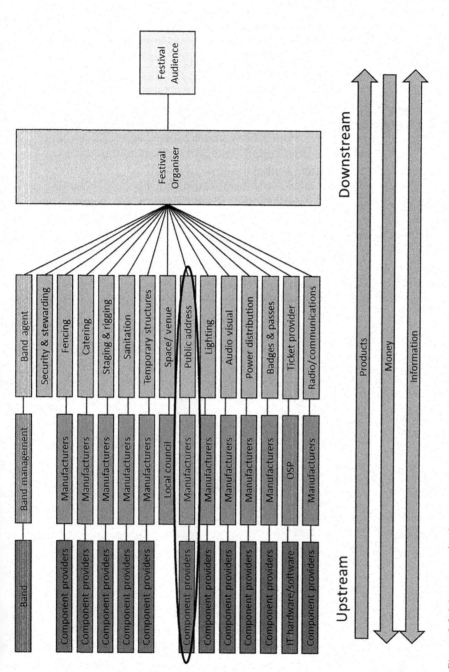

Figure 8.3 Macro supply chain representation for a large outdoor music festival
Source: Ryan and Kelly 2017

supply chains within supply chains emerges. To keep the supply chain diagrams at a manageable level, the links between festival suppliers have focussed on core supply, – i.e., the supply of products/services that relate to the direct products/services that the focus organisation provides to their customers. This means that areas of non-core supply and provision, which support the running of festival suppliers, such as electricity, furniture, stationery and shipping, are not included in these representations. However, it is recognised that these still play a role in the overall delivery, as they are indeed areas of expense for festival suppliers and they should still be appropriately managed with effective purchasing practices. It is important to point out that festival suppliers often supply multiple festivals within different supply chains at the same time (adding to the complexity), but for this initial study, each supply chain is considered a separate entity. Figure 8.4 shows a representation of a micro supply chain as it would be for a large outdoor music festival.

The data collected has been taken from a number of different organisations that constitute an individual supply chain in the larger representation shown in Figure 8.3 The focus of this study and supply chain is reconfigured in Figure 8.5 to show the range of organisations involved in manufacturing right through to the festival audience. The circled communication arrows

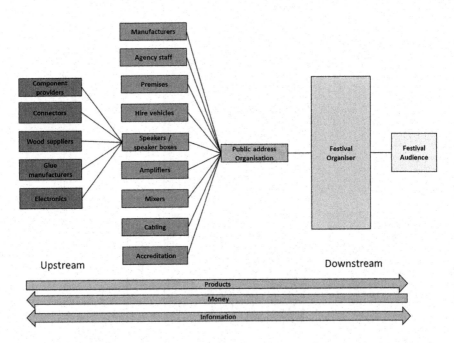

Figure 8.4 Micro supply chain representation for a large outdoor music festival
Source: Ryan and Kelly 2017

highlight the source of the primary data and can be organisationally represented as follows:

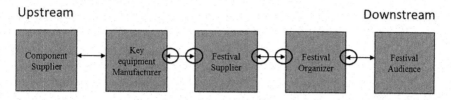

Figure 8.5 Organisations, primary research and communication points within the supply chain
Source: Ryan and Kelly 2017

Having established the specific nature and complexity of a festival supply chain, two key areas are revealed; the key role of information flow and purchasing behaviour, which are now discussed in turn.

The key role of information flows in the supply chain

As shown earlier, in the discussion of SCM, a key driver of co-ordination amongst supply chain members is the management of information flows (Lee et al. 2004) and in particular the flow of demand information – i.e., what and when products/services are needed (Lambert 1998). Some of the challenges identified in this study and mapping process showed that information flows, and their unpredictable nature, highlighted problems with the way the organisations functioned – for example, the impact of the Bullwhip Effect on the rest of the supply chain. The Bullwhip Effect was first observed between Proctor & Gamble and its suppliers where slow moving consumer demand created large swings in production for the suppliers at the other end of the supply chain (Wang and Disney 2016). This effect can lead to companies making unexpected changes to their working practices to counter these issues.

During the interview process, it was revealed that companies within the supply chain regularly have to review their purchasing activities. Previously, Organisation B had followed a purchasing process that allowed each department to order components as and when the need arose. While this gave more control to each department to deal with supply and demand issues, it created an environment that suffered from pressure purchasing, leading to a lack of control of inventory and finances within the business with problems such as double ordering of stock and oversights on what items readily available for use. In order to combat these and other issues, Director 2 of Organisation B was made responsible for all purchases to reduce waste, tighten up on financial expenditure and bring inventory under control. Director 2 explained,

> Purchasing on the whole is done more on opportunity now, taking advantage of when discounts are available [from our suppliers]. Only if

rigs are on the road and unavailable and a big hire comes in is a pressured purchase made.

Similarly, when reviewing purchasing activity after a long-term development programme to offer wider availability of their product in each territory, Organisation A observed better sales revenue, but a reduction in their profit margins. While this effort had created much greater access to their systems, the NAM detected that the increased competition between new and existing account holders was driving the price of their product down. More importantly, the available reserves that sustained the after-sales service and maintenance expected of a high-end product were being constricted. Considering an average purchase price of between £75,000 and £300,000, the after-sales maintenance was central to the ongoing customer satisfaction and the high-end status of the product. In order to counter this, Organisation A made the decision to reduce the number of points of sale (account holders) and introduce a global programme of Certified Providers (CPs) reducing the widespread access to their product in the United Kingdom from 35 account holders to 9 CPs with enlarged sales territories.

The NAM explained that by reducing the number of points of sale, they were not only able to maintain much more control over the final sale price, the trust levels between manufacturer and festival supplier increased substantially. The most notable development was almost complete visibility of the manufacturer's customer's customers. These improved levels of trust between manufacturer and festival suppliers led to closer engagement and collaboration with the customer's customers. The increased visibility provided new opportunities and levels of access that had never existed which led to direct discussions about the design of each project. Previously, communication would have ended one step further up the supply chain. By reducing the number of points of sale, the manufacturer was able to provide direct advice further down the supply chain on technical specifications. This new flow of information also created improvements up the supply chain such as informed design suggestions before the final proposal was submitted. The resulting impact both up and down the supply chain was ultimately enhancing the experience for the festival audience end user. The NAM stated, "Because we (Organisation A) became heavily involved [with our customer's customers] a much more informed understanding was created" improving the final product and virtually removing the Bullwhip Effect from the supply chain, which could have led to major implications at a later date.

With the increasing attendance at major festivals, greater demands are placed on everyone within the supply chain. Festival suppliers experience amendments in key aspects of the planning activities which then require an ability to respond rapidly to keep the event and supply chain on track. If we take a supply chain perspective of these, we can see that issues may arise as these challenges flow downstream towards delivery. We have described how the Bullwhip Effect means that as problems arise, they become amplified further up the supply chain. When these problems are not addressed, then the effect can lead to a tipping point in the organisation's ability deal with the problem, which as Akkermans and Vos (2003) suggest can lead to significant issues in delivering goods and service. Practices that may seem rational from a local and short-term perspective lead to issues in the overall supply chain and ultimately affect the end user experience (Anderson et al. 2005).

From the empirical data, further complexities were revealed that highlight the pressure not only to provide a quality experience but also to deliver on time and at a profit. Often, in festival and events management, there is a critical period of time just before a deadline, (assumed or agreed), when actual decisions are made. At the highest level, organisations will usually have a number of festivals and events to supply at the same time and ensuring all the necessary equipment is available and arrives in a satisfactory and working condition is dealt with on a regular – or as Director 2 of Organisation A suggests "as regular as is possible" – basis. This suggests there are a number of different demand patterns at multiple levels throughout the process.

Although demand patterns have a major effect on the events final 'experience' they appear downstream (closer to the customer) of the supply chain and can (or should) be fairly easy to predict in aggregate terms – for example, the actual date of the festival. As we discovered, this does not flow upstream until much later as signing contracts and agreements can be left until very late on in the process. Consequently, the risk and time pressure is pushed towards the festival suppliers in how they manage their capacity (e.g. buy, service or manufacture products, hire or lay staff off). The managing director of Organisation B stated, "We did a lot of festivals last year and it's not like you're given a 3 or 4-year contract even when you do supply a great experience. You've got to win each contract year-on-year".

This kind of activity manifests itself in pressure zones, contributing to the Bullwhip Effect on the final experience being created for festival suppliers during the day, the week and the year. For example, festivals are held at regular times throughout the year. Therefore, certain months are particularly busy and decisions at that time are affected by the added pressure. It was explained by Director 2 from Organisation A that pressure on repairs to equipment receives a rush towards the end of the week as the weekend is largely the busiest period for festivals and events. Then towards the end of the working day, pressure is increased on individual staff members as calls and enquiries both internally and from external sources increase. However, the type of demand and where it will come from is far less predictable making investment in personnel, equipment, servicing and new business much more complicated.

A typical example of this effect occurs when suppliers go back up the supply chain for corrections. These corrections can include reviewing 'to-do' lists, making repairs to equipment, reviewing inventory requirements and increasing the use of temporary labour.

Effect on purchasing behaviour – the purchasing portfolio model

Despite a number of studies on purchasing related activities of the festival audience – i.e., the consumer (Felsenstein and Fleischer 2003; Gripsrud et al. 2010; Kim et al. 2011; Alexander et al. 2012; Shone and Parry 2013), there is a distinct lack of research regarding the behaviour, practices and purchasing activities experiences of festival and event managers. When considering the importance of the festival manager's role in delivering 'an experience' (Berridge 2007), while at the same time generating a competitive advantage, it is clear that it is an increasingly important research undertaking to understand the influences over purchasing decision making in festival supply chains.

During the interviews, each organisation described how its own purchasing practices affected others in the supply chain, with both positive and negative consequences. Some areas have been discussed, such as the streamlining of internal activities to regain control of inventory and pricing and the importance of points of sale in maintaining profit margins for a high-end brand image that was maintained with the necessary support such products demand. Other factors included how contractual terms were agreed with major suppliers for high profile events and how replacing damaged items or the ordering of replacement parts to repair damaged items is maintained.

As specific purchases will be of differing importance to an organisation, in terms of their value, effect on customer satisfaction and strategic importance, it is clear that single purchasing practices involving the same behaviours will not be appropriate or desirable in all circumstances. It is therefore important to be able to distinguish between purchasing behaviours and the relative impact on the organisation. One commonly used approach in the SCM field is to link categories of purchase type to specific and suitable purchasing practices and ways of working are used depending on what products/services are being bought. There are a number of different variants of such a model, but the one developed by Kraljic (1983) forms the basis for many and is therefore adopted for this study. This classifies products or services along two axes; where they have different levels of impact on the event and different levels of supply risk or supply market complexity (as shown in Figure 8.6).

By positioning categories of supply (not single suppliers) into one of the four quadrants, different purchasing practices can be adopted which 'fit' with the type of category. These have been covered in some detail in both research papers (Gelderman and van Weele 2002; Padhi et al. 2012) and textbooks (Cousins et al. 2008; Trompenaars 2014). In principle, those that are in the non-critical items (routine), such as stationery and other office supplies, have a focus on efficiency and as the cost of moving from one supplier is low (as there are a number of suppliers in the market) the objective is to pay the most competitive price. Those at the opposite end of

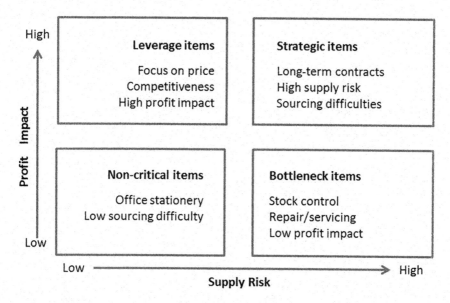

Figure 8.6 Kraljic's (1983) Portfolio purchasing model
Source: Kraljic 1983

the matrix, strategic items are those that have a high impact on the festival supplier's profitability, such as AV equipment, and are also characterised by high supply risk (monopoly supply, etc.), which suggests that a co-operative relationship is more suitable.

Having identified a number of pressures zones in the preceding section, we now turn to the effect these have on the purchasing practices of the organisations in the supply chain, through the use of a purchasing portfolio model as a lens through which to gather structured insights.

The actual impact on business can be seen on the organisation of the product/service as the internal effects create a tendency to view a purely financial (e.g. profit) impact. For example, considerations such as poor quality would consequently impact the ability of the organisation to sell to their own customers. However, in keeping with paradigm shifts in events, there may be broader considerations of health and safety, sustainability and ethics that may have a non-profit link. Examples of this include, maintenance of the supplier's equipment, attaining accreditations such as ISO 140001 or 20121, although this is of course a contested area in itself.

The supply risk can be seen as the external factors that may affect buying practices for festivals. These are, for example, how many festival suppliers operate in the marketplace, thus influencing the switching cost of moving between suppliers and the inherent complexity of the supply market. Of course, this is not a static reflection, as the external supply market will change as technologies are developed, when festival suppliers cease to trade or are unavailable or when new suppliers enter the festival market. Similarly, the internal impact factors could shift as the reliance on certain products or services change due to changes either in business direction or, as has been the case, the cancellation of multiple festivals (MusicWeek 2012; Thump 2016).

What the empirical data shows us is that this congestion of finance and information flow through the supply chain creates a heightened level of pressure in getting the experience for the end user right. These are manifested by the pressure zones, which suggest there is a greater impact on the festival supplier. This effectively *forces* the movement of categories of supply from routine items 'up' into the higher segments of the matrix and therefore forcing specific and less appropriate purchasing practices onto the festival supplier. This means that goods/services, which could be treated as non-critical items are 'forced' into the characteristics of a strategic one, which involves a considerable deployment of internal resources, which, if the pressure zones were managed more effectively, would not be necessary. Figure 8.7 illustrates our adaption of Kraljic's (1983) portfolio model for the events industry denoting the importance of strategic importance for all items in the supply chain.

This manifests itself in a number of potentially serious consequences such as ordering at short notice, postponing planned safety inspections until after

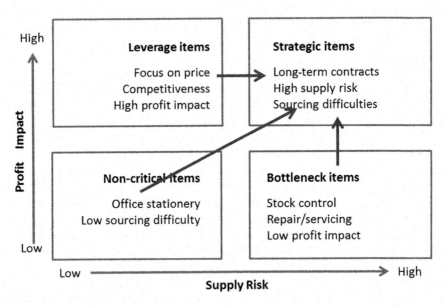

Figure 8.7 Kraljic's (1983) portfolio model (adapted).
Source: Kraljic 1983; adapted by Ryan and Kelly 2017

an event, not having time to make effective selections between suppliers leading to increased fees, loss of supply or the need to ensure the festival supplier has an even closer relationship with its own suppliers than it may, under normal circumstances, choose to do, resulting in unnecessary resource deployment. When such instances occur, complications can be sensed or amplified by knock-on effects that can eventually affect the festival audience experience of the event through the festival's management supply chain. A lack of effective demand management processes, compounded by a lack of clear information flows has a sizeable effect on the purchasing practices which means that the organisations cannot take advantage of the most effective and efficient purchasing practices, which would normally be associated with strategic purchasing behaviour. The most basic activities are creating potentially fatal consequences.

Implications and conclusions

It is clear that the current landscape of demands affecting the delivery of festivals provides a renewed set of supply chain challenges. This requires a new set of approaches from festival managers to understand the most appropriate, efficient and safe operations for their event. This section now summarises the findings to generate clear recommendations for practitioners in the festival field, as well as generating future research ideas for academics and providing learning opportunities for students in the area.

Firstly, clearly mapping an empirically based festival supply chain highlights the diversity of organisations involved and the complexity of managing supply chains in this field. Also, it shows that organisations beyond the direct control of the focal organisation may materially affect the delivery of high levels of customer service to the festival audience end user.

Secondly, the chapter highlights the importance of responding quickly to information that comes from the supply chain. Using the concept of the Bullwhip Effect as applied to an empirical festival supply setting, it has highlighted that the pressure zones created by the tapering of information flows may result in the adoption of inappropriate activities and practices. This could have the effect of poor performance at the level of the supply chain and a corresponding effect on the festival attendee's satisfaction. Not doing so can result in poor overall management of the supply chain (not necessarily at the level of an individual organisation) and lead to serious and, in some cases, fatal effects on the festival attendee's experience. Similarly, minor, incremental, often unintended or unforeseen incidents suggests the behaviour of one organisation can detrimentally effect another organisation in different parts of the supply chain. Increasing the timely availability and the amount and quality of information flows through the supply chain by making demand data available to suppliers, should positively impact the particular supply chain's ability to compete with others and increase the overall quality of the event.

Thirdly, if organisations consider the effect that their behaviour might have on the wider supply chain, then it should mean that the overall experience of a festival attendee will be improved. This does not require an overly altruistic perspective with the underlying thought that such actions might improve their competitor's performance, as there is enough variability in supply chain organisational selection to offer distinct advantages to the performance in their 'own' supply chain.

What becomes clear from discussions with the various organisations in this festival supply chain is that whilst they are operating in different goods/services markets, they are faced with similar challenges because of the overall supply chain they operate in. The time and resources that are devoted to festival delivery are considerable and, although this means that many events are a success, a more organised approach may provide an opportunity to make a more efficient use of internal management resources.

The turnover of each organisation in this supply chain is substantial (£100's of millions), and cash flow (money) continually affects purchasing practices as there is a sustained focus on budgets, which always have limits. This means that the timing of the different activities (both positive and negative) can have a knock-on effect further upstream or downstream in the supply chain. A critical skill that exists in festival management is the ability to anticipate and predict possible outcomes of any given situation, whether it is a risk or opportunity. This ability to make the right decision is a skill that can recognise possible advantages or prevent potential disasters.

It was observed throughout the interviews that the business of sound reinforcement or PA supply is fundamentally convivial and the passion expressed by those involved was clearly evident. Even though the work included long and often exhausting days, the nature of the work appears to provide a clear sense of job satisfaction for all those involved. However, while this was observed within this supply chain and is likely to be mirrored across other similar supply chains, there was evidence of serious rivalry between other festival supply chains and communication does not exist in any capacity across these divides.

The rationale for increased levels of SCM are the positive impacts that effective and efficient SCM can have on the overall supply chain, including; increased sales margins, greater levels of inter-organisational collaboration in terms of closer working relationships and the ability to adopt greater levels of strategic planning and purchasing behaviours.

While successful festivals are largely about varying levels of excitement for the end user, this research has highlighted that from an organisational or delivery perspective, festival management favours *uneventful* processes. Fewer surprises and greater levels of predictability allow for less complicated delivery procedures and the adoption of more suitable SCM practices. The chapter also highlights that there is a clear opportunity to build on this initial empirical research through the deployment of SCM concepts, theories, models and techniques in festival management, the classroom and other empirical festival settings.

References

Akkermans, H. and B. Vos (2003). "Amplification in service supply chains: An exploratory case study from the telecom industry." *Production and Operations Management* 12(2): 204–223.

Alexander, A. C., D.-Y. Kim, et al. (2012). "Individual and organizational characteristics influencing event planners' perceptions of information content and channel choice." *Journal of Convention & Event Tourism* 13(1): 16–38.

Allen, J., W. O'Toole, et al. (2008). *Festival and special events management*. Sydney, Wiley.

Aloini, D., R. Dulmin, et al. (2015). "Key antecedents and practices for Supply Chain Management adoption in project contexts." *International Journal of Project Management* 33(6): 1301–1316.

Anderson, E. G., D. J. Morrice, et al. (2005). "The 'physics' of capacity and backlog management in service and custom manufacturing supply chains." *System Dynamics Review* 21(3): 217–247.

Arcodia, C. and S. Reid (2005). "Event management associations and the provision of services." *Journal of Convention & Event Tourism* 6(4): 5–25.

Arnott, B. and A. Freire (2010). "Planning safe outdoor festivals and events." *Municipal World* 120(2): 19–23.

Babbie, E. (2001). *The practice of social research*. Belmont, CA, Wadsworth/Thomson Learning.

Basu, S., I. Bose, et al. (2013). "Lessons in risk management, resource allocation, operations planning, and stakeholder engagement: The case of the Kolkata Police Force and Durga Puja." *Decision* 40(3): 249–266.

Berridge, G. (2007). *Events design and experience*. London, Elsevier.

Bowdin, G., J. Allen, et al. (2011). *Events management*. London, Elsevier.

Source: Bratić, D. (2011). "Achieving a competitive advantage by SCM." *IBIMA Business Review*: 1–13.

Burgess, K., P. J. Singh, et al. (2006). "Supply chain management: A structured literature review and implications for future research." *International Journal of Operations & Production Management* 27(7): 703–729.

Calvin, J. (2012). "Festivals and events in emergent economies a sea change, and for whom?" *International Journal of Event and Festival Management* 3(1): 9–11.

Case, R. (2013). *Events and the environment*. London, Routledge.

Chen, S. C. (2011). "Residents' perceptions of the impact of major annual tourism events in Macao: Cluster analysis." *Journal of Convention & Event Tourism* 12(2): 106–128.

Christopher, M. G. (1992). *Logistics and supply chain management*. London, UK, Pitman Publishing.

Christopher, M. G. (2016). *Logistics and supply chain management*. 5th Ed. Harlow, UK, Financial Times/Pearson.

Cousins, P., R. Lamming, et al. (2008). *Strategic supply management: Principles, theories and practice*. Harlow, Pearson Education.

Croom, S., Romano, P. and Giannakis, M. (2000). "Supply chain management: an analytical framework for critical literature review." *European Journal of Purchasing & Supply Management* 6(1): 67–83.

Daniels, M. (2014). *Wedding planning and management: Consultancy for diverse clients*. Abingdon, Oxon, Routledge.

Elrod, C., S. Murray, et al. (2013). "A review of performance metrics for supply chain management." *Engineering Management Journal* 25(3): 39–50.

Emery, P. (2010). "Past, present, future major sport event management practice: The practitioner perspective." *Sport Management Review* 13(2): 158–170.

Felsenstein, D. and A. Fleischer (2003). "Local festivals and tourism promotion: The role of public assistance and visitor expenditure." *Journal of Travel Research* 41: 385–392.

Ferdinand, N. and P. J. Kitchin (2012). *Event management and internatiobnal approach*. London, Sage Publications Ltd.

Fields, K. and P. Stansbie (2007). Festival and event catering operations. In *Festival and events management: An international arts and cultural perspective*. I. Yeoman, M. Robertson, J. Ali-Knight, S. Drummond and U. McMahon-Beattie. Oxford, Elsevier: 171–182.

Gelderman, C. and A. van Weele (2002). "Strategic direction through purchasing portfolio management: A case study." *The Journal of Supply Chain Management* 38(1): 30–37.

Getz, D. (2007). *Event Studies: Theory, Research and Policy for Planned Events*. Oxford: Elsevier.

Getz, D. (2012). *Event studies*. Oxford, UK, Routledge.

Gioia, D. A., K. G. Corley, et al. (2013). "Seeking qualitative rigor in inductive research notes on the Gioia methodology." *Organizational Research Methods* 16(1): 15–31.

Goldblatt, J. (2008). *Special events: A new generation and the next frontier*. New Jersey, Wiley & Sons.

Grefrath, C., D. Wagner, et al. (2017). Development methodology for sustainable solutions. In *Value networks in manufacturing: Sustainability and performance excellence*. J. P. Liyanage and T. Uusitalo. Cham, Springer International Publishing: 193–221.

Gripsrud, G., E. Nes, et al. (2010). "Effects of hosting a mega-sport event on country image." *Event Management* 14(3): 193–204.

Kim, J., B. Crow, et al. (2011). "Relationship between corporate image and purchase behavior: Moderating effects of personal characteristics and situational factors." *Event Management* 15(3): 245–266.

Kraljic, P. (1983). "Purchasing must become supply management." *Harvard Business Review* 61(5): 109–117.

Lambert, D. M. (1998). *Fundamentals of logistics management*. London, Irwin/McGraw-Hill.

Lambert, D. M. and T. L. Pohlen (2001). "Supply chain metrics." *The International Journal of Logistics Management* 12(1): 1–19.

Lee, H., V. Padmanabhan, et al. (1997). "Information distortion in a supply chain: The bullwhip effect." *Management Science*, Apr 1997, 43(4), 546-558

Lee, J.-E., B. A. Almanza, et al. (2010). "Food safety at fairs and festivals: Vendor knowledge and violations at a regional festival." *Event Management* 14(3): 215–223.

Lincoln, Y. S. and E. G. Guba (1985). *Naturalistic inquiry*. Thousand Oaks, CA, Sage Publications Ltd.

Markwell, K. and S. Tomsen (2010). "Safety and hostility at special events: Lessons from Australian gay and lesbian festivals." *Event Management, Cognizant Communication Corporation* 14(3): 225–238.

Monczka, R. M. and J. Morgan (1997). "What's wrong with supply chain management?" *Purchasing* 122(1): 69–73.

Music Week (2012). *Three more festivals cancelled*. Retrieved from: www.musicweek.com/news/read/update-three-more-uk-music-festivals-cancelled/049005. Accessed 21st June 2012.

Okada, T., A. Namatame, et al. (2017). A Method to Reduce the Amount of Inventoried Stock in Thai Supply Chain. *Intelligent and Evolutionary Systems: The 20th Asia Pacific Symposium, IES 2016, Canberra, Australia, November 2016, Proceedings*. G. Leu, H. K. Singh and S. Elsayed. Cham, Springer International Publishing: 347–359.

Oosterhuis, M., V. T. van der, et al. (2012). "The value of upstream recognition of goals in supply chains." *Supply Chain Management: An International Journal* 17(6): 582–595.

Padhi, S. S., S. M. Wagner, et al. (2012). "Positioning of commodities using the Kraljic Portfolio Matrix." *Journal of Purchasing and Supply Management* 18(1): 1–8.

Pan, X., & Tian, Y. (2008). The Value of Downstream Information Sharing on Upstream Supply Chain. 2008 4th International Conference on Wireless Communications, *Networking and Mobile Computing*: 1–4.

Presenza, A. and S. Iocca (2012). "The weight of stakeholders on festival management: The case of music festivals in Italy." *PASOS: Revista de Turismo y Patrimonio Cultural* 10(2): 25–35.

Reid, S. and C. Arcodia (2002). "Understanding the role of the stakeholder in event management." *Journal of Sport & Tourism* 7(3): 20–22.

Riege, A. M. (2003). "Validity and reliability tests in case study research: A literature review." *Qualitative Market Research: An International Journal* 6(2): 75–86.

Ritchie, J. (1984). "Assessing the impact of hallmark events: Conceptual and research issues." *Journal of Travel Research* 23(1): 2–11.

Robertson, M. (2015). "Technology, society, and visioning the future of music festivals." *Event Management* 19(4): 567–587.

Rogers, T. (2013). *Conferences and conventions: A global industry*. Oxon, Routledge.

Rutherford-Silvers, J. (2012). *Professional event coordination*. New Jersey, Wiley.

Ryan, W. G. (2016). "How do you 'do' event management education (EME)? A case study of event management higher education awards." *Event Management, Cognizant* 20(1): 69–80.

Shone, A. and B. Parry (2013). *Successful event management: A practical handbook*. London, Thomson.

Slack, N. (2009). *Operations and process management: Principles and practice for strategic impact*. Harlow, Financial Times Prentice Hall.

Tandon, R., K. Agrawal, et al. (2012). "Firecracker injuries during Diwali festival: The epidemiology and impact of legislation in Delhi." *Indian Journal of Plastic Surgery* 45(1): 97–101.

Thump (2016). *The party is over: Cancelled festivals from around the world*. Retrieved from: https://thump.vice.com/en_us/article/the-party-is-over-cancelled-festivals-from-around-the-world. Accssed 10th February 2016.

Trompenaars, F. (2014). *100+ management models: How to understand and apply the world's most powerful business tools*. Oxford, Infinite Ideas.
Tum, J., P. Norton, et al. (2006). *Management of event operations*. Oxford, Elsevier.
Wang, X. and S. M. Disney (2016). "The bullwhip effect: Progress, trends and directions." *European Journal of Operational Research* 250(3): 691–701.
Yeoman, I., M. Robertson, et al. (2007). *Festival and events management: An international arts and culture perspective*. Oxford, Elsevier.
Yin, R. (2002). *Case study research: Design and methods*, 3rd Ed., Applied Social Research Methods Series, Vol 5, Thousand Oaks, CA, Sage Publications, Inc.

9 The importance of the stakeholder relationship for the success of an event
The case of Montreal

Mohamed Reda Khomsi

Introduction

Cities and metropolises have always benefited from major events (Olympic Games, World Expos, World Cup, etc.) to carry out large-scale urban projects. However, these cities must provide the facilities required by each type of event as well as the hosting, transport and communication infrastructures. Moreover, they must do so not only in keeping with the requirements of the international organizations managing such events (e.g. International Olympic Committee, FIFA, Bureau international des expositions) but also in ways that deliver the image which the event organizers wish to convey to the world. The city of Montreal was involved in the organization of a number of international events from the 1960s up until the beginning of the 1990s. Jean Drapeau, who was mayor of Montreal from 1960 to 1986, pursued these events as a means to demonstrate that Montreal, and through it French Canada, was capable of creating something significant and powerful (Dupuy, 1972: 25). Nevertheless, an analysis of the contemporary history of Quebec's metropolis shows that the two major events that were organized during this time (Expo 67, 1976 Olympic Games), had very limited spin-offs and a legacy that held very little support with the local population (Khomsi, 2014; Roult, 2011). By contrast, the celebrations of Montreal's 350th anniversary celebrations, which took place in 1992, had a considerable impact on the city's positioning as an international tourism destination. This raises the question of why events that are not as large-scale, such as celebrations of the founding of a city or other festivals, may have a greater impact on the destination than the organization of events such as the Olympic Games. Through the case of Montreal and using a historical-interpretative approach, this chapter will try to answer this question while also defining the conditions and dynamics that favour the success of a tourism development strategy focussing primarily on major events.

Theoretical framework

In a context of postmodernity, an event is regarded as a key activity insofar as the individual is both an individual and a collective actor in search of social and cultural interaction. As such, the consumption of events of all kinds appears to be an intrinsic characteristic of the postmodern city and an essential component in the thematization and staging of the urban space (Bourgeon et al., 2002; LeBel, 2011). In this regard, Pilette and Kadri (2005) consider that events, alongside their facilities and experiences, have quickly become an important marker of territories seeking to distinguish themselves. For the actors of the city, the hosting of major events is very often seen as an opportunity for urban development, as was the case in the 1992 Olympic Games in Barcelona and, much earlier, in Paris with the holding of the 1889 World's Fair.

However, before analysing the dynamics that favour the success of a tourism development strategy focused on major events, one should question the concept of major events. The latter is often used to refer to events of any kind without there necessarily being any commonalities or clear criteria for defining what constitutes such an event. This observation is shared by other authors such as Braudel (1985), Farge (2002) and Prestini (2006), who emphasize the importance of, in any scientific approach, first identifying the object of a concept before examining its trajectory. Nonetheless, alongside the broad usage of the concept, a dominant definition of major events has emerged, originating from information studies. According to Bensa and Fassin (2002), a major event is an event that enjoys international fame, regardless of its size, shape or budget. This definition focuses more on the media coverage of the event, since "in our contemporary societies, it is through these alone [the media and channels of diffusion] that the event strikes us and cannot escape us" (Bensa & Fassin, 2002: 5). For Prestini (ibid), a major event is considered "an important fact that deserves to be shared with the whole population," which explains its broad media coverage. Dosse (2010) underlines that the twentieth century was marked by a proliferation of major events, some of which formed the collective imagination. Building on that observation, Sarkis (1999, 2003 attributes the importance of an event to its space-time dimensions rather than to its media coverage. More explicitly, the qualifier "major" may be associated with an event when it is of importance, in time and space, to the actors involved in either creating it or participating in it. In other words, the importance of an event will largely depend on the context in which it emerges and on the value given to it by the local actors of a destination. This is the same position adopted by the *Regroupement des événements majeurs internationaux* of Quebec. This collective represents events of various sizes and types across Quebec that have in common that they are organized and anchored in their host communities. This attribute, which is more epistemological in nature, is important for at least two reasons. For one, if our objective is to understand the dynamics and success factors of an event, we need to look at the conditions that are specific to each territory. Linking the size of an event to the importance accorded to it by local actors makes it possible to identify these dynamics. Second, from a methodological point of view, the indicators used to describe the size of an event differ from one context to another, hence the irrelevance of calling on universal indicators that do not take into account the local specificity of each event.

It should be noted that a significant part of the event studies literature studying major events is interested in assessing the impacts of these events (Khomsi, 2014). This concern is becoming increasingly important given the impact, in particular the economic impact, of this type of event has upon its host environment. However, since at least the 1970s, the literature has also been examining other elements, such as the local governance structure, the culture of the actors and the objectives pursued. This shift is justified, or relevant, insofar as these elements can significantly influence the results of an impact assessment and that they reflect the fact that events take place in a wide range of different contexts (Ahlert, 2009; Bohlin, 2009; Soteriades, 2009; Varvaressos, 2009). According to Dimanche (2009: 275), "The diversity of these events, the various goals they seek to meet, the different geographical, social and economic contexts in which they are based, and the different markets they attract must all be identified for each event." This perspective is shared by Deery et al. (2012), who reject the nearly systematic recourse to economic impact studies on the grounds that the quantitative dimension is only one variable among others to be taken into consideration and quite rightly so. More specifically, Deery et al. (2012: 72) point out, "The adoption of more qualitative and innovative methods in social impacts research, following, to some degree, the path of organisational culture research is the proposed next stage of social impact of tourism on communities' research." This position is shared by Bauthier (2009), who also stresses the importance of understanding of the relationship between actors in order to better understand the consequences of an event. Therefore, one could argue that, it is the relationships between the actors involved in the various processes of planning and organizing an event that determine the success of the event and its legacies.

In short, the new stream of research emphasizes studying the governance of an event in order to grasp its impact. In this regard, Ballester (2009) advocates that analysis of the relationships between the various stakeholders involved in organizing an event should cover the time before, during and after the event.

Methods

In this chapter, focus is upon analysing the impacts of the celebrations of the 350th anniversary of the founding of the city of Montreal, which spanned over a period of six months from May to October 1992. In this sense, and based on the theoretical context outlined earlier, we will analyse the relationship between the actors involved in the planning and organization of this event before, during and after it took place. To achieve this, we mobilized a historical-interpretative approach that aims to explain historical facts taking into account their context of realization. Applied most often in architecture and heritage, this approach draws from an interpretative paradigm whereby the object of research is precisely the action of the actors (Lessard-Hébert et al., 1995). As such, the approach emphasizes the contextual dimension, as this allows to correlate research results to their context of study. As pointed out by Groat and Wang (2002), the historical-interpretative approach is even more appropriate when the objective is to find the meaning of a phenomenon within a specific and complex context. Thus, this approach allows one to go beyond an understanding that is restricted to quantitative facts, since the broadened scope of interpretation offers the possibility of detecting elements likely to significantly influence a process in a qualitative sense.

Analysis was carried out upon official documentation made public by the event's organizing committee as well as other documents such as minutes, correspondence, activity reports and internal notes of the various organizations or institutions involved in the planning and organization of the event. The latter include the city of Montreal, Tourisme Montréal, La Corporation du 350e and Quebec's department of tourism. These other less official documents reflected the positions, tensions and relationships between the influential actors in ways that are not necessarily reflected in the official documents. Subsequently, and given that our research approach is based on interpreting data in consideration of the context in which they originated, our analysis would not be complete without a triangulation of the data with other sources of information. For this, we consulted newspaper articles, historical accounts and monographs on the subject that were available to us.

The celebrations of the 350th anniversary of Montreal

Founded in 1642 by Sieur de Maisonneuve, Montreal celebrated its 350th anniversary in 1992. On that occasion, under the leadership of Mayor Jean Doré, the city of Montreal created a private corporation in 1988 to plan and organize the 350th anniversary festivities, with a budget of CA$14.1 million (Khomsi, 2014). The event occurred in a specific social, political and economic context. For one, after a 26-year reign as mayor, Jean Drapeau left office in 1986 to retire. He had been the architect of several major events that took place in Montreal during the 1960s, 1970s and 1980s, and was a major force behind the city's hosting of Expo 67 and the 1976 Summer Olympics. While these two events raised Montreal up the international city rankings, they were also the object of widespread criticism, in particular with regard to their planning and governance. In fact, Mayor Drapeau was even accused of creating and maintaining a monopoly of the planning and organizing process, since the other stakeholders were hardly consulted. Overall, the mayor's objective was to make Montreal a modern city and twentieth-century metropolis (Khomsi, 2014). However, his obsession with grandeur came at the expense of maintaining a good governance for these two major events. This could explain why planning for the post-event use of erected facilities was neglected and never figured among the main concerns of the Drapeau administration. For example, the Olympic Stadium, designed to host the 1976 Olympic Games, has since been usable for other sporting activities only a few months out of the year, due mainly to its lack of a roof (which was not built for another ten years) and Montreal's harsh winter climate. The same can be observed with regard to the facilities of Expo 67. In a report published in 1983, the Quebec economic development office emphasized the dilapidated state of the Expo facilities and called for a coordination between the different actors of the city in order to inject new life into the site. Thus, the event that had given Montrealers so much pride in 1967 became the source of the city's blemishing image only a few years later.

In economic terms, and despite the shift of the Drapeau administration in the early 1980s to scale down the focus on major projects, the financial structure of the city remained fragile (Pilette, 2009). The very slow restructuring of the Montreal economy, which began in the early 1970s, coupled with the economic recession of the 1990s and a high unemployment rate, gave a bleak picture of the metropolitan economic situation (Linteau, 1992). In this context, Mayor Jean Doré adopted a policy that promoted the accessibility of services and the integration of citizens in the management of municipal affairs, breaking with the practices of the previous administration that was centralized and not very open to inclusive consultation. For example, for the corporation in charge of organizing the celebrations, the Doré administration appointed a board of directors that was representative of the principal forces of the metropolis, as evidenced by its composition and diversity. The new corporation was more forward thinking and brought together representatives from academia, trade unions, community organizations and economic, tourism, political and media sectors. The mayor viewed these celebrations as an opportunity for growth and as symbolic of a new era and a new generation, as can be deduced from the large number of sites that were inaugurated, developed or renovated on the occasion of the 350th anniversary. Thus, unlike with the major events of the 1960s and 1970s, leadership, planning and event management were shared by local actors, even if the municipal government was the initiator of the project.

In terms of tourism development, the main stakeholders in the community were largely represented, thanks in particular to the contribution of Tourisme Montréal, which had been bringing together the city's tourism actors since 1986, the Régie des installations olympiques and the prestigious Ritz-Carlton Hotel. We also note the presence of representatives of the International Air Transport Association, the national railway company VIA Rail Canada and the Société historique de Montréal on the corporation's board of governors. Beyond representation on the corporation's decision-making bodies, the actors from the tourism industry were also actively involved in this preparatory phase. Their involvement was very visible in the field of communication, in particular those addressing international markets.

From the very beginning, the planning process worked towards ensuring the longevity and perpetuation of the event's legacy. As such, the various actors involved in organizing the event used the occasion of the 350th anniversary celebrations to redefine Montreal's position as an international tourism destination and to research the provision of the facilities required for such a new positioning. The latter was quickly determined insofar as Montreal's cultural landscape became very vibrant throughout the 1980s, making the choice of promoting Montreal as a cultural capital an easy one. To solidify this positioning, the activities proposed within the event's framework covered a wide range of means of media and cultural expression. Historic or heritage activities accounted for 23% of event programming, while street festivals and other festivities comprised 16% of the activities proposed in the programme schedule (Khomsi, 2014).

In terms of the facilities, the 350th celebrations enabled Montreal to develop new attractions that have since contributed to building the image and positioning desired by the city's tourism actors. Two new museums were created thanks to the event: the Musée des Hospitalières de l'Hôtel-Dieu and the Pointe-à-Callière Montréal Archeology and History Complex. The latter was, incidentally, built on the site on which archaeological excavations were carried out during the 1980s – and which evidenced that Montreal was founded on that very site. The Biodôme, which was built as velodrome for the 1976 Olympic Games, hosts a natural environment representative of the four ecosystems of the North American continent. The 350th anniversary celebrations also had an accelerating effect on the expansion of the Montreal Museum of Fine Arts, the move of the Musée d'art contemporain de Montréal to Place des arts and the renovation of the McCord Museum. As for the development of public spaces, the 350th anniversary gave rise to the creation of several parks and squares that have since become coveted locations of the Montreal cultural arts scene (CC350AM, 1992).

Findings and conclusion

Despite the scale of the two major events held in Montreal in the 1960s (Expo 67) and 1970s (Olympic Games), Montreal's 350th anniversary celebrations had a greater impact on the development of Montreal as a tourism destination. It is for this reason that the collaboration between the different stakeholders was exemplary. Indeed, the integration of several actors from economic, tourism, social and community development sectors in the planning and organizing process had concrete implications for the metropolis. This inclusive approach was in line with the definition of governance put forward by Kooiman (1993: 2), who defines good governance as the deliberate efforts by actors to guide, direct, control or manage activities to achieve a goal common. In the same vein, Lequin (2001: 85) explains, "Governance is based on a system or a network of actors whose logic revolves around negotiation and is focused on the realization of a common product." In the case of our event, there was a clear consensus around the objective of wanting to make the 350th celebrations a landmark moment in the city's contemporary history. That consensus was the result of a shared vision of the various actors, both public and private. Indeed, the approach was representative of one of the four types of governance among the actors of a tourism project or event proposed by the "Hall model" (2011). The model assumes a broader spirit of collaboration between public and private actors, allowing for greater policy coherence. Private interests are taken into account and the actors representing these interests have a special place in the decision-making process. In the case of Montreal, the problems that accompanied Expo 67 and the Olympic Games remained in people's minds, and from this the actors involved in the 350th anniversary celebrations drew lessons, which then contributed to the evolution of Montreal's tourism governance model in 1992.

In a postmodern metropolitan context where tourism and major events are an integral part of the city's identity, the involvement of all the actors responsible for tourism development in the organization of a major event can be considered essential for the event's medium- and long-term success. This constitutes a direct response to the question posed at the beginning of the chapter in regards to why an event that is smaller than the Olympic Games, for example, could nonetheless have a significant impact on a destination. Indeed, the more the process of organizing an event unifies all the actors and is integrated within the framework of a shared vision, the better the impact on the destination.

Finally, although the case of Montreal is certainly a special case, it serves as a lesson for other destinations on at least two levels. Firstly, while it may seem obvious that collaboration between the actors is an important condition for the success of an event, the majority of major events organized throughout the world often fail to reflect this awareness (Khomsi, 2014) as a result of conflicting objectives. Indeed, the establishment of a model aiming for an expanded partnership between public and private actors requires leadership from an organization that has credibility with stakeholders. As such, the issue of governance on a localized and inclusive level remains fundamental, as is the effort to ensure an ongoing partnership between actors when seeking to maximize the long-term positive impact of a major event. However, it should be stressed that this dynamic manifests not only in the integration of actors – an indicator in and of itself of the desire to unite all stakeholders in the process of organizing a major event – but also in the degree to which actions cohere, as this reflects the contribution of each of the actors towards reaching the common objectives of the destination.

Secondly, recourse to the historical-interpretative approach has given us the possibility to present a new reading of a subject that seems to have been exhausted. The main merit of this approach lies in the incorporation of the contextual dimension into the analysis of the studied phenomenon. In the case presented here, this dimension allowed us to situate the event in its social, political, historical and geographical context, and in so doing to offer a more in-depth understanding than an inventory of the facilities built for an event or the evaluation of its economic spin-offs could have afforded. Indeed, an understanding of the collaborative mechanisms of the actors involved in an event, in particular in the planning phase, offers great insight and may serve as a complement to the various economic, social and environmental impact studies.

References

Ahlert, G. (2009). Assessing the impact of the FIFA World Cup 2006 in Germany – some methodological and empirical reflections. In *L'évaluation de l'événementiel touristique*, Huron, D. & Spindler, J. (eds.). Paris: l'Harmattan.

Ballester, P. (2009). Barcelone face à la globalisation: comment penser la ville par l'organisation et l'évaluation de grands événements. In *L'évaluation de l'événementiel touristique*, Huron, D. & Spindler, J. (eds.). Paris: l'Harmattan.

Bauthier, I. (2009). L'analyse de l'événement: une approche par les acteurs. In *L'évaluation de l'événementiel touristique*, Huron, D. & Spindler, J. (eds.). Paris: l'Harmattan.

Bensa, A. & Fassin, E. (2002). Les sciences sociales face à l'événement. *Terrain*, vol. 38, 5–20.

Bohlin, M. (2009). Vasaloppsveckan: Assessing the apparent and hidden impact of a major ski event in Sweden. In *L'évaluation de l'événementiel touristique*, Huron, D. & Spindler, J. (eds.). Paris: l'Harmattan.

Bourgeon, D., Bouchet, P. & Pulh, M. (2002). L'expérience de consommation de spectacles vivants: De nouvelles perspectives de recherche. In *Proceedings of the first Norman consumer research days*. University of Bourgogne.

Braudel, F. (1985). *Écrits sur l'histoire*. Paris: Flammarion.

CC350AM (Corporation des Célébrations du 350e anniversaire de Montréal). (1992). *Rapport des Célébrations du 350e anniversaire de Montréal*. Montréal: Ville de Montréal.

Deery, M., Jago, L. & Fredline, L. (2012). Rethinking social impacts of tourism research: A new research agenda. *Tourism Management*, vol. 33, 64–73.

Dimanche, F. (2009). De la diversité des événements à une mesure généralisable. In *L'évaluation de l'événementiel touristique*, Huron, D. & Spindler, J. (eds.). Paris: l'Harmattan.

Dosse, F. (2010). *Renaissance de l'événement. Un défi pour l'historien: entre sphinx et phénix*. Paris: Presses universitaires de France.

Dupuy, P. (1972). *Expo 67 ou la découverte de la fierté*. Montreal: La Presse Edition.

Farge, A. (2002). Penser et définir l'événement en histoire. Approche des situations et des acteurs sociaux. *Terrain*, vol. 38, 69–78.

Groat, L. & Wang, D. (2002). *Architectural research methods*. New York: John Wiley & Sons.

Hall, M. (2011). A typology of governance and its implications for tourism policy analysis. *Journal of Sustainable Tourism*, vol. 19 (4–5), 437–457.

Khomsi, M.R. (2014). *Le rôle des grands événements dans le développement touristique des métropoles*. Ph.D thesis in Urban Studies, School of management, University of Quebec at Montreal.

Kooiman, J. (1993). Socio-political governance. In *Modern governance: New gouvernement society interac*, Kooiman, J. (ed.). London: Sage Publications Ltd.

Kraljic, P. (1983). Purchasing must become supply management. *Harvard Business Review*, vol. 61 (5), 109–117.

LeBel, P.M. (2011). Des mégasprojets aux mégas-événements: Le droit à la ville pour les citadins de deux quartiers montréalais et la question de la thématisation de l'espace. In *Proceedings of the XI Congresso Internacional de ABECAN*. Salvador-Bahia-Brasil, October 24–26, 1–8.

Lequin, M. (2001). *Écotourisme et gouvernance participative*. Québec: Presses de l'Université du Québec.

Lessard-Hébert, M., Goyette, G. & Boutin, G. (1995). *La recherche qualitative: Fondement et pratiques*. Montreal: Éditions nouvelles.

Linteau, P.-A. (1992). *Histoire de Montréal depuis la Confédération*. Montreal: Boréal.

Pilette, D. (2009). Embellie financière et fiscale à Montréal. In *Montréal, aujourd'hui et demain*, Pierre D. (ed.). Montreal: Liber.

Pilette, D. & Kadri, B. (2005). *Le tourisme métropolitain: le cas de Montréal*. Québec: Presses de l'Université du Québec.

Prestini, M. (2006). Une nouvelle grille de lecture: l'événement. *Pensée Plurielle*, vol. 3, (13), 81–90.

Roult, R. (2011). *Reconversion des héritages olymipques et rénovatganizatiion de l'espace urbain: Le stade olympique comme vecteur de développement*. PhD thesis in Urban Studies, School of management, University of Quebec at Montreal.

Sarkis, J.-G. (1999). *La notion de grand événement. Approche épistémologique*. Coll. Passages Cerf. Paris: Cerf.

Sarkis, J. (2003) A strategic decision making framework for green supply chain management. *Journal of Cleaner Production*, vol. 11, (4), pp. 397–409.

Soteriades, M. (2009). Les Jeux olympiques d'Athènes 2004: une première évaluation – Attentes, résultats et leçons. In *L'évaluation de l'événementiel touristique*, Huron, D. & Spindler, J. (eds.). Paris: l'Harmattan.

Varvaressos, S. (2009). Les Jeux olympiques et le tourisme. Étude comparative de trois villes organisatrices: Barcelone (1992), Sidney (2000), Athènes (2004). In *L'évaluation de l'événementiel touristique*, Huron, D. & Spindler, J. (eds.). Paris: l'Harmattan.

10 'Power wrestling'

The life and (untimely) death of the Real Food Festival

Trudie Walters

Introduction

The role of events and festivals in bolstering both the economies and the spirits of small rural communities facing hard times is an important but emergent area of research (see, for example, Davies, 2015; Gibson & Connell, 2015). However, the life cycles of such events and festivals and the attendant role of power in these life cycles is less well understood, particularly when a festival ceases to exist. This chapter examines the evolution of a local community food festival in Southeast Queensland, Australia, and investigates the changing nature of power relations in its life and (untimely) death. The chapter firstly provides a brief discussion of the nature of power and its application to tourism and event development. This is followed by a contextual section that examines the role of power in the birth of the Real Food Festival. Two different forms of power ('power to' and 'power over') and their influence during the remainder of the life course of the festival are then considered.

The nature of power and event evolution

The notion of power is highly contested and can be interpreted in a variety of ways, as evidenced by debates over the writings of Lukes (1974), Clegg (1989) and Foucault (1978, 1980). While a detailed review of the vast literature is not possible here, for the purposes of this chapter where power is viewed as a fluid force that may both enable and constrain, Foucault's notion of power is considered to be the most appropriate framework. Power in the Foucauldian sense is not 'possessed' by an individual or a group; rather it is something that is relationally constituted and thus an individual or group's position within a network is an essential component of power (Clegg, 1989; Foucault, 1978, 1980). Being dependent on circumstance, power is also temporally and spatially fluid, meaning that it can be possessed and dispossessed over both time and place rather than being static and localised (Foucault, 1980). Furthermore, even where there is no overt conflict in a relationship power may still be exerted and resisted (Clegg, 1989).

Power relationships have been the subject of some research in tourism development, particularly in relation to governance, politics and policymaking (Church & Coles, 2007; Cooper, Scott & Baggio, 2009; Doorne 1998; Thomas & Thomas, 2005). However, there are only a handful of analyses of power in festival and event research. In their seminal work, Clarke and Jepson (2011) examined power and hegemony within the Derby Jubilee Festival in the United Kingdom, finding that, firstly, the power wielded by the steering committee resulted in very little evidence of democracy during the festival planning process, and, secondly, their narrow definition of culture as 'high art forms' excluded the wider inclusive definition of culture as 'a way of life'. Therefore, despite the stated goal of 'embracing cultural diversity', large parts of the community were in fact excluded from participation in the festival. In other research, stakeholder (or network) theory has been used when examining power relationships in event decision-making and processes, and findings suggests that stakeholder power may be associated with the amount or level of critical resources held, including social and financial capital (see, for example, Batty, 2016; Onyx, Edwards & Bullen, 2007; Tiew, Holmes & de Bussy, 2015).

There is similarly only a limited amount of literature investigating the evolution and/or failure of festivals and events. It is held that events pass through a series of stages in much the same manner as organisations and tourism destinations are purported to do (Beverland, Hoffman & Rasmussen, 2001; Getz & Andersson, 2008). Furthermore, through their work on the evolution of regional wine events, Beverland et al. (2001) proposed that, in addition to going through stages, both the nature and the emphasis of events change over time. Although they identified decline and revival as the two final stages in event evolution, there was no inclusion or discussion of failed events where a revival did not occur for whatever reason. Getz (2002), however, noted that event failure is a common occurrence. Causes of event failure can be grouped into five areas: marketing and planning, human resources, financial resources, external forces (such as weather, lack of community support) and the culture of the organisation (Carlsen et al., 2010; Getz, 2002). While it is argued here that power is implicit in event planning due to its relational nature and the association with social and financial capital, to date, there has been little recognition of the role of power in the evolution or demise of an event.

Contextualising the research: power and the birth of the Real Food Festival

In order to understand power relations and how these are manifest in the life course of a festival or event (or indeed any phenomenon), it is important to first contextualise it within its specific social, economic, political and historical setting (Onyx et al., 2007). Maleny is a small town (population of approximately 3,500) in the hinterland of the Sunshine Coast, an hour's drive north of Brisbane in Southeast Queensland (Australian Bureau of Statistics, 2013). From the 1970s onwards, it became known for its 'alternative' communities as hippies and alternative lifestylers moved to the area in search of the good life. Over the years, Maleny has been (and remains) home to a high number of co-operatives – providing everything from organic food to dairy products, banking to book publishing, recycling, social and economic support for women and alternative currency trading (Green, 2010).

There is strong social capital within the community, which is both a reflection and a driver of the co-operatives; it has also manifested its presence in active (and frequently successful) resistance to a number of proposed developments over the past three decades (Green, 2010; Onyx et al., 2007). For example, against the 1989 proposal to build a large tourist and retirement village complex in the town, the 2003 proposal by national food retailing giant Woolworths to build a supermarket, and most recently the three-and-a-half year battle against the 2006 proposal to build the Traveston Crossing Dam on the Mary River – of these, only the supermarket development proceeded (de Rijke, 2012; Green, 2010; Keith, 2012). While these are positive narratives of power, resistance and social capital in Maleny, there are also negative narratives. In recent years deregulation, drought, increasing bureaucracy and compliance costs coupled with falling prices (and the threat of the Traveston Crossing Dam) meant many farmers in the region felt powerless and were struggling to maintain a viable business and remain on their land (de Rijke, 2012; Keith, 2012).

It was against this economically and socially tumultuous backdrop that the Real Food Festival was established in Maleny in 2011. Its purpose was to celebrate and support local Sunshine Coast hinterland farmers and food producers, to return some of their power and to demonstrate that they were valued by the local communities (Anon, 2011; Gration, 2014). The organisers' rationale for the festival was to provide an outlet for the farmers to sell their produce, and educate the public about the importance of local food producers at the same time. Thus, the very foundation of the Real Food Festival rested on the notion of power, in particular trying to restore power to farmers who were at the mercy of both natural (weather) and man-made (politics at national and state level) power dynamics beyond their control.

The festival was a single-day event in the first year, attracting approximately 4,000 attendees and 84 stallholders, and was expanded to two days from the second year. By 2014, attendance had increased to just over 8,800 and 100 stallholders, with 75% of attendees coming from the Sunshine Coast and 25% from the greater Queensland region – many of those were from Brisbane (Gration, 2014; Real Food Festivals, 2015). However after five years of successfully staging the Real Food Festival, the organiser announced in early 2016 to the surprise and disappointment of many that the event would 'take a break' that year, with the future of the event uncertain (Moffat, 2016).

The 12 participants interviewed for this study included 1 of the organisers plus 5 primary food producers, 2 value adders, 1 food wholesaler, 1 chef and 2 food retailers who had stalls and/or were sponsors or speakers at the Real Food Festival over the period 2011–2015. Reflecting upon the business environment in Australia where some 90% of businesses have an annual turnover of less than AUD$1 million and fewer than 20 staff, all participants in this study are defined as small-scale owner-operated businesses (McKerchar, Hodgson & Walpole, 2009). Ten were based in the Sunshine Coast hinterland, with just two from outside this area but still within the wider Sunshine Coast region. A number of the participants had attended the Real Food Festival every year, some had attended on a more irregular basis and a few attended for the first time in 2015. Interviews were semi-structured in order to keep the conversation on track but at the same time allow participants the flexibility to explore their ideas (McGehee, 2012), and as a result ranged from 25 to 90 minutes. All were audio-recorded for later transcription and the participants were de-identified.

Supplementing the interviews, an analysis was conducted of secondary information. This included confidential raw visitor and exhibitor survey data for 2011–2014 (supplied by the event organisers), Real Food Festival promotional material and local/regional newspaper commentary about the event from 2011–2016. This follows the examples of Beverland et al. (2001) and Batty (2016) who used similar mixed methods in order to triangulate their data in studies investigating the evolution of regional wine events and a community sports event, respectively.

Power wrestling and the Real Food Festival

Onyx et al. (2007) note the existence of two fundamentally dichotomous forms of power, 'power to' and 'power over', and both were identified over the life course of the Real Food Festival. The former provided the rationale on which the festival was established, while the latter was the site of the power wrestling that appears to have contributed to the (untimely) death of the festival.

'Power to'

Power (as an enabling force) was explicitly implicated in the conceptualising and creation of the festival. As discussed earlier, the festival organisers initially responded to what they saw as the needs of the local farmers and food producers, establishing the festival in order to support and empower this stakeholder group and demonstrate that the local community valued them. Unsurprisingly then, the media discourse reflected this:

> The Real Food Festival is the only event of this scale, in this region, that is genuinely dedicated to championing, supporting and promoting the best local food available.
>
> (*Hinterland Times*, 9 April, 2011: n.p.)

> [The organiser] said the short-distance, paddock-to-plate philosophy behind organising the festival had come from discussions with regional farmers who were having trouble selling their produce against the strong commercial market . . . many were actually living below the poverty line with very little income coming in from their efforts on the land.
> (Moran, *Sunshine Coast Sunday*, 26 May 2013: 17)

Interestingly, none of the media commentary featured quotes from the local food producers themselves about how they perceived the usefulness of the festival in empowering them. In the first year, the importance of the festival as a vehicle for the collective 'voice' of the local producers to gain political support was highlighted:

> Hopefully this festival will provide that vehicle to bring everyone together to create new networks, new ideas and have a bigger voice . . . If they are together, their voice is stronger and that might attract more support from councils and other organisations that can help.
> (*Sunshine Coast Daily*, 3 May 2011: 20)

By 2014, the discourse had changed slightly – as well as showcasing local food to local consumers, visitors (those from outside the local area) were also included in the target audience. This reflected the power and influence of the sponsors, which will be discussed in more detail next. Suffice to say here that most of the local producers operated on such a small scale that these visitors would in fact be unable to purchase the products in their local shops at home (Interviews with local food producers Robert, Rachel and Derek).

In addition to promoting local food producers and giving them a voice, in 2012 and 2013, the festival organisers successfully applied for local government funding to run a series of short workshops for exhibitors. The workshops were designed to empower the stallholders with practical business management skills such as presenting product lines to wholesalers, maximising opportunities in culinary tourism, and how to develop social media strategies. One interviewee was very positive about this initiative:

> I have to say one of the greatest things that were held in addition to the event was two pre-event workshops which [were] organised, and that was with a fellow who assisted us to develop our business plan. Very powerful, that was very powerful, so there was really a business education process that was taking place as well.
> (Interview with Rebecca, local food producer)

The second stakeholder group that the Real Food Festival sought to give 'power to' was the consumer, although this theme was strongest in the early years of the festival and had all but disappeared by the final year. This echoes the work of Beverland et al. (2001) on regional wine events, who found changes in event emphasis over the years. The Real Food Festival discourse centred on the notion of being empowered in terms of being able to make informed choices about what food to buy, where to buy it, and how to prepare it for the benefit of one's physical, social and environmental health:

> 'Research shows that an increasing number of people care about where their food comes from and want to understand why their food choices matter; for health, community and environmental reasons', [the organiser] said. 'Visitors will be able to discover how buying local subverts the centralised system that clocks up food miles and reduces food quality'.
> (*Hinterland Times*, 9 April 2011: n.p.)

> 'I'm not saying that everyone should buy only organically home-grown products, but it's important shoppers are informed so we can all make good choices about what we eat . . . Be empowered, don't be afraid to ask questions and don't be afraid to seek advice as to how best to prepare your food to ensure maximum nutrition', [the organiser] said.
> (Moran, *Sunshine Coast Sunday*, 26 May 2013: 17)

The voice of local consumers themselves was missing from the media commentary; therefore, it is unclear whether consumers felt empowered as a result of attending the festival. There is a sense that the festival was more a case of 'preaching to the converted' (Interview with Robert, local food producer), as was the case in another regional food festival in Australia, which was 'aimed at those wishing to celebrate a very particular kind of cultural capital' (Pacella, George & Roberts, 2015: 195). A number of interviewees in this study (Brendan, Cory, Ellen, Rachel, Tony) perceived a general increase in interest in recent years amongst their everyday customers in eating locally produced food – wholly independent of the Real Food Festival. They believed this was largely a response to the dominance of the two major supermarket chains (Coles & Woolworths) who were perceived to treat their small suppliers unfairly, mirroring the findings of Keith (2012).

The event organisers initially sought to empower both local food producers and food consumers, to provide 'power to' them, and, certainly, there was a strong discursive construction in the media about the need to support 'our local farmers' and the importance of 'educating ourselves' about eating well. Nevertheless, it is unclear how 'empowered' each group actually felt, and from the visitor survey data, it is doubtful whether the attendees changed their food purchasing behaviour as a result. The success of the Real Food Festival may have had less to do with reclaiming power and more to do with a serendipitous emergence of a critical mass of local producers who had diversified to take advantage of new niche markets to keep their businesses viable and an already-knowledgeable public ready to embrace a new type of food event in the region.

'Power over'

Whereas 'power to' was the driving force behind the birth of the Real Food Festival, it is argued here that 'power over' shaped its life course and contributed to its (untimely) death. As a number of studies have found, power can be coercive, repressive and a negative force – at the same time as it is enabling, it is also constraining (Onyx et al., 2007). Event stakeholders who held 'power over' were easily identifiable in the festival over the years and included the event organisers, sponsors and local government agencies – along with the local food producers and consumers.

The event organisers strongly felt the festival was 'truly a community event' (*Noosa News*, 9 August 2013: 28) but they chose to form a company rather than run the event through a committee or cooperative, with one of them stating in the interview:

> [I] didn't want to run it as a not-for-profit or a committee run thing – I was happy to look at moving it across to a social enterprise once it was established, but in the early years and I've had lots of experience with cooperatives, and I just know that if you want to get something up and running quickly, you've got to have a pretty tight control of the reins to move it forward in the direction that it's got to go.

However, she felt this decision to hold the power was misunderstood by some:

> I copped a bit of criticism around that because, being a private enterprise, there was a perception that it was all about earning profit for me, but I can tell you now [laughs] it's not been about the profit!

As a result of the organisational structure, the organisers were also in control of defining what constituted 'local' food; 'good, clean and fair' food; 'authentic' food; and for the selection of stallholders and speakers/topics:

> Good wholesome butter, milk and lots of chocolate – these are the kind of ingredients a weekend should be made of . . . Already 80 stall-holders have booked for the festival and many more have been turned away. Entry has strict criteria: the food must be local and no junk food or 'sideshow alley rubbish' allowed.
> (*Sunshine Coast Daily*, 25 August 2011: 8)

> Organisers have decided to extend this year's festival into a two-day feast that will include a Wellness space with advice on eating for good health; Food for Thought talks on subjects such as the carbon tax, organic vs local, and preparing food for babies . . . All food on display has been grown or produced in the Sunshine Coast bioregion according to the interconnected Slow Food principles of good, clean and fair.
> (Sinclair, *Kingaroy Mail*, 11 April 2012: 21)

> Sunshine Coast gluten and grain-free guru and author, Tania Hubbard will be sharing her love of local food and gluten- and grain-free living . . . leading a discussion about how to easily integrate raw foods into a gluten- and grain-free diet in the Jeffers Market Wellness Space.
> (*Caloundra Weekly*, 23 August 2012: 3)

The earlier extracts illustrate the organisers' power; they determined what constituted 'junk food' or a 'healthy diet'. It can be argued that chocolate is 'junk' food (irrespective of whether it is organic and produced locally or not), and there is scant scientific evidence that gluten-free and grain-free diets are beneficial for anyone other than those few who have a medically diagnosed intolerance (Gaesser & Angadi, 2012). Therefore, not only were the organisers acting as gatekeepers in deciding which food producers were eligible to exhibit at the festival but also dictated which were the 'key issues' and topics that would be discussed by speakers at the event (Clarke & Jepson, 2011; Getz, Andersson & Larson, 2007).

Sponsors also held 'power over' the event and this was evident through changing discourses in the media, from a strong focus on supporting local producers in the first year to more of a focus on promoting the Sunshine Coast as a food tourism destination in later years. Aligned with the Maleny community response to the proposed Woolworths supermarket discussed earlier in this chapter, a group of 14 local IGA supermarkets made a collective decision to sponsor the Real Food Festival from its inception. An early media article highlighted the strong connection between the IGA ethos, their commitment to local producers and their difference from the Coles and Woolworths duopoly:

> IGA will provide several thousand dollars to the organisers who will promote and celebrate links between the independent supermarket group and local producers . . . [one owner told us], 'We are all Sunshine Coast locals, supporting Sunshine Coast locals. IGA Supermarkets on the Coast sell many millions of dollars worth of locally grown and manufactured product. That money starts and stops on the Sunshine Coast, it does not get vacuumed through to Head Office in Sydney [alluding to Coles and Woolworths]; it stays within our local communities. It is just good business!'
> (*Hinterland Times*, 9 April 2011: n.p.)

Support from local business associations (the Maleny Commerce and nearby Montville Chamber of Commerce) was also announced on the Real Food Festival blog in mid-2011, and the notion of putting the region 'on the map' as a food destination was mentioned only in passing. The power held by these sponsors in the early years was not readily detected in the media commentary, and was not acknowledged as problematic at all by those interviewed.

Then in late 2014, the event organisers announced they had secured funding from Tourism and Events Queensland through the state-wide Regional Development Program (TEQRDP) to 'promote the festival to audiences outside the Sunshine Coast region' (Real Food Festival blog, 1 December, 2014). It marked a new phase in sponsor power, with more focus on the event's contribution to tourism and enhancing the area as a food destination. Nevertheless, while this illustrates a subtle change in the nature and emphasis of the Real Food Festival (Beverland et al., 2001), the influence of these sponsors was perceived by interviewees as less overt and challenging than that of one other stakeholder – local government agency Sunshine Coast Council (SCC).

Although they were also sponsors of the Real Food Festival (duly noted in some of the media articles over the years) and the mayor took part in a well-publicised cooking competition at the event, the SCC's power was seen by event organisers and the local food producers alike as being far more pervasive due to their broader policy and funding agendas. This was alluded to in the media discourse, at the time of the announcement to discontinue the festival:

> [The organiser] said the major events schedule organised by the Sunshine Coast Council for 2016, which has double the number of events this year compared to last year, was great for the region in many ways, but also had the potential to squeeze out smaller events. 'All these events are really great for the Coast but it's also making for a really crowded calendar', [the organiser] said.
> (*Sunshine Coast Daily*, 11 February 2016: 5)

However, during the interview for this project the organiser was very forthright, stating quite clearly their frustration that the SCC favoured (and thus funded) the larger, international sporting events held on the Sunshine Coast rather than smaller community-style events such as the Real Food Festival:

> So I struggled, and I'm probably going to sound a little bit bitchy here, but I struggled to put forward a case to win twenty thousand dollars worth of council money, and yet many many times that is allocated to some of these big sporting events because of the way the value is measured.

This was despite the tourism and agribusiness sectors (within which the Real Festival sits) being recognised as high-value industries in the SCC Regional Development Economic Strategy (Hill, 2014). Relatedly, Getz and Andersson (2008) note that competition amongst events in a region may result in less political support or funding, and thus an event may be unable to continue. Amongst the exhibitors and presenters/speakers interviewed here, there was a very real sense of a David and Goliath battle between the Real Food Festival organisers and the SCC:

> I think it's really sad . . . but I understand, [the organiser is] probably a little burnt out and . . . just . . . rules and regulations, red tape, government, bureaucracies, over-governed, the nanny state . . . So I can understand a hundred percent why [the organiser] would be sick to death of it because I know every year [they] had to fight with council.
> (Interview with Brendan, local food producer)

> What I see all over the place is the difference between individuals putting their money where their mouth is and running a food festival, and then you go to other places where the council, the economic development part of the council sees the value of doing it. Places like Maleny, which you'd imagine would have that council support to have a food festival, that was [the organiser] putting it all on single-handed.
> (Interview with Tony, presenter/speaker)

> Was the council supporting it, the council supported it but to what level, do you know what I mean? Could more have been done? Whereas it was sort of [the organiser] and [their] little team trying their hardest to market it and promote it and what-have-you.
> (Interview with Richard, local food producer/wholesaler)

These extracts demonstrate the power held by the SCC, not just in terms of obtaining funding (which was important) but also in terms of the amount of bureaucracy and paperwork needed to hold the festival, and in terms of in-kind support. Many of those interviewed perceived a lack of support as a major contributor to the (untimely) death of the Real Food Festival. Indeed, one implored the SCC to 'extremely strongly' underwrite the festival if it were to be held again in the future due to the 'great value' it held for them as local food producers (Interview with Rebecca, local food producer). It seems that in the case of the Real Food Festival, the decision to discontinue the festival was the ultimate (albeit extreme) assertion of power by the organiser. These findings echo those of others who have noted that higher-level organisations such as local government are generally perceived to hold more power than smaller entities – even where they are not directly involved in event-based decisions – and illustrate the complex nature of stakeholder power (Batty, 2016; Getz & Andersson, 2008).

The final stakeholders demonstrating 'power over' the event were the local food producers and consumers. This was not as apparent in the early years of the Real Food Festival, but became more evident in the later years through resistance. This was identified through the interviews and exhibitor/visitor survey data rather than in the media commentary. Analysis of the raw exhibitor survey data from 2011–2014 shows that the majority (57%) of exhibitors only attended for one year and just 9% participated every year. While this may have reflected a transitory nature of small food-related businesses on the Sunshine Coast, there may have been another more fundamental reason. Interviewee comments, supported by some of the feedback in the exhibitor survey, indicated that the 'power to the producers' premise the festival was based upon was somewhat misdirected:

> I think the Food Festival is more about promoting the region than about promoting individual food products . . . it's telling the story that Maleny or the Hinterland is a food destination.
> (Interview with Richard, local food producer/wholesaler)

> I think [the attendees] were looking more at the value-added product rather than the primary product. And I thought that was a disconnect within the festival itself, that actually [the organisers] should have been more about 'well this is actually where the food comes from and yes it's in a jar or bottle there but these are our primary producers and that emphasis didn't seem to be there.
> (Interview with Rachel, local food producer)

These comments appear to indicate a level of dissatisfaction amongst the exhibitors between the festival rhetoric and reality, which may have contributed to the lack of ongoing exhibitor attendance at the festival.

With regards to the consumers, there was a perception amongst some of the interviewees that the entry price of the festival was a barrier to attendance, particularly after it rose to $20 per adult in 2014 (An increase of $5 from 2013). This was supported by the visitor survey data gathered by the event organisers, with much feedback about a perceived lack of value for money, especially in 2014. Consumers had a fixed disposable income and exerted power through determining how they wished to spend it:

> It doesn't matter how good the festival is, if people don't have the dollars they won't come.
> (Interview with Derek, local food producer)

> As I said this [. . .] twenty dollars seemed to be a huge problem because most food festivals are free . . . I make a point of talking to people and finding out what they think, and it seemed to have been a lot of locals sort of went 'nup, we're not gonna go [to the festival]'.
> (Interview with Tilly, local food producer)

These findings suggest that even where the purpose of an event is to empower particular stakeholder groups, if not managed carefully these groups may also exert power in the form of resistance, which works against the event to constrain it. This supports Clegg's (1989) claim that power may still be demonstrated even in the absence of overt conflict. Furthermore, Getz (2002) noted that events may be highly substitutable. This appears to be the case with the Real Food Festival – it is argued here that consumers may have continued to attend the event had the 'empowerment' rhetoric, rather than entertainment, been the driving force for attendance.

Conclusion

This chapter has explored the complexities in power relations during the birth, life and (untimely) death of a local community food festival in regional Queensland, Australia. It provides an example of an event organisation that, while deliberately set up as a company in order to avoid the problems associated with a cooperative or committee structure, was nevertheless unable to challenge the established order of power (Jepson & Clarke, 2013). Despite their best efforts to give 'power to' local food producers and consumers, it seems this was not necessarily appreciated by these two stakeholder groups – or at least not sufficiently to overcome challenges faced by the festival. The organisers may have been better off taking a more inclusive approach to event management and decision making, and sharing the 'power over'.

The Real Food Festival had been lauded as a successful community food event, and the announcement of the decision not to hold it in 2016 was a surprise to many of those interviewed – there was no indication of falling attendance nor of financial mismanagement. Rather, it was the power held by local government that was perceived to be the most influential factor in the festival's demise. Security of ongoing funding from sources such as this is tenuous, and the level of bureaucracy and paperwork required to hold an event is increasing due to health and safety concerns. Local government selection of which festivals and events to support may change at whim, and in this case, a 'crowded calendar' of events provided the public with an abundance of options in how to spend their leisure time and money.

References

Anon. (2011) 'Hinterland to host real food festival', *Hinterland Times*, 9 April. www.hinterlandtimes.com.au/2011/04/09/hinterland-to-host-real-food-festival/ (Accessed 15 May 2016).

Australian Bureau of Statistics. (2013) *2011 Census QuickStats – Maleny*. www.censusdata.abs.gov.au/census_services/getproduct/census/2011/quickstat/SSC30999?opendocument&navpos=220 (Accessed 10 April 2016).

Batty, R.J. (2016) 'Understanding stakeholder status and legitimate power exertion within community sport events: A case study of the Christchurch (New Zealand) City to Surf', pp. 103–119 in Jepson, A. and Clarke, A. (eds.) *Managing and developing communities, festivals and events*. London: Palgrave Macmillan.

Beverland, M., Hoffman, D. and Rasmussen, M. (2001) 'The evolution of events in the Australasian wine sector', *Tourism Recreation Research*, 26(2), 35–44.

Carlsen, J., Andersson, T.D., Ali-Knight, J., Jaeger, K. and Taylor, R. (2010) 'Festival management innovation and failure', *International Journal of Event and Festival Management*, 1(2), 120–131.

Church, A. and Coles, T. (2007) 'Tourism, politics and the forgotten entanglements of power', pp. 1–42 in Church, A. and Coles, T. (eds.) *Tourism, power and space*. Abingdon: Routledge.

Clarke, A. and Jepson, A. (2011) 'Power and hegemony within a community festival', *International Journal of Event and Festival Management*, 2(1), 7–19.

Clegg, S.R. (1989) *Frameworks of power*. London and Thousand Oaks, CA: Sage Publications Ltd.

Cooper, C., Scott, N. and Baggio, R. (2009) 'Network position and perceptions of destination stakeholder importance', *Anatolia*, 20(1), 33–45.

Davies, A. (2015) 'Life after a festival: Local leadership and the lasting legacy of festivals', *Event Management*, 19(4), 445–459.

de Rijke, K. (2012) 'The symbolic politics of belonging and community in peri-urban environmental disputes: The traveston crossing dam in Queensland, Australia', *Oceania*, 82(3), 278–293.

Doorne, S. (1998) 'Power, participation and perception: An insider's perspective on the politics of the Wellington waterfront redevelopment', *Current Issues in Tourism*, 1(2), 129–166.

Foucault, M. (1978) *The history of sexuality: Volume 1: An introduction*. New York: Vintage Books.

Foucault, M. (1980) *Power/knowledge: Selected interviews and other writings*. London: Peregrine Books.

Gaesser, G.A. and Angadi, S.S. (2012) 'Gluten-free diet: Imprudent dietary advice for the general population?', *Journal of the Academy of Nutrition and Dietetics*, 112(9), 1330–1333.

Getz, D. (2002) 'Why festivals fail', *Event Management*, 7, 209–219.

Getz, D. and Andersson, T.D. (2008) 'Sustainable festivals: On becoming an institution', *Event Management*, 12, 1–17.

Getz, D., Andersson, T.D. and Larson, M. (2007) 'Festival stakeholder roles: Concepts and case studies', *Event Management*, 10, 103–122.

Gibson, C. and Connell, J. (2015) 'The role of festivals in drought-affected Australian communities', *Event Management*, 19(4), 445–459.

Gration, D. (2014) 'Food events in the Sunshine Coast, Australia: Paddock to patisserie and back', pp. 159–168 in Getz, D., Robinson, R. N. S., Andersson, T. and Vujicic, S. (eds.) *Foodies and food tourism*. Oxford: Goodfellow.

Green, E. (2010) *Maleny: An alternative history*. Maleny, QLD: Elaine Green.

Hill, J. (2014) 'Foodies flock to Maleny for local produce', *Sunshine Coast Daily*, 13 September. www.sunshinecoastdaily.com.au/news/foodies-flock-to-maleny-for-local-produce/2385845/ (Accessed 18 May 2016).

Jepson, A. and Clarke, A. (2013) 'Events and community development', pp. 6–17 in Finkel, R., McGillivray, D., McPherson, G. and Robinson, P. (eds.) *Research themes for events*. Wallingford: CAB International.

Keith, S. (2012) 'Coles, Woolworths, and the local', *Locale: The Australasian-Pacific Journal of Regional Food Studies*, 2, 47–81.

Lukes, S. (1974) *Power: A radical view*. London: Macmillan.

McGehee, N.G. (2012) 'Interview techniques', pp. 365–76 in Dwyer, L., Gill, A. and Seetaram, N. (eds.) *Handbook of research methods in tourism: Quantitative and qualitative approaches*. Cheltenham: Edward Elgar Publishing.

McKerchar, M., Hodgson, H. and Walpole, M. (2009) 'Understanding Australian small businesses and the drivers of compliance costs: A grounded theory approach', *Australian Tax Forum*, 24(2), 151–178.

Moffat, N. (2016) 'Don't give up on Real Food Festival: Farmers', *Sunshine Coast Daily*, 11 February. www.sunshinecoastdaily.com.au/news/hinterland-needs-the-real-food-festival-farmers/2928688/ (Accessed 12 February 2016).

Onyx, J., Edwards, M. and Bullen, P. (2007) 'The intersection of social capital and power: An application to rural communities', *Rural Society*, 17(3), 215–230.

Pacella, J., George, J. and Roberts, R. (2015) '"Taste"-ing festivals: Understanding constructions of rural identity through community festivals', pp. 187–196 in Jepson, A. and Clarke, A. (eds.) *Exploring community festivals and events*. London and New York: Routledge.

Real Food Festivals. (2015) *2014 Post-Festival Report*. http://realfoodfestivals.com.au/wp-content/uploads/2014/12/2014-RFF-Post-Festival-Report-small.pdf (Accessed 19 September 2015).

Thomas, R. and Thomas, H. (2005) 'Understanding tourism policy-making in urban areas, with particular reference to small firms', *Tourism Geographies*, 7(2), 121–137.

Tiew, F., Holmes, K. and de Bussy, N. (2015) 'Tourism events and the nature of stakeholder power', *Event Management*, 19, 525–541.

11 Religion and politics – event, authenticity and meaning
A dialogical approach

Ruth Dowson and Ian Lamond

This chapter transgresses the old adage, 'never discuss religion or politics'. Taking a dialogical approach, through a structured research-informed conversation facilitated by Professor Karl Spracklen, the authors consider the similarities and differences in how we can understand the articulation of events within church and social movement communities. The participants in this conversation are both academics and events practitioners; using both perspectives, the authors seek to explore how space is contested, physically, performatively and conceptually, with a view to establishing points of consensus and dissensus around planned and unplanned events and festivals, as utilised by churches and political activists alike, in their endeavours to achieve an authentic and meaningful community within a local area.

RD: So we were talking about dissensus giving us our rationale for this book chapter...

IL: And why we're doing it this way... Because from our conversations, I think we're very similar in perspective, but we approach it from two very different angles, so we're trying to see where the similarities and differences are – and whether similarities are genuinely similar, and whether differences are just ones that we construct.

RD: At the same time, those different angles are messy, because you have religious experience, and are a political activist, and I have political experience, and am a priest. So it's not like 'that's Ian' and 'that's Ruth...'

IL: There's not a wall between us...

RD: It's actually more like – a wiggly line?

IL: What I'm interested in trying to do is to think through those known knowns, known unknowns and so on – and what unknown unknowns will we discover, just by talking?

RD: Yes – for us, this is also about learning, isn't it?

IL: I think a lot of academic researchers say, 'This is what we've found. Hurrah! Learn from this'. Whereas we're saying, 'We don't know what we've found, let's learn from each other, let's go on a journey together and see what we see'.

RD: It's also 1+1=3. And Cartesian co-ordinates.
IL: And in terms of Descartes, it's about alternatives to Cartesian dualism – not just mind-body or spirit-matter. It's more about the messiness that is both and neither, at the same time. So it's a-dualistic – not anti-dualism, just 'not on the scene, man'.
RD: So it's not just one or the other . . .
IL: Ranciere talks about 'dissensus' but Mouffe tends to use 'agonistic'. What I get from them is the idea that real democracy needs a multiplicity of voices; it's not a done deal. It's not a finished project, where you've got an answer, and that's the end of the issue. It's looking at different voices, which becomes a creative process, offering alternatives, different ways of looking, different positions, options and possibilities, which forms the heart of democracy. So in a sense, it's a continual, creative 'otherness'. Where Habermas talks about deliberative processes, it's more that through the correct application of reason and thought, we'll come up with a solution. Dissensus is more about needing a plurality, a multiplicity of answers. Not just, 'this is the answer'.

For me, the idea of 'dissensus' ties in really closely with how I understand the concept of 'event'. Because for me, event is about disruption and the exposure of discourse as a result of disruption, and in part, how regimes of truth, power relationships, try to address that disruption, either to mitigate against it, or to shape it in some way to support a particular ideological end. So dissensus has a creative sense of ongoing difference, which ties in with 'event as disruption'. As somebody interested in studying events, I'm interested in how events disrupt, what kind of discourses are exposed, what kind of issues are raised because of that; who gets to create, curate and/or manage acts of disruption, and who tries to address and/or mitigate them. Who gets classed as a specialist, who gets classed as an expert?
RD: And we're thinking about this from two perspectives – political and religious acts and events.
IL: In terms of the political acts, for me, the focus is more on political acts by social movements and activist groups, rather than, say, political acts of MPs, or Parliament.
RD: It's activist groups in the religious context as well. And we recognise an element of celebration, of festival, in many protest events.
KS: So, how do political and religious events overtly challenge the hegemony of power elites and accepted discourse?
IL: For me, because of the philosophical underpinning of what 'event' means, which is essentially about contestation, it's about disruption – that events, by being events, have the potential for challenging the prevailing hegemony. What then becomes the issue is how that disruption is manifest. It can be evidenced in such a way that the dominant hegemony is actually shaping and twisting it, to commodify the

space that's being used, to imprint its own reproduction within the potential for disruption. But what fascinates me about protest events is that they are deliberately trying to disrupt the hegemony, to disrupt the discourse; to bring to the fore the prevailing power relations, through the very act of disrupting, by the act of the event itself. So how events do this becomes difficult to articulate, because that is the essence of event: the problem is that we have a hegemony that is trying to colonise that, and has colonised that, to a large extent.

RD: One of the things we might explore is what is the accepted discourse? To me, one of the accepted discourses is about being protective of everybody. For example, political correctness suggests that you shouldn't do things that might offend other people. That's the environment, the context, in which we live. Some of the things I've seen, that I've participated in, from the religious perspective and from the political perspective, have challenged that by saying, 'This is what's important, and we are going to do it' – but some people think you shouldn't do it because you might offend people, but actually the people who might be offended, aren't.

KS: Can you give us an example, please?

RD: Situations that I've seen around religious festivals, such as Easter or Christmas, where groups of Christians present the Easter or Christmas story in public, in a public space. So for example at Christmas, in Bingley, where my church is, there's a Nativity procession through the town, with a donkey. And we're telling the story as we go along. Easter is another one of those key times, and maybe it's more challenging, because you might have somebody playing the role of Jesus, carrying a cross. I have a vivid memory in the early 1980s of seeing a man, as Jesus, carrying a massive cross through Bradford city centre – claiming that space. I think there's a sensitivity around 'should that kind of thing be happening' – anywhere, but Bradford is multicultural, a diverse religious environment. And the reality is, that's not a problem, but some people think it is and that to me is the prevailing hegemony. It's being challenged, but not in an intentionally disruptive way. It's that we're doing what we need to do, rather than wanting to break any conventions. The churches are just doing what they think they should do.

IL: In terms of protest events, there's deliberate convention-breaking, but isn't that also the case with certain kinds of music event?

RD: Like raves? Absolutely.

IL: So there's something around disruption.

KS: Can you give me an example of a disruptive political event?

IL: The ones that interest me are those with a more performative element. Political events such as those that Greenpeace instigate, where they attend a shareholders' meeting, dressed as orangutans, to raise the profile of issues around sources for palm oil. Protests by loose activist collectives like those of UK Uncut, where they attend somebody's retirement dinner to give them an award for supporting businesses in their corporate tax avoidance. The essence of protest is to be disruptive, and to challenge people, both on what they think they know about the state of the world, but also their orientation to it, their ontology. But the ones that I find most interesting have a performative element, where there's an attempt to challenge mediated discourses as well as physical, spatial ones.

In Brazil recently, I observed a demonstration by centre-to-far-right-wing groups in the main street, the Avenida Paulista, that, at one level, felt much more like a party, and at some points, a bit like being in a mosh pit. It didn't feel like your standard street-based occupation-processional protest that we're used to in the UK. It was much more party-ish and festival-like.

Arriving at this demonstration, it felt like quite a pleasant thing to be attending. It was against corruption in government, in principle, a topic I could feel some resonances with. There were families carrying picnic hampers. I saw lots of concession stalls – selling crafts, baked goods. There were foods, different coloured popcorn, music playing, people dancing, having picnics in the street, lots of families. It wasn't a demonstration, it was an occupation of the street, so it wasn't actually moving anywhere. And the general feel was of a nice, cosy space, a comfortable space, and that people were just dissatisfied with the corruption in government. It was only when I began to look at some of the banners that were displayed, listen to some of the people speaking, look at some of the stands, other than the food and craft stands, that it actually became for me, very chilling. The banners were very homophobic, Islamophobic, some were calling for a return to the military junta. There were very few non-white people within the demonstration. There were people asking to sign up for quasi-military training, in event of the coup some wanted to take place happening, so they would be ready to take to the streets – armed. That felt very disturbing for me. The juxtaposition of one form of leisure, casual leisure – a, 'let's have a nice day out' form of leisure, with the very dark tension of something more serious or project based, that contestation came across really very strongly. It had a profound impact on me, just how easy it is to be swept up in an atmosphere, when we don't understand what the message is really about and what the discourse that is being articulated, is actually articulating. So that was my Brazilian experience.

I could identify close connections with what you talk about, Karl, as 'serious leisure', and activism as serious leisure. But activism is also, in the Sao Paulo example, casual leisure as well, with families having picnics in the middle of the street, people selling popcorn or craft jewellery. Particularly some of the early stages of the demonstration, it felt more like walking through the field at Glastonbury, than it did walking through a march in London.

RD: From some of the stuff I've seen on social media and heard people talk about PRIDE, from your description of what you saw in Brazil (and I've not been to a PRIDE event), there's the idea that PRIDE is a celebration, it is celebratory, festival-like. And for us, now, PRIDE is not so much a protest, but its roots were in protest. Though if you held PRIDE in some countries, you'd be locked up. So there is that evidence from PRIDE, of an atmosphere of celebration, but it is contesting the space of a city, in a way that we see as positive.

If you take the example of Leeds, it is that 'festival' feel; there's people asking questions, stalls selling things, like T-shirts, promoting things, very much buying into the values that it espouses. And to take a different position from the previous example, there was also a church stall that had activities like face-painting – similar to the Brazil demonstration. There were Christians with banners saying 'We are sorry for the hurt that we've caused. God loves you and so do we'. Not in a 'God loves you so we're going to pray for you to get better' kind of way, but saying, we stand with you, we stand alongside you. There was a special church service at All Hallows Church in Leeds, with the sermon preached by a transgender woman who is a minister. So that church is actually standing in solidarity with the people from PRIDE, and quite a few are also within the LGBTQ community. For me, that church is transgressing what is expected. But if you were outside of the church, you might expect the discourse of the church to be opposed to gay people.

To me, PRIDE is a similar type of event to the Brazilian event, but the values are quite different. And in a way, that's a dilemma that we hadn't really thought about before, had we? That it's ok for us to break the rules because we think something is wrong, because that's part of democracy and we can argue for that, and demonstrate that that's right, even though when demonstrations happen, perhaps the prevailing power elites are saying 'protest is wrong', we're saying 'protest is right'. But when the people who are protesting have values that are different from ours, that's a problem. And I don't think that we'd been aware of that before we started this process of dialogue.

IL: So there's something about discourse and contestation.

RD: Yes. And in Bradford the PRIDE event was moved from an open public event space because the organisers said they didn't have enough resources and were overwhelmed by the detailed administration imposed by the Council on holding the event – risk assessments, temporary event notices, etc. – and they didn't know how to do this. So a local inclusive church offered support, but even though there was the political will for the gay community and the church to collaborate together, the event couldn't happen in that space. Whereas ten miles away, it was a massive event, a big party and celebration, supported by Leeds Council.

IL: I've participated in the last four Leeds PRIDEs, being part of that community. The relationship that Leeds PRIDE has with the Council is very close, so that if that issue had arisen in Leeds, the Council would have said, 'here are people who can support you'.

RD: It seems that councils are now more aware of logistical issues, but they could consider helping people who want to use their City Park space. I remember Chris Howson (liberation theologian and Anglican priest), taking part in Bradford PRIDE in the past, wearing his clergy robes and rainbow-coloured stole.

IL: It brings to mind some thoughts about contrasting the differences between 'event' and 'ritual' (in a secular and theological sense). My construal of 'event' is that event is complex and porous and multiple, in that if you poke an event, what you get is lots of other events, and if you poke those events, you get lots more events. So, mathematically, it would be fractal; on the surface, it looks simple, but it's always more complex, when you dig down, there are multiple layers. So, when it comes to Leeds PRIDE and the Brazilian protest, many elements came across to me almost as 'ritual'. They've been done this way so many times that relationships have been set up; the conversations have been had; it's just a question of plug-in-and-play. But even though it's ritualised, to a certain extent . . .

RD: Even in the organisation of it . . .

IL: Yes, it's still an event for many of the participants, some of whom will be coming out for the first time, others will come out as a result of participating or observing, so it becomes an event for them. But because so many elements of it are ritualised, particularly within the current dominant hegemony of capitalism that we're in, it also becomes commodified. You get merchandising, branded products. Leeds PRIDE was dominated by orange this year, because so much came from Sainsbury's. It became Sainsbury's PRIDE, as far as I could tell. And you wouldn't get that, without a degree of ritual in there. Because if it was seat-of-the-pants scary protest, a company like Sainsbury's would really back away. And it was the same with the Brazil protest, a lot of what I saw was actually ritual, 'oh we've just run up this 500-metre flag of Brazil to process down the street'. No, that took a lot of planning, a lot of preparation, conversations. There were balloons for sale, emblazoned with pictures of Sergio Moro, the magistrate leading the Lava Jato ('Operation Carwash') inquiry into corruption in Brazil, dressed as some kind of superhero.

RD: which is commodification . . .

IL: And all that's only possible if you've got a comfortable space to work in, where things are commodified. So there's tension between 'event' as disruption, and 'ritual' as commodification. It's not that one replaces the other, both can exist simultaneously.

RD: Does the commodification make it ritual?

IL: I don't know, maybe?

RD: Looking at Falassi's typology of ritual, which was developed in terms of festivals – Falassi identifies a framing ritual that opens the festival – valorization – that makes the event like the sacred space – because the event is the sacred space, the liminal space.

IL: Peter Brooke talks about theatre in the same language.

IL: So what does Falassi mean by the term, 'rite?' Because when you mention rites of passage, I can picture that, because, particularly from a theological standpoint, there are certain forms of language, certain forms of authority that I can immediately associate with that.

RD: Falassi talks about them as 'ritual acts', that happen 'within an exceptional frame of time and space', with meaning beyond literal aspects.

IL: I would see 'event' as sometimes being a disruption of some rites. Thinking of the rite of passage of baptism, particularly for an adult, it may be a ritualised practice for the church that they go to, but for the individual it could be – and hopefully is – a profoundly life-changing moment, that means that everything about how they perceive the world before, alters. So that's massively disruptive. It might mean that their whole relationships that they have with other people radically changes. And surely that's the point of evangelism? I'm seeing 'ritual' as a consolidation, rather than a break, and that's why I'm contrasting it with 'event'. So it's more of a reification, a simplification, an abstraction, to something that is predictable, almost mundane: 'Oh we're here, we do this, we've come to this demonstration, so we've got to get dressed up. We've come to this protest, so we've got to buy the bow tie, we've got to buy the braces', because that's expected, through the 'ritual' of being there. Whereas the 'event' of being there is, 'I just saw these two policemen kiss, and it blew me away! That completely changed how I viewed the police, how I viewed same-sex relationships'. For me, that is the event.

RD: So that definition of 'event' is what we need to tie down.

IL: Yes, so that concept of 'event' is probably closer to a Platonic Pauline kind of moment, than something that's constructed. And then as events managers – we don't manage events; what we do is manage multiple narratives so that events can happen for people. So a good event is one that is transformational, because the narratives that the event manager has brought together, means that we can't be the same afterwards.

KS: And do the power elites use protest events? For example, the power elites in Brazil might be deliberately finding events and setting them up and giving them publicity, so there's more awareness of one event and not another that's more left-wing, which gets suppressed in the news?

IL: I think in some cultures that's the case, but in others it's not about news-suppression, it's about the imaginaries that are associated and articulated through the mediation of what protest is. So the event that I spectated on that Sunday was reported in the press as a very peaceful demonstration – how so many families were there, how it was good to see so many children, and so on. But there was very little in the press about the themes that we could see whilst we were there, and the photographs in the press were principally of people with Brazil flags processing up and down the street, carrying a huge Brazilian flag. The following Sunday, which was sadly the day I was returning, so I couldn't attend, there was a demonstration of a number of Black Bloc groups, where they smashed windows of some of the state banks, because they wanted to protest against the poverty and violence that they saw the banks as sustaining. They wanted to protest against police violence and government corruption that they saw as a simple characteristic of the state. In the media, that wasn't suppressed; that demonstration was described as a horrific outburst of violence. And yet, the violence articulated within the 'peaceful' demonstration, was against families, people of different cultural groups. But the violence articulated by the Black Block was against a few corporate windows. So the peaceful protest was intensely violent, symbolically, whereas the Black Bloc protest was quite peaceful in terms of its relationship to people, but was violent in terms of its relationship to concepts and institutions, through breaking windows.

RD: There's something about the role of the media here, isn't there? I recall the raves and freeparties that we've studied, where the organisations that develop and organise these illegal events, make sure they tidy up afterwards. But this was presented in the press, with a photograph taken from the organisers' website of a pile of full black bin liners, as the people who had attended the (illegal) freeparty had cleaned up the whole place, and the bin bags are there, ready to go into the van, to be taken away and properly disposed of by the organisers. And this is transformed by the press into violence against property and a public space and beautiful nature, 'and look what they did because there's all this rubbish everywhere'. So this role of the media in explaining why things are happening and how things are happening, and the effects of them, appears to be biased against protest.

KS: Moving on: How does community culture manifest itself within the planning process around these events? How does community work to construct these events? And how then is community manifested in the creation of these events? Is that a good example of the thing you just mentioned – cleaning up the bin bags?

RD: Bradford Apple Day is one of my favourite events that I've never been to. That is a small community sharing really generous hospitality with the wider community, and trying to engage with the wider community in that hospitality. The local allotment society has apple trees and the fruit is used to develop activities; it's creative, it's co-creation, it's an incredibly positive and happy day. But what they're doing is celebrating, saying 'let's share stuff'. And there are groups all around the world who do guerrilla gardening – where you plant stuff and say 'it's free'. And anybody can have this food. And that is, in a sense, a protest. It's saying, 'As a community, we want to share what we have'. But also as a community, it's engaging with the wider community, bringing people in – creating that sense of belonging that's really important to our well-being.

IL: And in social movements, there are quite closed communities as well as those open ones. So you get very tight-knit communities within certain activist groups. Perhaps the Greenham Common protest was like this? They were very tightly bonded with each other, and whilst outsiders could come in, they had to find some way of integrating into that community concept, in order to be able to stay as part of that protest. But then there are other social movements where community and looking outwards, become ways of drawing people into a more fluid sense of their presence. Though 'knitivism', where people engage in knitting – the example that comes to mind is when the Faslane base was surrounded by a huge scarf that had been knitted – a demonstration through knitting that was about drawing people in and raising awareness of those issues, rather than saying, 'Well now you've knitted a square, you've got to be part of our group forever'. So it was opening that conversation up and linking into wider communities.

RD: It's kind of evangelism, isn't it?

IL: Yes. My understanding of evangelism is that its purpose is to change people's worldview – and that's what protesters are trying to do as well.

KS: Are these protests about sacralisation? Is that the right word? Creating something special, sacred?

RD: Durkheim says that community, society, happens when people come together, and people come together to celebrate. And, originally, celebration was about things that were part of the religious environment, births and marriages and deaths, and harvest. These are all 'sacred time'. And there is something about events that become sacred time. So perhaps for people who are politically motivated, as those who are religiously motivated, that protest is sacred time, because it's not 'ordinary' time, it's not the 'profane' time.

IL: There's definitely something about ritual that is associated with community. But there's something about political action that has to be disruptive of that community, as well, for it to be effective.

KS: What do you mean?

IL: A protest, an act of civil unrest, where people go, 'Oh yeah, six o'clock, now we're doing this. Six thirty, we've finished it', isn't a demonstration. It isn't a protest, because it's not having any consequences. It's not challenging anything. It's just 'this is what we do, because this is the day, this is the time – this is what we do on this day, at this time, all the time'. So even having a church service on a Wednesday, that involves bringing food and sharing a meal, if that happens every Wednesday at 7.30, as it did when I was a child, and my dad used to go to the Men's Supper Club, becomes a routine. And, for me, it stops being an event. It can still be an event if somebody goes there and, suddenly, their world changes. But then it's both ritual and event? When you were talking about the Easter procession with somebody carrying a cross – if that happened every year – and I don't know if it did – but if it happened every year, since 1870, and you were seeing it in 1960, or 1970, then, for most people there, it would have been experienced as 'Oh look, it's our Easter Good Friday procession. How lovely, let's have a chat, let's catch up with our neighbours'. But from what I understand, for you . . . it was life-changing.

RD: Yep

IL: So for you, it was definitely an event. Because it disrupted your world.

RD: It did.

IL: And gave you a completely new orientation to it. For myself, when I was not even a teenager, I was 11 or 12, I really had a crush on somebody in school. And they were going on a CND demonstration, and I wanted to sit next to them on the coach. So I went so that I could sit next to this person that I had a crush on. Got there, made sure that I was next to them on the parade, all the way through, so we could have a really nice chat. I could get to know them really well. Hopefully ask them on a date afterwards. But then I heard Tony Benn speak. And whilst I was hearing Tony Benn speak, I thought 'Shit! This is really scary! We could just blow up the planet and every living thing on it!' And my whole world changed then. I became much more politically conscious, much more politically active. But it was something that hadn't even entered my radar. What was entering my radar, was people that I had crushes on. That was about the limit of it. But for many people on that demonstration, it would have been semi-ritual; we do this every year. We get on a coach. We drive to London. We walk along this road. We end up in this park, or outside this bit of public artwork, and we hear people talk.

RD: And we see the same people . . . We might go in community, but we see people that we know: 'Oh, you're here again this year'.

IL: So there is a relationship between ritual and event, but it's not as simple as saying it's either ritual or event, and that things are just rituals or are just events. They're incredibly messy and tangled and layered, complex, multiple, fractal, and whatever other fancy metaphor you want to use.

KS: But it's essentially this phenomenology of experience at work here, isn't it? It's about the mundane, every day, normative stuff versus the transformative.

RD: I recall an example of a young man who experienced that transformative politicisation when he was in London, and a friend invited him to a demonstration outside Parliament. He didn't know that it wasn't a legal demonstration. He didn't know the rules, regulations, legislation. But he did know that he thought the war was wrong. So he went along, and because it was an illegal demonstration, the police were waiting for the demonstrators. And the people who organised it ran away. And other people, who perhaps didn't know what was going to happen, decided to go anyway, and were kettled. And some of them were arrested – one of them was this young man. And that was transformative for him, because he became much more political. He asked 'Why did they arrest us, when we weren't doing anything? The police picked on an old guy . . . they picked people out of the crowd'. And that changed his life. I remember one of his grandmothers saying, 'Well I hope he's learned his lesson now, he won't do that again.' But his other grandmother said, 'Yes, he's learned his lesson now; he's going to do that all the time'. The experience transformed him, but now he knows the law. So he can decide to break the law, or not – because he knows the law. That event changed his life, in a political sense, and in other ways too.

IL: We work on multiple levels, but within that there are levels of knowledge of the world, which we can have lots of, but that doesn't necessarily change what we do. But we can have those worldviews, at an ontological level, with a level of values, and of ethics, and it does take some form of disruption, some form of break in that, which means that we have to confront the discourses that we've been living within. And it's only through that break that those discourses become apparent.

IL: One of the CAAT campaigns against the National Portrait Gallery's hosting meetings for arms dealers, had 15–20 people dressed as artists, outside the Gallery, painting . . .

RD: This reminds me that now, everywhere is a venue – and that's to do with commodification? capitalism? So, for example, a church can be hired out, or a university. Church House in London, St Paul's Cathedral – everywhere is now a multiple-purpose venue, not just for its initial purpose, but for 'you can hire us out'. And once you start to think about 'you can hire us out', you actually have to think about – who can't?

IL: Yes. And that's particularly troubling when you get to public space – like Millennium Square, like Briggate, where it becomes 'if you want to demonstrate, fine, but you've got to pay for the cordons, for the police cover'.

RD: So there's public space too . . .

IL: And 'venuefication!'

RD: It is venuefication! But there are massive ethical issues. So Church House is the administrative centre of the Church of England, in London, next to Westminster Abbey, but it has meeting facilities that anybody can hire out. And when they hired it out to the arms traders, there were people outside, protesting, 'You can't use this, because it's sacred space'. It's not a church, but because it belongs to the church, should it embody the values of the church? And the same thing happens with actual churches – and your view of what is sacred space and what isn't, depends on your theology. So some churches would say, 'No, you're not allowed to do that in here, because it's a church'. So you wouldn't host certain activities there.

IL: It's the same narrative around the National Portrait Gallery – this is not a sacred space, but a space of culture . . .

RD: It's civil sacred space. And it clashes with our values.

KS: So how can event planners provide that space to break, to transform? Is there such a thing as a good practice guide for events management on disruptive events, and if so, what would you put in it?

RD: I think that it depends how you define 'event planners'. Getz would say you need to be professional, you need to have these skills and these competencies, and use these processes. And Getz would say that there are 'planned' events and 'unplanned' events. But the problem we find, is that the events that Getz says are 'unplanned', are actually more planned. Because if you're planning a rave, you need to know the venue, you need to secure the venue, well in advance. You have an hour in which to communicate the location to the audience. And even less time to set up and establish the space as a viable venue. If you think about most events, most are planned weeks, months in advance, sometimes years. So, I would say that there are skills to being a planner of what Getz calls 'unplanned' events, which is about communication, and planning.

I remember one of the anti-war demonstrations going on in London, and people were being kettled. And because of social media, everybody knew what was going on. So it might not be visible on official, traditional media, but because of social media, everybody knew what was happening, that people were being kettled, and what was happening to them. And there is an element in which social media allows, enables, helps people to subvert that traditional power structure. It doesn't necessarily stop them from being beaten, or stop them from being kettled, but it means that everybody knows, because it's out there, you can't hide it anymore, you can't pretend that it doesn't exist. But in terms of event managers and what they do, there

IL: are similar skills, but it's a mind-set which is about trying something new. Not, 'What did we do last time? How do we do this normally?' Instead, 'Let's do it differently'. It's about breaking, isn't it?

IL: Yes it is. There isn't a universal set manual for planning an event ever, but I think there should be an organic, living manual for protest event planners. One that's always updating, always changing.

RD: Because processes shouldn't just always be the same. It's not like 'this is the way to do it'. If events were that easy, we wouldn't be teaching events management, I don't think. Or maybe that's what people think – events are easy to organise. But the problem with events is that things go wrong. And so you have to be in a position whereby you can address issues as they arise, or predict them.

KS: So just concluding, do you believe that the same counter-hegemonic opportunities are there in both types of events that we've been discussing?

IL: The more I talk to Ruth about it, the more I think, yes. I think before we started talking, I thought that protest events were a very distinct kind of transformational event. But the more I speak to Ruth, the more I see them as having a family resemblance to certain forms of religious events.

RD: Yes, certainly not all religious events, but there are some similarities between religious and political activism events, and so we're trying to learn more about their close connections, their similarities – and how much is out there, as well, because the more you learn, you come across more examples. For us, going through this process, has been a learning experience. We've learnt from each other. We've also co-created – this concept of venuefication is something we can take out of it. And the idea that these events take more time and more planning, than 'planned' events.

IL: We need to see where we agree and where we genuinely do differ; where we think we agree, but differ; where we think we differ, but actually agree; and all points in between.

RD: And this idea of the importance of values is that we think it's ok for us to believe and to act in a way that fits our values, but if somebody disagrees with us – that's a dilemma.

IL: Who said morality should be easy?

Summary of discussion

The nature of this research-informed conversation underlines the importance and the role of dialogue. Mouffe's (2000) concept of the 'agonistic' encourages ongoing discussion and debate, recognising that real democracy requires a multiplicity of voices. The process of dialogue enabled the authors to explore existing concepts in an innovative way, and through learning from each other, to develop new ideas and concepts.

Rancière's (2013) 'dissensus' connects with the critical events approach to defining what an event is. In contrast to traditional views of events management, where researchers such as Getz (2016) focus on logistics and management of processes, critical events identifies events as transformational opportunities. The authors suggest that Falassi's notion of ritual acts connects more with a traditional definition of events, whilst a critical events perspective sees events as disruptive of those rituals.

Continuing research questions include the following:

How do we understand the meaning of 'event' from a critical events perspective?
How do political and religious events overtly challenge the hegemony of power elites and accepted discourse?
How does community culture manifest itself within the event planning process around church and political or social movement events?
How is shared meaning and experience created, reinforced or replicated in church and political or social movement events?
How do decisions associated with the event planning process impact the experiential and transformative aspects central to many church and political or social movement events?
How do political or social movement and religious events address contested space through resolution containment in order for planned events to take place?
What are the impacts of power relationships and discourse on the construction of events in church and political or social movement communities?

Bibliography

Boal, A. (1998) *Legislative Theatre*. (Translated by A. Jackson). Abingdon, Routledge.
Bourdieu, P. (1984) *Distinctions*. (Translated by R. Nice). Abingdon, Routledge Kegan & Paul.
Brook, P. (2008) *The Empty Space*. London, Penguin.
Dowson, R.R.; Lomax, D.; Theodore-Saltibus, B. (2015) Rave culture: Freeparty or protest? In. *Protests as Event: Politics, Activism and Leisure*. Ed. Lamond, I.R.; Spracklen, K. London, Rowman & Littlefield International.pp. 191–210.
Durkheim, E. (1972) Religion and ritual. In *Emile Durkheim: Selected Writings*. Ed. Giddens, A. Cambridge, Cambridge University Press. pp. 42–59.
Falassi, A. (1987) *Time Out of Time: Essays on the Festival*. Albuquerque, University of New Mexico.

Foucault, M. (1986) Of other spaces. (Translated by J. Miskowiec). *Diacritics*, 16 (1), 22–27.
Getz, D. (2016) *Event Studies: Theory, Research and Policy for Planned Events*. Abingdon, Routledge.
Habermas, J. (2004) *Between Facts and Norms: Contributions to a Discourse Theory of Law and Democracy*. (Translated by W. Rehg). Cambridge, Polity Press.
Mouffe, C. (2000) *The Democratic Paradox*. London, Verso.
Putnam, R. (2001) *Bowling Alone: The Collapse and Revival of American Community*. New York, Simon & Schuster.
Rancière, J. (2013) *Dissensus: On Politics and Aesthetics*. (Translated by S. Corcoran). London, Bloomsbury.
Sabatier, P. (1993) *Policy Change and Learning: An Advocacy Coalition Approach*. Boulder, Westview Press.
Turner, E. (2013) *Communitas: The Anthropology of Collective Joy*. New York, Palgrave Macmillan.
Wittgenstein, L. (1973) *Philosophical Investigations*. (Translated by G.E.M. Anscombe). Oxford, Blackwell Publishing.
Zizek, S. (2015) *Trouble in Paradise: From the End of History to the End of Capitalism*. London, Penguin.

12 Commemoration, celebration, and commercialisation
Akaroa's French Festival

Joanna Fountain and Michael Mackay

Introduction

Since 1992, the small rural settlement of Akaroa on the South Island of New Zealand has held a community festival celebrating its historic French connection. The town's association with France has its origins in the nineteenth century when a small band of European colonists, mainly French nationals, sailed into Akaroa Harbour on the ship the *Comte de Paris* and made the area home, despite New Zealand having been declared a British colony by the time they arrived (Fountain, 2002; Fountain & Mackay, 2017). Today, the town's French festival – also known as 'French Fest' – provides Akaroa's base population of 624 (CCC, 2014) with an opportunity to learn about, celebrate, maintain, and reinforce *their* town's French cultural heritage. However, the well-publicised events held over festival weekend are also a drawcard for international and domestic tourists, who often outnumber locals in attendance during the weekend's celebrations.

This chapter draws upon a thematic analysis of in-depth interviews with French Fest stakeholders to explore and interpret the multiple, shared, and contested meanings they associate with the event. Our analysis points to a mixed set of meanings attached to the occasion, ranging from the largely commercial to the personally significant, with a clear distinction evident between meanings framed around 'celebration and spectacle' and those centred on 'commemoration'. The study builds on research on the meanings of festivals (e.g. Carnegie & McCabe, 2008; Crespi-Vallbona & Richards, 2007) and extends the allied scholarly literature on the evolution of rural festivals, the role of community festivals in place making and destination-promotion, and the link between community festivals and local identity creation and maintenance (e.g. Fountain & Mackay, 2017). Before presenting the findings of our research, we provide a short summary of the research literature, a description of the research setting (Akaroa Harbour), an historical commentary on the origins of French Fest, and a brief methodological note, and finally we present our findings and conclusions.

A review of the literature

Since the 1990s rural festivals and events in New Zealand have flourished (Higham & Ritchie, 2001; Mackay & Perkins, 2013), echoing a trend that has been closely researched in the Australian context (e.g. Gibson & Connell, 2011; Roberts et al., 2014). The genesis of the proliferation of festivals in rural New Zealand can be interpreted as part of a local response to a set of economic challenges brought about by 1980s rural restructuring – including the wholesale removal of long-standing agricultural subsidies (Mackay et al., 2014; Perkins et al., 2015; Sandrey & Reynolds, 1990). The changing and challenging economic milieu of the 1980s and early 1990s forced many communities in New Zealand to think carefully about ways to diversify their economic base beyond the traditional mainstay of agricultural production (Perkins, 2006), while also seeking to attract new residents to replace those lost to urban migration. While a diverse range of local responses materialised, one common community strategy was to develop appealing and distinct – and often quirky – place-based identities in an attempt to attract tourists to town, while also providing enhanced amenity value to existing residents (Bell & Lyall, 1995; also see Mackay & Perkins, 2013; Perkins, 2006). As articulated by Bell and Lyall (1995), many communities sought to fight marginalisation by promoting local claims to fame in order to put their town on the tourist map. Developing local festivals was part of this process. Community events were a mechanism to promote and reinforce these new and emerging place-based identities, generate new revenue, and provide an opportunity for communities to develop a sense of pride in their community and, simultaneously, build and maintain a sense of collective identity.

The evolution of rural festivals in New Zealand over two decades has led to significant shifts in their management and organisation. For example, there is evidence of a growing sophistication and professionalism in the organisation and management of these events, and an ever-present need to find a unique point of difference or 'hook' to entice the visitor (Fountain & Mackay, 2017). Some rural communities are opting to develop and host a *portfolio* of events over the calendar year, rather than investing all their time and energy in one hallmark event (Shone & Mackay, 2016; also see Ziakas, 2011, 2014). Further to this, there is a marked diversification in the types of festivals hosted by rural communities, which include a range of novel lifestyle events, including annual music festivals in vineyards and other areas of high amenity value (e.g. Hoksbergen & Insch, 2016).

Notwithstanding the work pointed to earlier, there has been limited academic attention paid to this phenomenon of rural festival development in New Zealand, particularly from a theoretical standpoint. However, valuable insights into the evolution, meaning and significance of these events are available from other contexts, including Australia, where questions about the link between rural festivals and small town regeneration have been at the centre of a large body of work (Gibson & Connell, 2011). These studies of rural festivals provide valuable insights into the processes at work in local communities, offering, "A concentrated time- and place-specific lens through which to examine how rural communities define themselves, both internally, and to those outside the community" (George et al. 2015: 79).

Important considerations in this context are questions of identity: of places, of communities and of individuals. Often the aim of festivals is to provide opportunities for people to express a particular sense of place, community pride, connectedness and belonging, and for the preservation of local heritage and culture (de Bres & Davis, 2001; Derrett, 2003; Duffy & Waitt, 2011; Gibson et al., 2011). Festivals provide also a place – a moment in time and space – to display and celebrate personal heritage and one's connection to a locale. However, as de Bres and Davis (2001) acknowledge, community festivals may not only reinforce existing place and personal identities, but can provide the opportunity and space to challenge such constructions, particularly when the festival is important to the identity of only some sections of the community (e.g. Clarke & Jepson, 2011; Frost et al., 2009; Paradis, 2002; Quinn, 2006).

While notions of individual and community identity and sense of place are important to understanding the meaning and purpose of rural festivals, as a result of the postmodern condition, economic meanings are never far from the surface. Many rural festivals have a commercial imperative; some must attract visitors and capital from elsewhere if they are to be feasible and sustainable in the long term, while others act as a device to promote local businesses and/or locally produced commodities. Such commercial imperatives may mean that a community festival, through the process of commodification (Perkins, 2006; Mackay & Perkins, 2013), comes to represent a particular *version* of place, history, and culture that appeals to the potential visitor at the expense of gaining resonance amongst some, or all, local residents (Clarke & Jepson, 2011). For example, festival organisers may place emphasis on spectacle and entertainment, overriding the deeper meaning that attendees or participants desire (Getz, 2012). Over time, however, the perception of a festival can shift. Visitors may become suspicious of the authenticity of the frivolity that first seemed fun, while local residents may gradually come to identify with the version of place represented in the festival, or begin to recognise the important benefits the festival brings to the community, whether these be social or economic (Paradis, 2002; Brennan-Horley et al., 2007). In these terms, festivals are multi-faceted phenomena, having both an instrumental profit-making function and role in production of community. They are settings for social interaction in which place and cultural identities are at once commercialised, celebrated, and negotiated (Ruting & Li, 2011).

Akaroa and the origins of 'French Fest'

Akaroa is a small harbour town located on the east coast of New Zealand's South Island. Getting to Akaroa by road involves a 75-kilometre drive from Christchurch city, New Zealand's second largest metropolitan area, on a road that initially winds around the edge of Lake Ellesmere/Te Waihora before climbing steeply up the side of an ancient volcano to a point known locally as 'Hilltop'. This elevated position provides the first panoramic view of Akaroa Harbour and has thus become a popular site for tourist photography. The road then descends sharply, before meandering through coastal farmland and the small settlements of Barry's Bay, Duvauchelle, Robinsons Bay, and Takamatua, before reaching Akaroa. In recent years, cruise liners have also started to transport large numbers of tourists to Akaroa Harbour – a recent phenomenon that has stimulated vigorous community debates about the impacts of this form of tourism on the small town. The population of Akaroa increases very significantly over the summer months when domestic and international tourists arrive in their greatest numbers for daytrips or longer stays. Holiday home ownership also boosts the town's population during this period, and holiday homes (or 'baches') make up two-thirds of the housing stock in the town.

The area appeals to tourists for a variety of reasons, including the high natural amenity values based on striking volcanic formations, a marine reserve, sea caves, and steep cliffs, which together provide the habitat for bird life and sea mammals, including the rare Hector's Dolphin. The harbour setting is appealing also to recreationists who use the environs for sailing, kayaking, caving, fishing, walking, cycling, and water skiing. Another tourist drawcard is the attractive built environment of the village itself, which comprises British and French colonial architecture, cafés and restaurants, craft stores, and boutique hotel accommodation. The Māori, French and other European settlement history of Akaroa adds a further dimension to the area's appeal, but it is the French connection which is positioned at the core of the area's tourism promotion activities and town-branding initiatives which includes the Akaroa French Festival (Fountain, 2002).

The first official French festival took place in October 1992, at the instigation of the local promotions association, Akaroa District Promotions. The primary objective of the inaugural event was to extend the tourist 'shoulder season' in Akaroa and give local businesses a financial boost heading into summer. This first festival was a single-day event with market stalls and musical performances, the centrepiece of which was a re-enactment of the French landing on the main beach in the town from the *Comte de Paris* in 1840 – an event that remains central to the festival. Since then, the festival has undergone various strategic modifications; the timing of the event has changed from one to two days and from spring to the summer months and back again. Furthermore, since 2011, the festival has shifted from an annual to a biennial affair. The emphasis on French heritage has changed also, as community attitudes in the town have shifted in light of political events. For example, the 1995 festival faced significant community opposition in light of a resumption of French nuclear testing in the Pacific, resulting in the cancellation of the event the following year.

Arguably, the most significant change to the Festival has been an organisational one. This occurred because of the amalgamation in 2006 of the long-standing local authority – the rural Banks Peninsula District Council – with Christchurch City Council (CCC). Two years later, the Akaroa Heritage Festival committee signed a Memorandum of Understanding with CCC, with the latter agreeing to provide funding and a team of festival specialists to manage the event for an initial three-year period. This new arrangement culminated in the 2015 festival that marked and celebrated the 175th anniversary of French settlement in the area.

French Fest 2015 occurred over three days and was considerably more elaborate than previous editions of the event. This was in large part due to an additional funding boost from council and the provision of the specialist events team who helped mobilise resources and develop promotional material, including the commissioning and distribution of stunning posters, which have become highly sought after by residents and tourists. The volunteer members of the Akaroa Heritage Festival committee were involved in the running of the anniversary event also. This committee comprises residents of the town (both long-time residents and newcomers), local business owners, and Māori representatives from the local Ōnuku marae (indigenous meeting ground). Members of the *Comte de Paris* descendants group, a cultural organisation located outside of Akaroa who position themselves as stewards of the town's French heritage, are also significant members of the committee.

Over the weekend of French Fest 2015, the symbolic markers of the French heritage of the town were ubiquitous. Red, white, and blue bunting and balloons lined the streets, and cancan dancers and men with berets and suspicious moustaches patrolled the town. The event's unabashedly French flavour was neatly characterised in a review article in the Christchurch newspaper, the *Press*:

> It was a weekend, which celebrated life, love, and everything French in the harbour town of Akaroa. Thousands donned berets and clutched baguettes for Akaroa French Fest, an event celebrating the town's heritage. The festival . . . includes everything from Pétanque and language lessons to crêpes and historical re-enactments.
>
> (Mitchell, 2015)

More long-term observers might question the extent to which the 'French flair' on display genuinely reflected modern day Akaroa, and the people who now call it home. These observers might conclude that it was little more than a commodified image of place designed to lure the visitors who now make up the majority of festival spectators. Such scepticism has surfaced episodically throughout the event's history. Most years, prior to and after the Festival, a debate ensues among some members of the community, often played out in the local print media, about the value and meaning of the event, the continuing relevance of the town's French connections and the authenticity of its portrayal during the festival (Fountain, 2002, Fountain & Mackay, 2017).

The significance of French Fest – as a marker of community identity, a commemoration of an important period of Akaroa's history, and as a drawcard for visitors to a small community reliant on tourism – drew us to study the event. We were fascinated particularly by the fact that few current residents in the town had French ancestry or a personal connection to the events of that day in 1840 when the *Comte de Paris* sailed up Akaroa Harbour. Due to the somewhat turbulent history of the festival over 20 years, we were interested in looking beneath the glossy promotional material and posters to reveal the meanings the event held for festival stakeholders. There is no doubt that an important imperative for the event – as it had been since its inception – is a commercial one; Akaroa needs visitors. The exuberant display of 'Frenchness', however, suggested that this was not the only motive for organisers, participants, or spectators.

Methods

In order to elicit the meaning of the event for festival stakeholders, qualitative social research methods were employed, and semi-structured in-depth interviews were used as the primary empirical data gathering technique. The interviews also facilitated the testing of ideas emerging from an analysis of historical and documentary sources, and academic literature. Documentary analysis included a close reading and simplified content analysis of the local newspaper, the Akaroa Mail, as well as promotional material and meeting minutes of local organisations such as Akaroa Heritage Festival committee. Periods of fieldwork in 2015 and 2016 to Akaroa provided additional opportunities to engage with local residents in a range of commercial and non-commercial settings. Our main strategy was to walk around and engage with the township, so to become intimately familiar with the research setting (Lofland & Lofland, 1995). During these interpretative walks, we visited the town's services and facilities, such as the information centre and local hospitality and retail stores, while observing and photographing sites of relevance and interest (such as evidence of the town's French heritage – street signs and monuments, for example). We used this time 'on the move' to inspire and develop new questions, which we pursued in the interviews which followed. During this process, we encountered many local residents, some of whom were known to us through previous research in the town. Many of them took an interest in our work and offered unprompted views and perspectives on issues, albeit in a casual unstructured manner. These observations were recorded in field notes for our future reference.

In all, we formally interviewed 14 people, including current and past members of the festival organising committee and event performers. Seven of the interviewees had been involved with the French festival for more than ten years and were able to reflect on the evolution of the event over this period. More recent arrivals offered a newcomers' perspective. All but one of the interviewees occupied voluntary roles in the festival. Each interviews took between an hour and two hours to complete. All interviews were audio-recorded and transcribed verbatim, prior to manual thematic content analysis by each researcher separately. The themes identified by the researchers were discussed, revised and refined collaboratively to ensure credibility of the results, which ensured a high level of investigator triangulation (Wallendorf & Belk, 1989). The results of this analysis from interviews, documentary analysis and personal observations in the township, culminated in the following assessment of Akaroa's French festival, which is structured around three main themes: commemoration, celebration, and commercialisation.

The meaning of French Fest: stakeholder perspectives

Commemoration

The first theme to emerge from our analysis is that French Fest is seen as an historical commemoration of the making of a French settlement. This theme emerges most strongly in discussions around the re-enactment of the French landing on the Saturday morning of the festival. This re-enactment has been an element of French Fest since the 1990s, but in 2015, it involved, for the first time, a substantial contingent of local Māori welcoming the new arrivals as they disembarked from small boats on the beach. All participants in this re-enactment wore period costumes (under health and safety-regulated life jackets for those on boats). Accompanying the re-enactment was an historical commentary outlining the significance of the event and the context in which it occurred. A free flyer which contained historical facts about the landing, including a list of the names of the settlers who came out as passengers on the *Comte de Paris*, was also made available to those attending the re-enactment. The flyer, designed in the shape and style of a vintage scroll, points to both the historical and continuing cultural significance of the landing and establishment of a 'French colony':

> We would like to welcome you here today to watch our re-enactment of the disembarking of our ancestors from the French ship *Come de Paris* onto the Akaroa beach – their new home, half way around the world . . . we would like to acknowledge and show respect for our brave and adventurous ancestors who fled their homelands of poverty and war

and endured many months of uncomfortable conditions on the sea to settle in what was to be Nouvelle-Zelande – their new French colony.

(From printed festival flyer, 2015)

As outlined earlier, this element of the festival has been organised largely by *Comte de Paris* descendants and Ōnuku representatives on the event's organising committee. While stakeholders had much to say about the commemorative re-enactment, overall it was this element of the festival that drew the most discussion from interviewees in response to questions about the meaning of French Fest. A number of interviewees told us that they found the re-enactment emotionally moving and noted how important it was to remember those events of 1840, which were central to the identity of Akaroa. The following quotations encapsulates this perception:

> We had a wonderful landing including the local rūnanga [Māori village], there was a warrior there, we had a waka which we'd brought in from Christchurch and a crew and it was just a very special ceremony or I thought it was and I think that's a very important perspective that we need to maintain and promote as well . . . I had a lump in my throat when I watched it, it was great.
>
> (Heritage Festival Committee member)

> I think it was actually so emotional, really was a beautiful re-enactment and we'd worked hard to make it. . . . It really brought that whole historical thing alive and that's something that we can really work on because in the past I think it's all just been a little bit of a fun French thing and a theme really, put your berets on, red, white and blue but now it seems to be much more important.
>
> (ADP representative)

It is interesting to note this second interviewee observing the need to treat this commemorative ceremony with respect – a point returned to next. For direct descendants participating in the landing, it had especially significant resonance. One participant reported on the feedback she received from descendants in the re-enactment:

> It means so much to the people involved, that was really the feedback that I got from the people who got participated, it was both Māori and the European/Pakeha descendants, they all said that it just brought tears to their eyes and that's because there they were seven generations on playing their own ancestors meeting for the first time, it was powerful.
>
> (Festival participant)

As one re-enactment participant explained, "Our focus has always been to remind the public about the history of Akaroa, to keep our ancestors alive . . . that's what Akaroa is based on". The need to keep the heritage alive is supplemented by the need to share this history, particularly with new residents who may be unfamiliar with the stories:

> It's an opportunity for community to tell its story and the way the community has chosen to tell its story is through this re-enactment thing which is great because . . . it means that what you do is you take all the visitors to this place, that's your theatre.
>
> (Festival participant)

In this way, this commemorative event helped shape how this community "see themselves, their heritage and their identity" (Frost & Laing, 2011: 37) and how they portray themselves to the world.

Celebration

The second theme emerging in analysis of Akaroa French Fest 2015 is that the festival offered an entertaining spectacle for residents and visitors. As one respondent explained, "It's a great excuse to get dressed up and for the town to go into carnival mode". This meaning primarily emerged when respondents talked about the attractions and activities offered at the recreation ground during the Saturday afternoon, which included food and drink stalls, music, and fun 'French-themed' competition and games, which together created a festive and fun atmosphere. Two participants involved in different elements of the festival explained the celebratory feel of these activities, and the role of French heritage in this:

> All the . . . 'oh la la' froggy stuff is hilarious, especially when people come up with all the wacky creative stuff like waiter races and snail races and all that kind of stuff.
>
> (Festival participant)

> I think that the whole idea is to have a big party and celebrate that fact that you've got the French coming and the odd German or two and a couple of Italians.
>
> (Festival participant)

These celebratory events were spatially removed from the more serious commemorative atmosphere associated with the landing re-enactment by being situated at the other end of town, and the importance of making this spatial, as well as symbolic, distinction was realised:

> I think it's that fine line you see, I think it's all very well when you've got oh la la froggy stuff happening at the recreation ground, that's fine but not the landing itself.
>
> (Festival participant)

This distinction was highlighted when some respondents reminisced about a landing re-enactment at an earlier festival which they felt was spoiled and degraded by a comic making fun of the event in his commentary – an approach which was clearly unacceptable.

While most respondents were relatively relaxed, and even pleased, with the caricatures of Frenchness on display at the recreation ground, a few interviewees felt less comfortable, seeing them as superficial. One past committee member felt:

> They rather sort of played to clichés about French culture and French people and didn't seem to be particularly grounded in anything of Akaroa or the place.
> (Former French Fest committee member)

At the same time, she recognised the appeal of these activities:

> Anything old and quirky seemed to get in there so to my mind that sort of dilutes the authenticity of it but on the other hand it's a big community event and it involves the community and if it draws more people from outside Akaroa from Christchurch to come and have a look and a day of fun where's the harm?
> (Former French Fest committee member)

The theme of celebration related not only to the carnival atmosphere but also to the opportunity the festival provided to celebrate community. This meaning was revealed in discussions about the organisation of the festival and the event itself. This meaning was perhaps less tied to a specific element of the festival, but related more to the camaraderie and social capital which emerged through working together – a theme that is consistent with the findings of past research on community festivals (e.g. Arcodia & Whitford, 2006; Moscardo, 2007). Participants in the re-enactment specifically talked about the opportunity this occasion provided for building relationships between representatives from Ōnuku and the wider community. As one *Comte de Paris* descendant described:

> It was just great and . . . this is what it would have been like . . . it would have been the Māoris [sic] and the people off the ship and the odd person that already lived there and it really brought it together and made it whole, it was so good.
> (Comte de Paris descendants' group representative)

One event encapsulated the community theme for respondents during the festival itself perhaps more than the landing re-enactment. This event was a relatively informal street party held on the Friday evening of festival weekend, where local residents could relax and socialise before the influx of visitors to the town began:

> Lots of those people are working on the Saturday, they're all involved in it in some way or another, so it was a nice chance for us to just kick it off and be excited about the festival.
>
> (Ōnuku representative)

Some respondents spoke with bemusement about the fact that the Council events team was not informed about a highlight of the evening – a light projection of the *Comte de Paris*, which appeared like a ghostly apparition out in the harbour. This spectacle was possible due only to the coming together of a couple of local residents drawing on their professional skills and know-how, and the work of the volunteer fire brigade, who sprayed a jet of water on which the projection appeared. As one of the creators explained,

> I think that how we organised that apparition was a good example of what you can do in a community and with that kind of spirit the whole thing can be alive and well.
>
> (Festival activity organiser)

Another respondent concurred:

> That was really good actually and that wasn't the events team, that was a local initiative and done by virtue of the fact there were people here with the skills to execute it, to see it through.
>
> (Former French Fest committee member)

A number of respondents reflected on the fact that the degree of involvement by the Council events team over the past seven years had perhaps limited the opportunity for the community to get involved in this way. In this context, a number of respondents viewed the withdrawal of council support for future events as a potential opportunity to reinvest the event with social capital and greater community togetherness, as these quotations suggest:

> I think it has to come back to the community because it is a community event and I think when the Council did get involved it [took] away from the heritage aspect in terms of it [being] just an event like any other event.
>
> (Ōnuku representative)

> My thinking is that . . . [when the council were running it] . . . the local people sort of fell away completely from being active on the committee. Now that the council are pulling out again it seems there's been a bit of

a reawakening and we've got a larger group of people in Akaroa back on the committee than I've seen for a while.

(*Comte de Paris* Descendants' Group representative)

It is often the case with heritage, or in this case, a heritage festival, that the local community most clearly recognise its value when it is threatened or at risk of being lost (Hewison, 1987). There is no doubt that the future of this heritage festival is in the balance, due to the removal of council funding and logistical support. In this situation, it seems stakeholders have become more attuned to the festival's role in celebrating community. Commercial considerations, however, remain critical for the future of the festival.

Commercialisation

The final theme emerging from discussions related to the commercial imperative for the event, including the cost of running the event and the economic spin-offs, such as the benefits of promoting the town to visitors. As discussed earlier, rural towns in New Zealand are well aware of the importance of attracting tourists as a source of income and employment, and Akaroa is no different, with the visitor industry being an important source of revenue for the town. In this context, the theme of commercialisation was never far from the surface in discussions with respondents, although it was framed in differing ways by the different interest groups we interviewed. For example, the ADP representative, who was the only respondent paid for their involvement in the festival, acknowledged that the peripheral location of the town acted as a barrier to visitation and felt that the festival was a way to address this: "To get people over the hill, we have to have an interesting enough event programme, so the French festival [is important]".

All the stakeholders we interviewed recognised that Akaroa's French connection is its unique selling point and that the festival was a means to promote that image of the town to the outside world:

For me Akaroa is the only French settlement in New Zealand and it gives it a single difference and I think it's important that we try and celebrate that and promote . . . this little part of Banks Peninsula.

(French Fest committee member)

Some of our interviewees felt that the need to attract visitors to Akaroa had diluted the meaning of the event as experiences became more commodified, particularly since the involvement of the council. There was a sense from respondents that the council's focus on the return on investment to the town, if not to their own coffers, had intensified this situation. As a member of the *Comte de Paris* descendent group explained,

[The council] want then the festival to be a business success and a successful day out so they're happy then to organise the French games and the other entertainment and the stalls and food and all the things that go together to make a festival, so that's the business side of it and they're really almost quite divorced [from the landing re-enactment].

(Comte de Paris Descendants' Group representative)

There was a clear sense too that the business community looked to get a significant financial boost from the weekend and that this was their clear goal:

For us [the festival] is to promote the history and the heritage of Akaroa. If you ask the Akaroa community they will say it has to bring money into the community and keep the businesses buoyant.

(*Comte de Paris* Descendants' Group representative)

It is interesting to note, however, that at the time of the 2015 event, there was very little representation from the business community on the festival organising committee.

Other respondents spoke about the financial challenges ahead, given the Council's imminent withdrawal of the majority of funding from the event. This had resulted also in an urgent reconsideration of the French Fest's purpose and meaning going forward, and a reinvigoration of the festival organising committee. One recently appointed French Fest committee member pondered the future of the event thus:

I think the anniversary of the landing will always be there and that should be an event almost of its own, the additional thing of having a big tent and . . . something you control the entry to will allow us to make some money and have some other entertainment as well . . . I think that how we organise that apparition was a good example of what you can do in a community and with that kind of spirit the whole thing can be alive and well and work really well but whether it means there'll be an influx of 10,000 people from Canterbury or something to come and look at it is another matter.

(French Fest committee member)

In this deliberation, the interplay and juxtaposition between the three themes outlined earlier – commemoration, celebration, commercialisation – is revealed, and the future of the event depends in part on how stakeholders come to prioritise these meanings.

Conclusion

To conclude, our study of Akaroa's French Fest points to the multiple meanings attached to any one event. In the current case study, these meanings can be mapped onto the various spaces of the festival – some set aside and respected as sites of commemoration, others prepared for and accepted as sites of spectacle, fun, and frivolity. It is clear also that different groups of stakeholders prioritise different meanings and that the prioritisation of these meanings can change over time. Our study also points to role of festivals in the building and maintenance of (a sense of) community – the sum of the effort and (inter)actions of local residents who, for many months, work together to plan and successfully orchestrate an event.

Our interviews revealed also that the meaning of the festival has changed over time, as funding sources and the organising committee has changed. The 2015 French Fest marked the final festival to have guaranteed funding, and support personnel, available from the CCC. This fact gives rise to questions regarding the future management, and focus, of French Fest. From a festival emerging as a local initiative – with planning and decision-making processes in the hands of a small group of enthusiastic local volunteers – to a much slicker and more professional affair heavily funded and supported by the local authority, the festival is returning to its roots. The next stage of our research will examine this process and consider how different stakeholders collaborate in order to produce a successful community event, and how, in this process, outsiders, newcomers and long-time residents negotiate the meanings of place.

References

Arcodia, C. and Whitford, M. (2007). Festival attendance and the development of social capital. *Journal of Convention & Event Tourism*, 8(2), pp. 1–18.

Bell, C. and Lyall, J. (1995). *Putting Our Town on the Map: Local Claims to Fame in New Zealand*. Auckland: Harper Collins.

Brennan-Horley, C., Connell, J. and Gibson, C. (2007). The Parkes Elvis revival festival: Economic development and contested place identities in rural Australia. *Geographical Research*, 45(1), pp. 71–84.

Carnegie, E. and McCabe, S. (2008). Re-enactment events and tourism: Meaning, authenticity and identity. *Current Issues in Tourism*, 11(4), pp. 349–368.

CCC (2014). Akaroa Community Profile. [online] Available at: www.ccc.govt. nz/assets/Documents/Culture-Community/Stats-and-facts-on-Christchurch/CommunityProfile-BanksPeninsula-Akaroa.pdf [accessed 25 Jan. 2017].

Clarke, A. and Jepson, A. (2011). Power and hegemony within a community festival. *International Journal of Event and Festival Management*, 2(1), pp. 7–19.

Crespi-Vallbona, M. and Richards, G. (2007). The meaning of cultural festivals. *International Journal of Cultural Policy*, 13(1), pp. 103–122.

De Bres, K. and Davis, J. (2001). Celebrating group and place identity: A case study of a new regional festival. *Tourism Geographies*, 3(3), pp. 326–337.

Derrett, R. (2003). Making sense of how festivals demonstrate a community's sense of place. *Event Management*, 1(1), pp. 49–58.

Duffy, M. and Waitt, G. (2011). Rural festivals and processes of belonging. In: C. Gibson and J. Connell, eds., *Festival Places: Revitalising Rural Australia*. Bristol: Channel View Publications, pp. 44–57.

Fountain, J. (2002). *Behind the brochures: The (re) construction of touristic place images in Akaroa, New Zealand*. PhD dissertation. Murdoch University, Australia.

Fountain, J. and Mackay, M. (2017). Creating an eventful rural place: Akaroa's French Festival. *International Journal of Event and Festival Management*, 8(1), [online] Available at: www.emeraldinsight.com/doi/pdfplus/10.1108/IJEFM-06-2016-0043

Frost, W. and Laing, J. (2011). *Strategic Management of Festivals and Events*. 2nd ed. South Melbourne, Australia: Cengage, pp. 30–42.

Frost, W., Wheeler, F. and Harvey, M. (2009). Commemorative events: Sacrifice, identity and dissonance. In: J. Ali-Knight, M. Robertson, A. Fyall and A. Ladkin, eds., *International Perspectives of Festivals and Events: Paradigms of Analysis*. Oxford: Elsevier, pp. 161–172.

George, J., Roberts, R. and Pacella, J. (2015). Whose festival? Examining questions of participation, access and ownership in rural festivals. In: A. Jepson and A. Clarke, eds., *Exploring Community Festivals and Events*. London: Routledge, pp. 79–91.

Getz, D. (2012). *Event Studies: Theory, Research and Policy for Planned Events*. Oxford, UK: Butterworth-Heinemann, pp. 189–220.

Gibson, C. and Connell, J. (2011). *Festival Places: Revitalising Rural Australia*. Bristol: Channel View Publications.

Hewison, R. (1987). *The Heritage Industry*. London: Methuen.

Higham, J. and Ritchie, B. (2001). The evolution of festivals and other events in rural southern New Zealand. *Event Management*, 7, pp. 39–49.

Hoksbergen, E. and Insch, E. (2016). Facebook as a platform for co-creating music festival experiences: The case of New Zealand's Rhythm and Vines New Year's Eve Festival. *International Journal of Event and Festival Management*, 7(2), pp. 84–99.

Lofland, J. and Lofland, L. (1995). *Analysing Social Settings: A Guide to Qualitative Observation and Analysis*. Belmont, CA: Wadsworth Publishing Company.

Mackay, M. and Perkins, H. (2013). Commodification and the making of a rural destination: Insights from Cromwell district, Central Otago, New Zealand. In Proceedings of CAUTHE 2013: Tourism and Global Change: On the Edge of Something Big. Lincoln University, Christchurch, New Zealand, 11–14 February, pp. 494–496.

Mackay, M., Perkins, H. and Taylor, N. (2014). Producing and consuming the global multifunctional countryside: Rural Tourism in the South Island of New Zealand. In K. Daspher, ed., *Rural Tourism: An International Perspective*. Newcastle upon Tyne: Cambridge Scholars Publishing, pp. 41–58.

Mitchell, C. (2015). French Fest frivolity returns to Akaroa, [online] *The Press*, 10 October. Available at: www.stuff.co.nz/the-press/christchurch-life/72868902/French-Fest-frivolity-returns-to-Akaroa [accessed 28 May 2016].

Moscardo, G. (2007). Analysing the role of festivals and events in regional development. *Event Management*, 11(1/2), pp. 23–32.

Paradis, T. W. (2002). The political economy of theme development in small urban places: The case of Roswell, New Mexico. *Tourism Geographies*, 4(1), pp. 22–43.

Perkins, H. C. (2006). Commodification: Re-resourcing rural areas. In P. Clarke, T. Marsden and P. H. Mooney, eds., *Handbook of Rural Studies*. London: Sage, pp. 243–257.

Perkins, H. C., Mackay, M. and Espiner, S. (2015). Putting pinot alongside merino in Cromwell District, Central Otago, New Zealand: Rural amenity and the making of the global countryside. *Journal of Rural Studies*, 39, pp. 85–98.

Quinn, B. (2006). Changing festival places: Insights from Galway. *Social and Cultural Geography*, 6(2), pp. 237–252.

Roberts, R., George, J. and Pacella, J. (2014). There's not a hot dog van in sight: Constructing rural ruralities through South Australian Events. In: K. Daspher, ed., *Rural Tourism: An International Perspective*. Newcastle upon Tyne: Cambridge Scholars Publishing, pp. 79–95.

Ruting, B. and Li, J. (2011). Tartans, kilts and bagpipes: Cultural identity and community creation at the Bundanoon is Brigadoon Scottish Festival. In: C. Gibson and J. Connell, eds., *Festival Places: Revitalising Rural Australia*. Bristol, UK: Channel View Publications, pp. 265–279.

Sandrey, R. and Reynolds, R. (1990). *Farming without Subsidies: New Zealand's Recent Experience*. Wellington, New Zealand: MAF.

Shone, M. and Mackay, M. (2016). Creating an eventful rural town: Insights from Geraldine, Timaru District, New Zealand. Unpublished working paper presented at the New Zealand Tourism and Hospitality Research Conference, 29 November – 1 December, University of Canterbury, New Zealand.

Wallendorf, M. and Belk, R. W. (1989). Assessing trustworthiness in naturalistic consumer research. *Interpretive Consumer Research*, pp. 69–84.

Ziakas, V. (2011). The use of an event portfolio in regional community and tourism development: Creating synergy between sport and cultural events. *Journal of Sport and Tourism*, 16(2), pp. 149–175.

Ziakas, V. (2014). Planning and leveraging event portfolios: Towards a holistic theory. *Journal of Hospitality and Marketing Management*, 23(3), pp. 327–356.

13 Managing community stakeholders in rural areas

Assessing the organisation of local sports events in Gorski Kotar, Croatia

Jelena Đurkin and Nicholas Wise

Introduction

One could argue that the purpose of organising sport events is to create high quality experiences for participants and to contribute to the image, branding and development of destinations. However, it is essential to recognise the range of impacts which sport events could potentially have on communities and local stakeholders. Positive economic impacts that sport events generate are immediately visible, from increased demands for transportation, accommodation and food and beverage, to media promotion, as well as increased overall consumption. Economic impacts can have long-term positive legacies through enhanced image of destination, the creation of viable business relationships, and new investment, enterprise and employment opportunities (Cheung et al., 2016; Daniels et al., 2004; Weed & Bull, 2009). Apart from economic effects, increasingly important are social impacts and a focus upon communities which surround events (Jepson & Clarke, 2015, 2016; Kim & Uysal, 2003; O'Brien & Chalip, 2007; Richards et al., 2013; Wise, 2016; Wise & Perić, 2017). According to Reid (2008), and later emphasised by Smith (2012), important social impacts of events could include the potential for urban regeneration, enhancement of community spirit, improved quality of life, provision of leisure/recreational opportunities, promotion of civic boosterism and educational (and cultural) understanding. Social impacts can also become a primary motive for organising sports events (see Perić et al., 2016a), this is evident from sport-for development initiatives which use sport events to exert positive influences on public health, socialization, the social inclusion of disadvantaged, economic development, and to foster intercultural exchange and peace (Schwery, 2003; Sherry et al., 2015). Jointly, positive economic and social impacts produced by sport events are sometimes successfully united in a leveraging framework, based on strategic planning objectives in order to maximise the benefits for local communities through sustainable events organisation (Chalip, 2006; O'Brien and Chalip, 2007; Perić et al., 2016a; Schulenkorf & Edwards, 2012).

In research it is important to investigate the potential for combining and maximising the positive benefits of sport events through the strategic management of different community stakeholders (e.g. organisers, participants, inhabitants, civil society organisations, private sector) (Weed & Bull, 2009). Collaboration among stakeholders can mobilise community resources and create synergies between different organisations, which is thought to be critical when it comes to successfully hosting sport events (Dredge, 2006; Getz, 2005; Provan et al., 2005; Yaghmour & Scott, 2009). This chapter gives a critical analysis of stakeholder management and the challenges of organising small-scale local sports events in rural communities. 'Small scale' refers to events which are minor in size, (often) held annually, where competitors may outnumber spectators, and receives little media interest (outside the local or immediate region) compared to 'larger-scale' events (Gibson et al., 2012; Hall, 1992; Rojek, 2013; Wilson, 2006). However, whilst 'small-scale' events see overall limited economic results, economic impacts on host communities tend to provide proportionately more benefits than if they were held in a larger city (see Veltri et al., 2009). The term 'local' in this context means sport events organised by local community organisations (mainly by non-profit sport and/or tourism organisations) with significant support and involvement of the local public and private sector. Rural communities often have unique characteristics and dynamics, with often limited financial and operational capacities – which can significantly influence the overall objectives of the sport event, its organisation and stakeholder management. The main purpose here is to conceptually examine the role of various community stakeholders when considering the organisation of and participation in local sporting events. This chapter will also focus on rural communities with limited financial and operational capacities in order to analyse particular strategies when dealing with the challenges of planning and organising local sporting events.

The next section offers a discussion of literature surrounding leveraging frameworks as a model for the strategic organising, managing and planning of events and outlines primary sport event stakeholders. This is followed by an elaboration of specific characteristics and of rural communities, related theory on sense of community and potential relations between those characteristics. Finally, theoretical contributions and concepts elaborated in the sections discussing the case of Gorski Kotar in Croatia.

Leveraging, organising and managing community stakeholders

Models of social and economic leveraging are important to consider when planning, organising and managing sport events for the purposes of identifying and implementing various strategies for stakeholders and to maximise community benefits (see Chalip, 2006; Chalip & McGuirty, 2004; O'Brien & Chalip, 2007, 2008). An important element of leveraging is including various stakeholders in the planning process – so to better identify and work towards desired economic and social outcomes (Chalip, 2014). Speaking of desired outcomes, economic leveraging includes strategies for optimising both trade and event revenues by enticing visitor spend, minimising the booth effect, fostering business networking/enhancing business relationships and using events to promote and build a destinations brand (Chalip, 2014). Social leveraging through sport events should be achieved through the process of generating and cultivating liminality, aimed at fostering social integration (and cohesion) and feelings of celebration (or place pride) as part of the event atmosphere (Chalip, 2006; O'Brien & Chalip, 2008; Wise, 2015a). Enabling socialisation by facilitating informal social opportunities and producing ancillary events and/or theming can be a useful strategy for social leveraging (Chalip, 2006). These preconditions should lead to creation of liminality and *communitas*, two important concepts aimed at contributing to the fulfilment of indicators related to the specific social strategies organisers want to promote when delivering a sport event (O'Brien & Chalip, 2008). Empirical work has been analysed in respect to social and economic leveraging, focusing on model implementations in general (e.g. Chalip & Leyns, 2002; Taks et al., 2013), the use of event portfolios (Ziakas, 2010) and have addressed organisers' perspectives and intentions in rural communities (Perić et al., 2016a).

Delivering and achieving a high quality sport experience requires generating economic and social benefits for the host community (see Chalip, 2006; Perić et al., 2016b; Wise & Perić, 2017). It is therefore essential that sport events are organised through partnerships and cooperation among various stakeholder groups. The importance of stakeholders (as organisations, groups or individuals) is fundamental as they can affect (or be affected) by an organisation's actions (Freeman, 1984), which is mainly assessed on the level of interest and impact they have on the actions of the focal organisation/enterprise. Therefore, primary and secondary stakeholders should also be considered – but there are many other classifications of stakeholders. Primary stakeholders are those groups and individuals formally connected with and invested in a project; in terms of sport events, the important primary stakeholder is the organising committee. Organising committees can be divided into manager(s), paid staff and volunteers, or can be considered as one homogenous group. Other important stakeholders include various levels of government; residents, sponsors, businesses, schools, community groups and sport organisations; the print, radio, television and Internet media; and athletes, coaches, officials and support staff composing the delegations (see Emery, 2002; Masterman, 2004; Parent, 2008). Depending on the complexity, nature and size of a planned sport event, the composition of the organising committee and the number of stakeholder categories involved may vary. Similar to the organisation of festivals, many sport events are the result of collaboration among governmental bodies, private sector enterprises and non-profit sector organisations, which is termed 'mixed industry'

(Andersson & Getz, 2009). In terms of partnerships and common goals in sport events organisation and delivery, all three sectors should, in parallel with their own special interests, pursue 'public goods', which include entertainment, economic growth, identity reinforcement and healthy lifestyles (Getz et al., 2015). These can also be extended to particular social and economic opportunities to benefit host communities as well.

Stakeholder relationships in sport events can be also observed through studies on inter-organisational networks and their impact on event organisation and collaboration with communities in general (Dredge, 2006; Provan et al., 2005; Yaghmour & Scott, 2009, Ziakas & Costa, 2010). Contributing to this discussion, categories of sport event stakeholders proposed by Getz et al. (2015), outlined in Table 13.1 are referred to in this chapter. The categories listed in Table 13.1 are not mutually exclusive and can be shared by the same organisation. It must be noted that emphasis was added in Table 13.1 *to the host community* as 'others impacted' because the host community is the key focus of enquiry in this chapter. Getz et al. (2015) also discuss the topic of event ownership and that community ownership of the event(s) relate to sense of community and legitimacy building. These concepts, as well as discussion on implementation of this stakeholder typology for the purposes of rural communities as event organisers will be elaborated

Table 13.1 List of sport event stakeholders

Stakeholder	Description
Sport-related stakeholders	Governing bodies, clubs/associations, athletes, participants, officials and judges.
Co-producers	Independent organisations actively involved in the event's production; they can be allied permanently with the event organisers or collaborate with them on an event-specific basis.
Regulators	Local authorities, essential services like police, fire, health.
Internal stakeholders	Owners, directors, members, paid staff, volunteers.
Audience and customers	The audience, often referring to paying customers; crucial to an event financial success, especially concerning consumer participation where profit has to be made by attracting and satisfying event tourists.
Media	Have an economic interest in the event – based on demands of live and television viewing audiences.
Facilitators	Grant providers, sponsors, allies and collaborators.
Suppliers	Facility owners, merchants, catering, accommodation, entertainment, technical support, insurers.
Others impacted	Groups receiving benefits, the host community and environment.

Source: Adapted from: Getz et al., 2015: 100

on more in the next section, focusing on rural communities, their characteristics, strengths and constraints.

Rural communities and the local sport event organisation

Rural 'areas' can be described in regards to their geographical and demographic characteristics; but rural 'communities' are more complex to explain. For the purpose of this chapter, a community is described as "a group of people with common interests, living in the same geographic area, and frequently feeling a sense of belonging to the community" (Shucksmith, 2000: 48). Spatially, rural communities are situated outside towns and cities, and rural areas are situated in what is considered the periphery (Osborne et al., 2004). Dimensions including population density, accessibility, settlement patterns and existence of local facilities are sporadic and relate to widely accepted descriptions of rural areas by national governments and policy makers. Such identified rural areas and communities are eligible for special financial (and funding) development programmes and other types of assistance (depending on the country and available funding). Rural areas are often associated with isolation, with relatively homogeneous populations and cultures, but people are linked through a strong sense of community and the local/regional economies are based on natural resources; however, globalisation, connectivity and lifestyle changes have changed this image (Butler & Flora, 2008).

The notion of sense of community is important to discuss here because it reinforces conceptual understandings addressed in this chapter. Wise (2015b: 922) notes, "Research on community suggests that even despite local conditions, people will strive to achieve a sense of community," and while this point in made generally speaking, organising events can challenge this statement when outlining community cooperation later in this chapter. Adding further conceptual insight, McMillan and Chavis (1986: 19) suggest, understanding "sense of community can provide the foundation for law makers and planners to develop programs that meet stated goals by strengthening and preserving community," which is necessary when it comes to joint collaboration and organising events. The same authors also outlined four conditions of sense of community: membership, influence, integration or fulfillment of needs, and shared emotional connections (McMillan & Chavis, 1986). Membership is often recognised based on location, connecting people who reside within close proximity or may share similar ideals that connect collective groups through mutual understanding (Dunham, 1986; Poplin, 1979; Suttles, 1972; Wise, 2015b). Influence within a community involves social capital accumulation, which can be bias of local politics, economics and culture. Place politics, concerning involvement and interactions, especially, have profound influence that can either create or limit integration and fulfillment of needs based on influential factors/variables that reinforce individual or group networks (Jenkins, 2008). Numerous research has supported this conceptualisation because integration and fulfillment are requirements to promote and sustain shared emotional connections (Gibson et al., 2012; Provan et al., 2005; Schulenkorf & Edwards, 2012; Wise, 2015a), which is highly relevant to this study as they can influence involvement and participation in event organisation.

In the context of this study, pertinent to the sense of community and likewise important for small-scale sport events is the complex issue of event ownership, not so much in terms of legal rights on event name, structure, brand and broadcasting, but more related to intangible "community ownership" as "sense of commitment (through political and sponsorship support) and engagement (volunteering, attendance, organisation) that translate into tangible, sustainable benefits" (Getz et al., 2015: 98). As discussed in this chapter, local event organisation can foster individual and community capacity building and help rural communities develop and better make use their own potentials rather than relying on external support and funding (Reid, 2011). Referring to discussions earlier, it is important that principles of economic and social leveraging are introduced in the planning stage so that rural community stakeholders build on their expertise, skills and human and community capital. Involving a range of stakeholders in planning process of the sport event can ensure stakeholder satisfaction and their acceptance of the event, which leads to increased legitimacy. Apart from gained legitimacy, attracting and retaining willing and capable individuals from various stakeholder groups in the process of planning and organisation of events is crucial to sustain events and improve them over time. Without them, the organising and planning process could be threatened, so it is essential that stakeholders build on existing collaborations so the community experiences success as opposed to failure. A lack of collaboration and participation could result in lost potential, decreased economic and social benefits, and diminished social and recreational opportunities for residents of rural communities (Reid, 2011).

Analysing the characteristics which all rural communities share is equally important when managing stakeholders and sport event organisation, rural communities can suffer from a number of limitations, challenges and issues (Butler & Flora, 2008; Osborne et al., 2004; Reid, 2008, 2011), outlined in Table 13.2. The limitations outlined in Table 13.2 have significant impact on previously listed event stakeholder categories, as well as their relationships and collaboration. Due to the lack of financial resources, transport and accessibility, local event management further relies on volunteers, sponsors and donors (sourced in the immediate region). This does, however, lead to a higher number of partnerships between and across the various organisations from the public and private sector, which might strengthen their long-term cooperation but at the same time risk associated with the events success is increased.

Strategies that involve providers of all necessary infrastructures and services, needed to deliver a successful sport event, can use more or less

Table 13.2 Limitations, challenges and issues facing rural communities based on the findings from this study

Generally tight local budgets and financial limitations	Rural communities in many countries are subject of various government support programmes, but their economic situation (particularly in low-populated areas) is not prosperous enough to ensure sufficient funding for all social services that are usually available in urban areas.
Transport and accessibility issues	Many less-developed rural communities, due to the low population density, great distances and potential natural barriers (e.g. unfavourable landscape and climate conditions) suffer from the lack of quality and reliable public transportation, connecting rural communities among themselves, but also connecting them with 'hub' towns of an area.
Lacking social and human capital	Emigration of young people due to the weak prospects and overall quality of life in rural community causes decrease in social and human capital available in community. Human capital is comprised of talents, skills, knowledge and potentials that each individual in a community can offer. Social capital deals with mutual trust, reciprocity, collective identity and a sense of a shared future.
Insufficient strength of the local voluntary and community infrastructure	In relation to the previous problem, rural also communities often do not have developed mechanisms of identifying and employing existing social and human capital – in terms of organisations/centres/networks equipped for work on community issues and provision of support for individuals and groups interested in creating community initiatives/actions and/or volunteering in them.
Local political relationships	As key factor in strategic decision making, rather than interests of the overall community, keeping in mind that rural communities are characterised by great socio-economic differences among the inhabitants of the same area. There are evidences of general distrust among community members and the strong influence of local government representatives which exert specific interests not necessarily strictly oriented on well-being of entire community, but rather on the vision and particular interests of individuals/groups closely related to the political representatives.

power distribution. If all providers are directly included in organisation as a part of the organising committee, it might complicate and slow down decision-making process. Alternatively, leaving service providers out of the formal decision-making process might increase costs and may have severe consequences on an event delivery. Problems associated with insufficient human and social capital available in the community can often lead to the 'usual suspects' phenomenon – one that situates a limited number of people (usually those with strong internal motivation or some kind of accepted legitimacy among community members) who take the lead. As Jepson and Clarke (2013: 26) further argue, "Stakeholders align themselves within particular power structures". These individuals (as stakeholders) become further involved as community representatives, which may result in various conflicts of interests, cultural elitism, or simply burn-out when it comes to organising and delivering an event on schedule and within budget (Osborne et al., 2004). The real challenge for the organisers and the collective local community is to identify and motivate 'new' individuals willing and able to become involved in community activities and event planning. Involving members of the community will help ensure that efforts are made to raise people's self-efficacy and to ensure longer-term social sustainability. Keeping in mind limitations facing rural communities, it is expected that those involved in planning and organisation across the range of stakeholder categories significantly overlap; especially in terms of regulators and facilitators, as well as community members which can be part of the organising committee (as volunteers or event managers), sport-related stakeholders and co-producers. The complex nature of stakeholder categories and associated relationships will now be explored more critically as the chapter focuses on the case study of Gorski Kotar in Croatia.

Evidence from practice: local sport events organisation in Gorski Kotar, Croatia

This chapter will now discuss the case and stakeholders involved in organising small-scale local sport events in rural communities. The content presented on the case study of Gorski Kotar in Croatia is based on local reports, conversations (informal interviews, or conversational analysis) with local sport event organisers and observations of field visits to five small-scale sport events held in Gorski Kotar. Discussions and observations address practical delivery and challenges associated with organising and delivering of sport events and managing stakeholders in remote rural areas.

Gorski Kotar is a rural mountainous area in western Croatia located between two major Croatian tourism markets – the national capital (Zagreb) and coastal tourism destinations (along the northern Adriatic Sea). Regardless of its favourable position and great natural resources it is among the least economically developed regions in Croatia with very low number of inhabitants (with a population just over 23,000 residing in an area of 1,275.05 km²); the region has been experiencing depopulation and proposals and investments to spur tourism aim to promote new opportunities for residents. This results from a lack of employment opportunities and overall living standards resulting from a lack of infrastructures and the remote location. Depopulation is not limited to younger generations, people of all age cohorts are seeking opportunities in larger urban areas, such as Rijeka or Zagreb. Gorski Kotar comprises three towns and six municipalities, each has its own representing body (assembly in towns or council in municipalities) and executive bodies that perform local administration. Most of the economic generation comes from forestry and wood processing, but tourism based on nature and outdoor activities shows great potential. To build the destination and promote events, each of the nine local self-administrating units in Gorski Kotar have established local tourism boards, but the development of its tourist (and event) offering and visitation figures are progressing slowly.

The delivering of sport event programs and services in Gorski Kotar, similar to across Croatia, is organised through network of various non-profit organisations – mainly sport clubs and associated alliances. At the community level, these clubs are very important for introducing sport options for children and young people; however, still they struggle with limited budgets and lack of adequate infrastructure to train and organise events. For the area of Gorski Kotar the most popular sport/recreational activities are mountain biking, sport fishing, sledding, hiking, trail running and skiing, around 55 related small-scale sport event activities are organised (Perić et al., 2016b). Previous research has also identified that sport event organisers are associated with sport clubs, supported by tourist boards in partnership with municipalities and towns, as well as a few private sector event organisers from specialised enterprises who can support planning and delivery (Perić et al., 2016b).

Community stakeholders and organisational challenges in Gorski Kotar

Since all of the analysed local sport events in Gorski Kotar are small scale, organised by local public, private and civil sector, with the help of local volunteers, it can be argued that the (rural) community in this case is the primary stakeholder. Still, not all community members, or their respective stakeholder categories, were equally involved in the process of planning, organising and delivering the events. It is important to highlight difference between the two main sport event organisers in Gorski Kotar: sport clubs (and associations) and local tourist boards. Differences in their approach, desired outcomes and stakeholder inclusion, as well as management approaches indicate issues associated with sport event organisation in rural communities.

Sport clubs are mostly interested in organisation and delivering quality sport events with as many participants as possible (because fees are charged), but their services do not typically cater to the full tourist offer (e.g. choice of food and beverage, accommodation options, souvenirs). Sports clubs tend to plan for and include basic supporting services, such as parking, toilet facilities and catered meal (included in the fee), not giving much attention to those elements outside the primary participant motives – that being attending sport events. Sport events might have attractive sponsors (for instance, sport equipment producers), but not much is offered to potential audiences (non-active spectators) accompanying participants. With sport clubs as the main event organisers, they work with a small number of internal stakeholders, preferring suppliers over co-producers, and (depending on the sport activity) are not very interested in organising additional offerings or cooperating with external stakeholders who provide additional tourist services, as well as local residents, the media or local government (unless they are directly sponsoring the event). Therefore, they are failing to utilise the presence of participants form local, regional, national and often international participants and spectators to project the regions image, destination brand or contribute a positive economic impact on the host community. Still, social benefits aimed at including young people in sports, retaining them in community and promoting sport in local communities through national and international competitions gives sports clubs important social roles in rural areas. During conversations and observations, it was noted that all sport club members involved in sport event organisation emphasised the need for greater financial resources in order to maintain and upgrade the service quality of sport activities and events.

Tourist boards as sport event organisers have very different visions than sport clubs. They are more concerned with recreational activities suitable for larger numbers and promote a 'fun for all' principle aimed to attracting not just active participants, but also an audience of spectators and visitors. By using events as additional motives to visit Gorski Kotar, the tourist boards place more effort into media promotion and event coverage to increase consumption. Tourist boards also have vested interests in collaborating with local accommodation, food and beverage providers, differing from the sports clubs. Their organising committees also consist of more people and they rely on an extensive base of volunteers and supporting organisations, especially from public sector. Tourist boards aim to integrate the local communities to promote shared emotional connections through involvement; this fulfils social opportunities whilst attempting to impact the region economically, in theory. Local public communal services providers are therefore often co-producers of these events and play important role in event logistics. What was observed was sport events organised by tourist boards were not highly visited (as expected), nor they had satisfied short-term and long-term economic effects. The reason for that might be as a result of these events mainly being supported and attended by community residents who remain the main source of audience as well as participants. Additionally, within the private sector, local enterprises working in the field of tourism and hospitality did not involve their businesses in the events as sponsors or contributors, but mostly as contractual suppliers. Some of these enterprises did not have any interest in participating in event delivery due to the rather small numbers of attendees. In this case, results from another study on rural community event stakeholders conducted by Reid (2011) are not confirmed in terms of the involvement of local sponsors. While Reid (2011) argued that local private sector enterprises are not just profit-oriented, they are also interested in philanthropic and altruistic approaches; however, this was not the case with the enterprises of Gorski Kotar.

Bearing in mind that both dominant approaches to local sport event organisation suffers from problems associated with stakeholder management, it is important to analyse and provide recommendations and insights based on the causes of such problems, and the potential impacts upon residents in rural communities. Firstly, common to both the organisation approaches is the fact that even though they both significantly depend on the support of community members and groups in terms of volunteers, audience and infrastructure owners, neither have active cooperation strategies that promote the involvement of community groups and members in direct decision making. Most of the collaborations and partnerships are grounded in personal relationships, often the case in small rural communities. Alternatively, private animosities between members of various stakeholder groups often make otherwise logical (and logistical) cooperation of complimentary organisations/groups difficult (or impossible). Combined with the 'usual suspects' phenomenon, meaning only a small number of individuals carrying various functions and involvement in many activities, this creates a vicious 'circle' rather than an iterative one and with it a rather unfavourable situation aimed at promoting change when it comes to extending the base of stakeholders actively involved in organising events. Limiting involvement in the organisation process and decision making can quickly escalate distrust among different community stakeholders (especially in rural close-knit rural communities), this is also evidenced by the existence of various mutually opposed groups among community inhabitants (usually based on political status, ethnic group or some other difference). Since there is no transparent system of stakeholder management in organising sport events in Gorski Kotar, building on Reid's (2008) argument that organising committees are usually overly representative of one of community or a particular social group, and they often lose the support of community members. In the case of Gorski Kotar, it is vital that organisers (whether sports clubs or local tourist boards) maintain positive relationships with the community as a primary stakeholder, because they are often involved in events as active participant and spectators and therefore their support is essential in the long run.

Overlapping stakeholder groups and representatives, along with scarce financial resources and infrastructures in a municipality/town imposes the need for inter-community cooperation. Creating a synergic effect in Gorski Kotar is necessary, but such practical cooperation does not currently exist. The reason can be found in strong micro-local identities, similar to findings of Osborne et al. (2004), more precisely, the inhabitants and organisers in municipality A might find themselves completely separated from municipality B or C, and although they all might only be separated by a few miles, they both face the same problems/issues. A sense of belonging locally can contribute to community cohesion and social capital, but resistance to extend cooperation, and sharing ideas across and with neighbouring communities makes it difficult to establish larger forums/platforms for event organisation. Political factors are also often engrained in these problems, especially since all municipalities and towns have completely separate legal identities, budgets, representatives and local administrative bodies. Local government representatives are more interested on ensuring short-term political gain by investing in resources within their own administrative boundaries, opposed to considering long-term sustainable partnerships/collaborations. Uniting to organise and deliver events, and to promote a system to better manage community stakeholders and shared resources means investments across the region. Those investments have the potential to encourage cohesive involvement aimed at creating benefits for all included communities (and stakeholders) in the future.

There are favourable ideas that promote the inclusion of various local stakeholder groups to get involved in organising sport events. It might be fair to argue that an inclusive strategy to increase sense of community and ownership of events means promoting local social capital that will further capacity building within and across rural communities. Moreover, it is important to note that the often voluntary nature of most event organisers limits available time for a democratic consultation process.

Conclusions

Rural communities are faced with many limitations and constraints that negatively influence sport event organisation. There exist numerous challenges associated with delivering and creating sustainable events that will have a significant economic impact and generate social benefits. These can however be addressed through careful and transparent stakeholder management. Referring back to the conceptual insights offered earlier, achieving economic and social leveraging is even more important, knowing that there are limited resources available for planning and organisation of sport events in rural areas which should generate quality experiences for not only participants and visitors from outside a region but also for community members.

In order to achieve maximum positive benefits, create legitimacy and build, maintain or strengthen a sense of community, when it concerns ownership over organising sport events, there is a need to conduct and raise awareness though capacity building across the range of stakeholders. This will better introduce and allow community members to realise potential event benefits and can increase their support and involvement. Although it is impossible to avoid overlapping of stakeholder categories and issues associated with organising given the multiplicity of event stakeholder roles, transparent cooperation and quality combination of sport event and wider tourism goals should help overcome some of the distrust among stakeholders. It is essential to break down the boundaries that separate interest groups within communities by including neutral experts or organisations from outside of the community who may be part of (or even head of) the organising committee. Researchers have argued that external facilitators are useful and can increase trust and credibility when it comes to gaining support of mutually confronted stakeholder groups (see Babiak, 2007; Schulenkorf & Edwards, 2012). Increasing social capital and confidence through new formal and informal cooperation (aimed at promotong relationships) within particular micro-communities, as well as combining resources and potentials of neighbouring administrative units, would create positive synergic effects aimed at sustaining events by improving the quality and service offerings.

To conclude, understanding the complex nature and characteristics of rural communities, in terms of transparent stakeholder identification and management systems for the purpose of planning and organising local sport events, is crucial. Rural areas definetly have the space and given opportunities to utilise natural resources and environments suitable for sport and events. However, they need to maximise strategic advantages and promote cooperation to devop destinations that can generate sustainable long-term benefits based on joint cooperation among stakeholders to increase social and economic benefits for communities.

Acknowledgements

This work has been supported in part by the Croatian Science Foundation under the project UIP-2014-09-1214.

References

Andersson, T., and D. Getz. (2009). Tourism as a Mixed Industry: Differences between Private, Public and Not-for-Profit Festivals. *Tourism Management* 30: 847–856.

Babiak, K. (2007). Determinants of Inter-Organizational Relationships: The Case of a Canadian Nonprofit Sport Organization. *Journal of Sport Management* 21: 338–376.

Butler, C., and J.L. Flora. (2008). *Rural Communities: Legacy and Change*. Boulder, CO: Westview Press.

Chalip, L. (2006). Towards Social Leverage of Sport Events. *Journal of Sport Tourism* 11: 109–127.

Chalip, L. (2014). From Legacy to Leverage. In *Leveraging Legacies from Sports Mega-Events: Concepts and Cases*, ed. J. Grix. London: Palgrave Macmillan, 2–12.

Chalip, L., and A. Leyns. (2002). Local Business Leveraging of a Sport Event: Managing an Event for Economic Benefit. *Journal of Sport Management* 16: 132–158.

Chalip, L., and J. McGuirty. (2004). Bundling Sport Events with the Host Destination. *Journal of Sport Tourism* 9: 267–282.

Cheung, S.Y., J.Y. Mak, and A.W. Dixon. (2016). Elite Active Sport Tourists: Economic Impacts and Perceptions of Destination Image. *Event Management* 20: 99–108.

Daniels, M.J., W.C. Norman, and M.S. Henry. (2004). Estimating Income Effects of a Sport Tourism Event. *Annals of Tourism Research* 31: 180–199.

Dredge, D. (2006). Networks, Conflict and Collaborative Communities. *Journal of Sustainable Tourism* 14: 562–581.

Dunham, H.W. (1986). The Community Today: Place or Process. *Journal of Community Psychology* 14(4): 399–404.

Emery, P.R. (2002). Bidding to Host a Major Sports Event: The Local Organising Committee Perspective. *International Journal of Public Sector Management* 15: 316–335.

Freeman, R.E. (1984). *Strategic Management: A Stakeholder Approach*. Boston: Pitman.

Getz, D. (2005). *Event Management and Event Tourism*. 2nd ed. New York: Cognizant.

Getz, D., D. MacDonald, and M.M. Parent. (2015). The Sport Event Owners' Perspective. In *The Routledge Handbook of Sports Event Management*, eds. M.M. Parent and J.-L. Chappelet. London: Routledge, 91–108.

Gibson, H.J., K. Kaplanidou, and S.J. Kang. (2012). Small-Scale Event Sport Tourism: A Case Study in Sustainable Tourism. *Sport Management Review* 15(2): 160–170.

Hall, C.M. (1992). *Hallmark Tourist Events: Impacts, Management and Planning*. London: Belhaven Press.

Jenkins, R. (2008). *Social Identity*. New York: Routledge.

Jepson, A., and A. Clarke. (2013). Community Festivals and Community Development: Inclusive or Exclusive Events. In *Research Themes for Events*, eds. R. Finkel, D. McGillivray, G. McPherson and P. Robinson. Wallingford, UK: CAB International, 6–17.

Jepson, A., and A. Clarke (Eds.). (2015). *Exploring Community Festivals and Events*. London: Routledge.

Jepson, A., and A. Clarke (Eds.). (2016). *Managing and Developing Communities, Festivals and Events*. Basingstoke: Palgrave Macmillan.

Kim, K., and M. Uysal. (2003). Perceived Socio-Economic Impacts of Festivals and Events among Organizers. *Journal of Hospitality and Leisure Marketing* 10: 159–171.

Masterman, G. (2004). *Strategic Sports Event Management: An International Approach*. Oxford, UK: Elsevier.

McMillan, D.W., and D.M. Chavis. (1986). Sense of Community: A Definition and Theory. *Journal of Community Psychology* 14(1): 6–23.

O'Brien, D. and L. Chalip. (2007). Executive Training Exercise in Sport Event Leverage. *International Journal of Culture, Tourism and Hospitality Research* 1: 296–304.

O'Brien, D., and L. Chalip. (2008). Sports Events and Strategic Leveraging: Pushing towards the Triple Bottom Line. In *Tourism Management: Analysis, Behaviour and Strategy*, eds. A.G. Woodside and D. Martin. Wallingford, UK: CAB International, 318–338.

Osborne, S., R. Beattie, and A. Williamson. (2004). Community Involvement in Rural Regeneration Partnerships: Exploring the Rural Dimension. *Local Government Studies* 30: 156–181.

Parent, M.M. (2008). Evolution and Issue Patterns for Major-Sport-Event Organizing Committees and Their Stakeholders. *Journal of Sport Management* 22: 135–164.

Perić, M., J. Đurkin, and N. Wise. (2016a). Leveraging Small-Scale Sport Events: Challenges of Organising, Delivering and Managing Sustainable Outcomes in Rural Communities, the Case of Gorski Kotar, Croatia. *Sustainability* 8(12): 1–17.
Perić, M., S. Skoric, and V. Jurcevic. (2016b). Sport Tourism Supply in Gorski Kotar (Croatia) – Analysis and Possible Recommendations for Providers. *Acta Turistica* 28(1): 49–71.
Poplin, D.E. (1979). *Communities*. New York: MacMillan Publishing Co., Inc.
Provan, K.G., M.A. Veazie, L.K. Staten, and N.I. Teufel-Shone. (2005). The Use of Network Analysis to Strengthen Community Partnerships. *Public Administration Review* 65: 603–613.
Reid, S. (2008). Identifying Social Consequences of Rural Events. *Event Management* 11: 89–98.
Reid, S. (2011). Event Stakeholder Management: Developing Sustainable Rural Event Practices. *International Journal of Event and Festival Management* 2: 20–36.
Richards, G., M.P. de Brito, and L. Wilks (Eds.). (2013). *Exploring the Social Impacts of Events*. London: Routledge.
Rojek, C. (2013). *Event Power: [How Global Events Manage and Manipulate]*. London: Sage Publications Ltd.
Schulenkorf, N., and D. Edwards. (2012). Maximizing Positive Social Impacts: Strategies for Sustaining and Leveraging the Benefits of Intercommunity Sport Events in Divided Societies. *Journal of Sport Management* 26: 379–390.
Schwery, R. (2003). The Potential of Sport for Development and Peace. *Sport, Science and Education Bulletin* 39: 15–25.
Sherry, E., N. Schulenkorf, and L. Chalip. (2015). Managing Sport for Social Change: The State of Play. *Sport Management Review* 18: 1–5.
Shucksmith, M. (2000). *Exclusive Countryside? Social Inclusion and Regeneration in Rural Areas*. New York: Joseph Rowntree Foundation.
Smith, A. (2012). *Events and Urban Regeneration*. London: Routledge.
Suttles, G.D. (1972). *The Social Construction of Communities*. Chicago: The University of Chicago Press.
Taks, M., L. Misener, L. Chalip, and B.C. Green. (2013). Leveraging Sport Events for Participation. *Canadian Journal of Social Research* 3: 12–23.
Veltri, F., J. Miller, and A. Harris. (2009). Club Sport National Tournament: Economic Impact of a Small Event on a Mid-Size Community. *Recreational Sports Journal* 33: 119–128.
Weed, M., and C. Bull. (2009). *Sport Tourism: Participants, Policy and Providers*. 2nd ed. Oxford, UK: Elsevier Butterworth Heinemann.
Wilson, R. (2006). The Economic Impact of Local Sport Events: Significant, Limited or Otherwise? A Case Study of Four Swimming Events. *Managing Leisure* 11: 57–70.
Wise, N. (2015a). Football on the Weekend: Rural Events and the Haitian Imagined Community in the Dominican Republic. In *Exploring Community Festivals and Events*, eds. A. Clarke and A. Jepson. London: Routledge, 106–117.
Wise, N. (2015b). Placing Sense of Community. *Journal of Community Psychology* 43(7): 920–929.
Wise, N. (2016). Outlining Triple Bottom Line Contexts in Urban Tourism Regeneration. *Cities* 53: 30–34.

Wise, N., and M. Perić. (2017). Sports Tourism, Regeneration and Social Impacts: New Opportunities and Directions for Research, the Case of Medulin, Croatia. In *Tourism in the City: Towards and Integrative Agenda on Urban Tourism*, eds. N. Bellini and C. Pasquinelli. Berlin: Springer Vieweg, 311–320.

Yaghmour, S., and N. Scott. (2009). Inter-Organizational Collaboration Characteristics and Outcomes: A Case Study of the Jeddah festival. *Journal of Policy Research in Tourism, Leisure and Events* 1: 115–130.

Ziakas, V. (2010). Understanding an Event Portfolio: The Uncovering of Interrelationships, Synergies, and Leveraging Opportunities. *Journal of Policy Research in Tourism, Leisure and Events* 2: 144–164.

Ziakas, V., and C.A. Costa. (2010). Explicating Inter-Organizational Linkages of a Host Community's Events Network. *International Journal of Event and Festival Management* 1(2): 132–147.

14 Concluding remarks on power authenticity and meaning

Alan Clarke and Allan Jepson

These epilogues are always difficult to write as we have a great deal invested in the work. We have worked closely with the contributors; we believe in their issues as central to the critical understanding of communities and their events, and we hope that you have been engaged in the reading of our efforts. You may have read through the whole volume or dipped into those chapters which caught your interest, but which ever approach you have taken, we hope that you have been stimulated and challenged by the contributions to critical event studies literature.

We feel that critical understandings underpin our work whether we are practitioners, academics or even attendees. Our participation, at whatever level, should not be unreflective but humanistic, participatory and even co-creative. We should have the tools to question our experiences and explore how the things we are doing have been put together and exploited.

Our work has been based on the examination of power since we first started exploring the ways in which community festivals and events were put together during the early 2000s. In those days, we were able to say with some confidence that there were not many studies of how power plays out in the things we do. We had to justify claims of elitism in cultural and the devaluing of popular and ethnic forms. Now we can see how the issues of power are becoming clearer and widespread in research. We now have moved beyond power as a concept to do something to something which is more complex and is felt through the range of stakeholder relationships and the discourses which legitimate the positions taken up and championed within the production of events. We are working in a field which recognises the discourses of class, gender, ethnicity and professionalisation in the ways in which they contribute to the production of meanings.

We are also pleased to say that this approach has challenged the economistic readings which have provided a dominant rationale for evaluating events. Our critical gazes force financial accounts to have to deal with the meanings that people construct within their own accounts of what has value to them in the events. We see the chapters in this volume as encouraging deeper readings of events. It is not enough to know what the bank statement says at the end of the events to know whether it has been a success. Not losing money is, of course, significant but it may not be enough to guarantee the feeling of success of the event if it does not connect with values in the community. We feel that the organic connections are to be valued more than those events which are simply grafted on to communities.

We have a tradition within the literature that argues that festivals and events can contribute to the well-being of communities by enriching the life blood of the people living there, but by taking a value led analysis, we can see that such claims can only be supported if the values expressed in the events fit with those of the communities involved.

What has impressed us as the editors of this volume is the wide range of backgrounds of the contributors – not only where they come from, but the disciplines they represent and their sense of understanding of the events they have been analysing. The more we can bring together ethnically diverse and multi-disciplinary teams of authors, the more difficult it becomes to maintain any one simple reading of events. This volume champions the need to understand events within the cultural and historical contexts in which they are shaped and come into being. If we had only ever seen events from one perspective it would be easier to see one version as the normal way things are done, how they are produced and how they are consumed. The more we present alternatives to this single view of the world, the more we recognise that the events are produced in a context of differences and consumed by participants with different expectations and different values.

Critical readings are the way forward to ground our understanding of values and meanings in communities. We will continue to encourage further analyses and research which continues to challenge simplistic dominant ideologically based readings. The growth of our study area cannot rest on the work already done, as we must continue to probe and question the superficial. We believe that the chapters here have made great contributions to these critical readings.

However, we would urge you as a reader of this volume not to accept this as the final word. Every one of the chapters makes a case for a particular reading of the events discussed. We would suggest that this volume has a second level of relevance which goes beyond the narratives about the events. There is a meta level of analysis which is suggested by and supported by these narratives. We recognised that the processes involved are worthy of consideration, no matter where the location. The concepts are valuable in their own right but have more meaning when applied in cultural contexts. At first glance, we can settle for a description of events but we need to look more closely and deeper. At second glance, events are more complex. The events are embodiments of different cultures and different values of production and consumption. By examining events through a series of critical perspectives, we can see more of what events perform or, you could say, actually about. When we sit an audience, does it matter what the gender divide of the producers and the performers was? Or the ethnicity of those involved? Do we actually notice those excluded from the processes in and around the events?

We believe that the significance of the contributions presented here lies not only in their accounts but also in the ways in which those accounts were constructed. We hope this volume with its focus on power and meaning will reshape the way events are seen. As critical researchers, we cannot only look at the superficial face of the event that is presented to us. There are processes that allow these presentations to come to the fore and which also prime us, as audiences, volunteers and participants, to accept this at face value. How closely do 300,000 people at Glastonbury think about what is happening, even when Jeremy Corbyn is invited on stage?

We live in a society where simple readings are presented and accepted without question. Our political discourses are lacking, the debates in civil society are lacking and we accept that having an event is better than not having one. This volume is based on questioning that too easy acceptance of the everyday taken for granted narratives of our lives. By looking for the ways in which meanings are created and given value, we want to explore the issues behind the front stage. Power permeates all the debates going on behind the scenes – power can even make some alternatives appear to be the only ones whereas others become unthinkable. Where you cannot think them, you do not have the opportunities to do anything about them.

A critical view of events will mean exploring the discourses that shape them (and equally those discourses which are excluded from the construction of events). Our authors have shown how these critical gazes can unpack the events that they have been studying and we believe that these approaches should become part of our first sight evaluations. Some would say that this is an idealistic or theoretical quest, especially where we have already drawn attention to the lack of critical skills in civil societies. However, we all work in the world where events are asked to justify themselves in financial terms. Yet not all of us have been trained as accountants. We can address this by sharing and publicising critical accounts more widely. There is no reason why the societies we live in have to be critically repressed. Our agendas can be opened to critical thought just as easily – or with as much hard work – as it took economists to form a largely unquestioned hegemony in how we evaluate events. It is a work for cultural and intellectual efforts, but if we are to increase our understanding of differences in our societies, we need to share the ability to read the value of other culture's meanings with wider audiences. Media studies, as it was labelled, became an easy target for jokes aimed at diminishing its significance. We live in a world where many still believe what is put in front of them without any means of questioning those narratives. These critical skills are very important, as our authors have demonstrated here.

We welcome the growth of the network involved in critical events research and we see this volume as another meaningful contribution in developing this network. For it to work, we need to take the accounts from the pages included here and in the way people see the world and recognise value in their own experiences.

With Best Wishes,
Alan and Allan

Index

accepted discourse 155
activism 156–157
agonistic 154, 165
Agresti's IQV 79
Airey, David 1
Akaroa 172; see also Akaroa French Festival
Akaroa District Promotions 172
Akaroa French Festival: community identity of 174; cultural heritage 169; organisation of, changes in 173; origins of 169, 172–174; significance of 174; stakeholders perspectives on 175–182; symbolism of 173–174
Akaroa Harbour 169, 172
Akaroa Mail 174
alienation of community see community alienation
All Hallows Church 157
alliances 99–100
alter central tendency 79
alter dispersion 79
arrogant introducers 100
attachment of festival 96
attendance/attendees 41, 141
authentic food 145
autonomy of managerial/management 12–13
Avenida Paulista 156

Banks Peninsula District Council 173
Barcelona 130
Barry's Bay, Duvauchelle 172
behaviour, purchasing 120–124
belonging, sense of 51–52
Benn, Tony 162
Biodôme 134
Black Bloc groups 160
Blau's index 79

Bradford Apple Day 161
Bradford city centre 155
branding of Iceland 55–57
Brazil 158–160
Brazilian flag 160
bridging structures 95, 104
Briggate 163–164
British Laws 25
Brooke, Peter 159
Bullwhip Effect 110, 114, 117, 119, 123
buyer-supplier relationships 113–114

CAAT campaigns 163
capital, social 141
Cartesian 154
case studies on ego network based research 74–78
Cassel, Susanna Heldt 2
CCC see Christchurch City Council (CCC)
celebration 177–180
Christchurch City Council (CCC) 173, 182
Christians 157
Christmas 155
church events 153
Church House in London 163–164
Church of England 164
Clarke, Alan 7, 21–22, 32, 52, 74, 91–94, 103, 140, 146, 150, 171, 185, 192
cohesiveness of host community 31
command-and-control approaches 14
commemoration 175–177
commercialisation 180–181
commodification 158–159
communal social experiences 51–52
Communitarians 13; see also community

community: creative 66, 73; culture of, manifestation of 160, 166; defined 189; empowerment in 103; festival success, perspective on 13–14; host 188; identity within 171, 174; imagined 51; networked 66, 85; power over events in 145; relations in 95; rural 189; sense of 189; social movement 153; sporting events, impact on 185–188; *see also* community alienation; host community; rural community
community alienation: concept of 24; events and, failure of 23–25; festival and, failure of 23–25; Glastonbury Festival and 32; physical impacts of 24–25; powerlessness as result of 24
compensation of host community 29
Comte de Paris 169, 172, 174–176, 178–181
connectivity, regular forms of 68
connectivity index 96
connotation 51
consumers/consumption: of events 130; power over 148–149; power to 143–144
contributor, meaningful role of 65
Corbyn, Jeremy 203
cost-effective reductions 112
creative communities 66, 73
Crete tourism 5–6
Critical Management approach 26; to events, organisers of 21; to host community 21, 31–32
Croatian tourism market 192
cultural celebrations 91
cultural events 49
cultural heritage 169
culture: attractiveness of 36–37; of community, manifestation of 160, 166; of Finland, national 35; of Glastonbury Festival 25; Montreal, landscape of 134; segregation of 36

Dalarna University, Sweden 2
Danish rural festival 96–97, 102–103
David and Goliath battle 148
demands of supply chain 118–119
democracy, real 154, 165
Denmark festivals 91–92; *see also* Danish rural festival
denotation 51
Derby Jubilee Festival 140

Descartes 154
diet, healthy 146
disadvantaged groups 95
dissensus 153–154, 166
Doré, Jean 132–133
Doré administration 133
Dowson, Ruth 3–4
Drapeau, Jean 129, 132–133
Drapeau administration 133
Dupre, Karine 1

Easter 155
Easter Good Friday 162
Eavis, Michael 25, 28–29
economic leveraging 186–187, 190
economy: events, impact of 131, 139; festival, importance of 91, 139; festival success, contribution to 5–6, 13–14; New Zealand, challenges in 170; sporting events, impact on 185
ecosystems 66
Edinburgh Napier University, United Kingdom 2
ego-alter similarity 79–80
ego network based research 65; case studies on 74–78; in creative communities 73; data analysis of 79–84; defined 65; individual interviews as foundation of 71; justification of 74; name generators for 71–72, 74–75; name interpreters for 72–73, 76–77; name interrelators for 73, 76–77; resource generators for 72, 75–76; social network analysis and 65–66; whole network *vs.* 69–70
EI index 79–80
empowerment 94–95; alliances and, importance of 100; community 103; dimensions of 95; of disadvantaged groups 95; of organisations involved in festival 101, 103; power of Real Food Festival 149–150; power to 143–144; self- 95, 103
E-NET 79–84
enthusiasm of host community 23
equestrian sports 54, 57–58
ethical/ethics 25, 70
European Capitals of Culture 35
evangelism 161
Event Management 7
event planners 164–166
events: belonging, sense of 51–52; within church 153; communal

social experiences during 51–52; community alienation and 23–25; consumption of 130; Critical Management approach to, organisers of 21; cultural 49; development of, challenges of 112; economic impact of 131, 139; evolution of 140; facilities for 129; failure of 140; "feel-good" factor for hosting 23; final experience of 119; governance of 131; hegemony of 154–156; identities in 49; large-scale 186; life cycles of 139; participation in 6–7; political 155–156; portfolio of 170; power broker for 22; PRIDE 157–158; protest 155–156, 159–162; public rituals performed at 52; reflective management practices for organisers of 32; ritual vs. 158–163; within social movement communities 153; social network analysis of 68; sports 91; stakeholder for 22–23, 67, 85–86; theoretical framework for 129–131; tourism, development strategy for 130–131; urban development, incentive for successful 37; see also festival; sports/sporting events; specific types of
Events and Urban Regeneration (Smith) 37
evolutionary trend in Housing Fair in Finland 38–44
evolution of events/festival 140
exclusion of imagined community 51
Expo 67 132–133

facilities 129, 134
failure of events/festival 140
Falassi's typology of ritual 159
Federation of Finnish Financial Services 39
"feel-good" factor for hosting events 23
female identities in Landsmót 60–61
festival: attachment of 96; belonging, sense of 51–52; challenges of 109; communal social experiences during 51–52; community alienation and 23–25; defined 5; in Denmark 91–92 (see also Danish rural festival); economic importance of 91, 139; evolution of 140; failure of 140; food (see Real Food Festival); as gatekeeper 31; geographical issues important for 52; harvest 91; heritage 180; home-grown 97; identities in 49; life cycles of 139; Likert-type scale for surveying data on 96; management of 110–113, 119; market for 91; national heritage 52; organisations involved in 97–103; organisers of, defined 9–10; partnerships in collaborating 97–98, 100–104; as political minefield 31; power broker for 22; profile characteristics about 11; public rituals performed at 52; social network analysis of 68; stakeholder for 22–23, 67, 85–86, 109–110; supply chain for 109, 113–117 (see also Supply Chain Management (SCM)); tractor-pulling 99; types of 52; volunteers involved in 98–99; see also events; festival success; Glastonbury Festival; rural festival; types of
festival feel 157
festivalisation 72, 103
Festival Republic 25
Festival Steering Committee 22
festival success 7–13; communitarian/person-oriented perspective on 13–14; economic contribution to 5–6, 13–14; literature on 7; managerial perspective on 6, 11–13; Q-factor interpretation of 11; Q-methodology for 9; see also host community and festival success
FHFCO see Finnish Housing Fair Cooperative Organisation (FHFCO)
FIFA 129
final experience of events 119
financial structure of Montreal 133
Finland 35–36; see also Housing Fair in Finland
Finnish Architectural Review 46
Finnish Fair Foundation 39
Finnish Housing Association 39
Finnish Housing Fair Cooperative Organisation (FHFCO) 39–41
Finnish Housing Reform Association 39
Finnish Savings Banks Association 39
flexibility of Housing Fair in Finland 45
food 145–146
food festival see Real Food Festival
Foucauldian concept 22–23, 139
Fountain, Joanna 4

free tickets for host community 30
French colony 175–176
French heritage 177
French settlement 175
fun for all principle 194

gatekeeper, festival as 31
gender identity 49, 54
geographical issues 52
Glasgow Action 39
Glastonbury Festival: community alienation and 32; culture of 25; host community for 21, 29–30; shared vision for, lack of 32; stakeholder objectives of 27–29
God 157
Golden Age 35
good, clean and fair food 145
Gorski Kotar, Croatia 192–196; geography of 192–193; non-profit organisations for 193; organisational challenges of 193–196; sports clubs 193–194; stakeholders for 193–196; tourism in 192, 193; tourist boards 194–195
governance of events 131
Grand Duchy of Russia 35; see also Finland
Greenfield Music and Performing Arts Festival 21; see also Glastonbury Festival
Greenham Common 161
Greenpeace 25, 27, 155
Griffith University, Australia 1

Hall model 135
hard bodies 44–45
harvest festival 91
healthy diet 146
hegemony of events 154–156
Hellenic Open University 1
Helsinki Festival 35, 38
heritage 53, 177
heritage festival 180
heritage tourism 53
high salience statements 11
Hinterland Times 144
hippie ethics 25
Hjalager, Anne-Mette 2
Holar 58–59
home-grown festival 97
homophily 73
horses *see* Icelandic horses

host community 188; compensation of 29; for Glastonbury Festival 21, 29–30; Housing Fair in Finland, guarantees given to 40–41; local pride of 29–30; *see also* host community and festival success
host community and festival success: cohesiveness of 31; Critical Management approach to 21, 31–32; enthusiasm of, factor for 23; free tickets for 30; meeting needs of 21; powerlessness of 31; professional organisers *vs.* 25; shared vision of 26–29
Housing Fair Finland Co-operative 38
Housing Fair in Finland 36; attendance to 41; evolutionary trend in 38–44; Finnish Housing Fair Cooperative Organisation, host of 39–41; flexibility of 45; host community, guarantees given to 40–41; literature on 46; location for 41; longevity of 45; permeability of, to trends and social issues 42–44; residential development, advertising of 38; retrofitting, benefit of 38–39; Seinäjoki as host of 38; sideway outcomes of 45–46; theme of 39–42; urbanisation, benefit of 38–39
Howson, Chris 158

Iceland 55–57
Icelandic horses 50, 55–57
identity: community 171, 174; in cultural events 49; in events 49; female 60–61; festival 49; gender 49, 54; of Iceland 55–57; individual 171; in Landsmót 50, 52–53, 58–61; local 52; male 60; New Zealand 171; participant 60–61; in sports 49; of stakeholders 66–67; in tourism 50; visitors 60–61; *see also* identity in Landsmót; national identity
identity in Landsmót 49; female 60–61; male 60; national 50, 52–53, 58–59, 61; participants *vs.* visitors 60–61
IGA 146
images of spectators at Landsmót 59
imagined community 51
inclusion of imagined community 51
individual identity 171
individual interviews 71
influence and power 94, 104

information flows in SCM 117
Instagram 50–51, 57–58
inter-community cooperation with stakeholders 195–196
International Air Transport Association 133
international friends 57
International Olympic Committee 129

Jarman, David 2
Jepson, Allan 7, 21–23, 25, 32, 37, 52, 74, 91–94, 103, 140, 146, 150, 171, 185, 192
Jesus 155
junk food 146

Kelly, Stephen 3
Khomsi, Mohamed Reda 3
knitivism 161
Knitting Festival 99–100
knowledge, Foucauldian concept of 22–23
Koszalin University of Technology, Poland 2
Kotka Maritime Festival 35
Kraljic's Purchasing Portfolio Model 110, 114
Kwiatkowski, Grzegorz 2

Lake Ellesmere 172
Lakeside Blues Festival 36
Lamond, Ian 3–4
Landsmót: in Holar 59; Icelandic horses, competition of 50; images of spectators at 59; social media posts on 50–51, 57, 61–62; symbolism of 52–53, 57, 59; visitors for 58–59; *see also* identity in Landsmót
large-scale events 186
Leeds 157–158
Leeds Beckett University, United Kingdom 3–4
leveraging 186–187, 190
LGBTQ community 157
life cycles of events/festival 139
Likert-type scale for surveying data on festival 96
Lincoln University, New Zealand 4
LittTalk 104
Liverpool John Moores University, United Kingdom 4
local food 145
local identity 52

local pride of host community 29–30
location for Housing Fair in Finland 41
longevity of Housing Fair in Finland 45

Mackay, Michael 4
male identities in Landsmót 60
Maleny 141
managerial/management: autonomy of 12–13; of festivals 110–113, 119; festival success, perspective on 6, 11–13; rural festival, aspects of staging 97; standard functions of 12
mapping supply chain 123
market: Croatian tourism 192; for Danish rural festival 102–103; for festival 91
Mary River 141
McCord Museum 134
meaninglessness 32
media coverage of protests 160
Memorandum of Understanding 173
Men's Supper Club 162
MGRI *see* multiple generator, random interpreter (MGRI)
Millennium Square 163–164
misuse of power 23
mixed industry 187–188
Montreal: cultural landscape of 134; Drapeau administration in 133; financial structure of 133; founding of 131–132; Olympic Stadium in 133; partnerships in, public *vs.* private 135; 350th anniversary 131–136; tourism in, development of 133
Montreal Museum of Fine Arts 134
multiple generator, random interpreter (MGRI) 76–77, 80–81
Musée des Hospitalières de l'Hôtel-Dieu 134

NAM *see* national account manager (NAM)
name generators 71–72, 74–75
name interpreters 72–73, 76–77
name interrelators 73, 76–77
narrative of sports 53
national account manager (NAM) 114, 118
national heritage festival 52
national identity 49; in Landsmót 50, 52–53, 58–59, 61; in sports 53
National Portrait Gallery 163–164

Index

network: partnerships and 100; personal 70, 76; two-mode 70; whole 69–70
networked communities 66, 85
network society 68
New Zealand 22, 170–171; *see also* Akaroa French Festival
non-profit organisations 193
nonreplicable stakeholder 93
Noosa News 145

Olympic Games 35, 53, 129–130, 133–135
Olympic Stadium 133
OP-Pohjola Group Central Cooperative 39
ordinary time 161
organiser/organisations: collaborative structures 94; empowerment 94–95; empowerment of 101, 103; festival, involved in 97–99; of festival, defined 9–10; French Festival, changes in 173; functioning, multi-level layers of 92; Gorski Kotar, Croatia, challenges of 193–196; non-profit 193; power 92–93; power over 146; purchasing, turnover and impact of 124; purchasing behaviour, impact on 120; purpose of 100–102; resource competition 94; rural festival, innovation in 92–95; sporting events, purpose of 185; stakeholders 92; supply chain, involved in 114, 116–117
ownership of sports/sporting events 190
Oxfam 25, 27

PA *see* Public Address (PA) system manufacturer
Paris 130
participants identities 60–61
partnerships: festival, in collaborating 97–98, 103–104; in Montreal 135; networks and 100; public *vs.* private 41, 135; purpose of 100–102
Pearson correlation 100
Pehlivanidou, Eirini 1
people power 85
permeability of Housing Fair in Finland, to trends and social issues 42–44
personal networks 70, 76
personal relationships 68

person-oriented perspective on festival success 13–14
Pilton 26
Platonic Pauline 159
Pointe-à-Callière Montréal Archeology and History Complex 134
political activism 165
political events 155–156
political minefield, festival as 31
Pori Jazz Festival 35–36
portfolio of events 170
power: concept of 22; Foucauldian concept of 22–23; influence and 94, 104; misuse of 23; of organiser/organisations 92–93; people 85; in rural community, distribution of 190–192; in rural festival, centralization of 100; of stakeholder 22–23, 85; *see also* power of Real Food Festival; specific types of
power broker 22
power elites 159–160
powerlessness 24, 31–32
power of Real Food Festival 139, 150; contexualising research on 140–142; empowerment 149–150; Foucauldian sense of 139; interviews on 141–142; notion of 139; social capital and 141; stakeholders 149–150; Sunshine Coast Council 148; tourism, relationship with 140; types of 139, 150 (*see also* power over; power to); wrestling of 142–150
power over 32, 139, 145–150; community events 145; consumers 148–149; food producers 148–149; organisers' 146; Regional Development Program (TEQRDP) 147; sponsors 146; stakeholders 145
power to 139, 142–144, 150; consumers 143–144; empowerment 143–144; sponsors 143; stakeholders 143–144; workshops 143
PPP *see* private-public partnerships (PPP)
PQMethod 10–11
pragmatic managerial perspective on festival success 11–13
pressure zones 110, 119, 121–122
PRIDE event 157–158
pride of host community, local 29–30
Principal Component method 10
pristine nature 55

private entities 11
private-public partnerships (PPP) 41
Proctor & gamble 117
professional organisers *vs.* host community 25
profile characteristics about festival 11
protests 155–156, 159–162
Public Address (PA) system manufacturer 114, 124
public rituals 52
public space 163–164
purchasing: activities of, review of 117–118; organisations, turnover and impact of 124; positive *vs.* negative consequences of 120; pressure zones, impact on 121–122; supply risk, effect on 121–122; *see also* purchasing behaviour
purchasing behaviour 120–124
purebred status of Icelandic horses 55
purity 55

QFA *see* Q-factor analysis (QFA)
Q-factor analysis (QFA) 9
Q-factor interpretation of festival success 11
Q-methodology 6, 9–10
Q-methodology for festival success 9
QOL *see* quality of life (QOL)
Q-perspective 13
Q-sorts, features of physical 10
qualitative research on SCM 113
qualitative social research methods 174–175
quality of life (QOL) 37
Quebec 130

real democracy 154, 165
Real Food Festival 139; attendees to 141; purpose of establishing 141; success of 150; Sunshine Coast Council for 147–148; tourism, impact on 139; *see also* power of Real Food Festival
reflective management practices for organisers of events 32
Regional Development Program (TEQRDP) 147
relationships 68, 70, 113–114
replaceable stakeholder 93
research *see* ego network based research
residential development 38
resource competition 94

resource generators 72, 75–76
respondent fatigue 76
retrofitting 38–39
Reykjavik 52–53, 57
Rijeka 192
ritual: events *vs.* 158–163; Falassi's typology of 159; public 52
Ritz-Carlton Hotel 133
Robinsons Bay 172
rural community 189–192, 197; challenges of 190 196; geography of 189; notion of the sense of 189–190; power in, distribution of 190–192
rural festival: alliances built in 99–100; Danish 96–97, 102–103; defining 95–96; evolution of 91; influence in, centralization of 100; innovation of 104; managerial aspects of staging 97; in New Zealand 170–171; organiser innovation in 92–95; power in, centralization of 100; stakeholders in, reality of 104; types of 91, 104; *see also* festival
rural gender identity 54
Ryan, W. Gerard 3

sacralisation 161
sacred space 164
St. Paul's Cathedral 163
Sampo Bank 39
SCC *see* Sunshine Coast Council (SCC)
SCC Regional Development Economic Strategy 147–148
SCM *see* Supply Chain Management (SCM)
Scotland 66
Seinäjoki 38
self-empowerment 95, 103
self-esteem 95
semi-structured interviews 114
serious leisure 156–157
shared vision 26–29, 32
sideway outcomes of Housing Fair in Finland 45–46
Smith, Andrew 37
SNA *see* social network analysis (SNA)
social capital 141
social leveraging 186–187, 190
social media posts on Landsmót 50–51, 61–62; contextual analysis of 51; Instagram 50–51, 57; semiology of interpreting 51
social movement communities 153

social network analysis (SNA) 65, 86; academic research on 69; ego network based research and 65–66; ethical considerations on 70; of events 68; of festival 68; of personal networks 70; of personal relationships 68
social relationships, ownership of 70
Société historique de Montréal 133
soft bodies 44–45
Southeast Queensland, Australia *see* Real Food Festival
spectators, images in Landsmót 59
sponsor 143, 146
sports clubs 193–194
sports/sporting events 91; stakeholder for sporting events; community, impact on 185–188; economy, impact on 185; equestrian 54, 57–58; heritage of 53; identity in 49; narrative of 53; national identity in 53; organising, purpose of 185; ownership of 190; in rural communities 189–197 (*see also* rural community); *see also* Gorski Kotar, Croatia
Spracklen, Karl 153
Stadler, Raphaela 1, 37
Staffordshire University, United Kingdom 3
stakeholder: for events 22–23, 67, 85–86; for festival 22–23, 67, 85–86; French Festival, perspectives on 175–182; Glastonbury Festival, objectives of 27–29; for Gorski Kotar, Croatia 193–196; identity of 66–67; management of 109–110; nonreplicable 93; organiser/organisations and 92; power of 22–23, 85, 149–150; power over 145; power to 143–144; replaceable 93; in rural festival, reality of 104; value of 67; *see also* stakeholder for sporting events
stakeholder for sporting events: capacity building across 196–197; impact on 185–186; inter-organisational networks and 188–189; leveraging of 186–187, 190
standard management functions 12
Stergiou, Dimitrios P. 1
structural holes 84
subworld, Icelandic horses as 57
Summer Olympics 132

Sunshine Coast Council (SCC) 147–148
Sunshine Coast Sunday 144
suppliers 112–113
supply chain: Bullwhip Effect for 123; categories of 120–122; challenges of 123; corrections in 119; defined 110–111; demands of 118–119; for festival 109, 113; mapping 123; organisation of 114; organisations involved in 114, 116–117; supply chains within 114–116; *see also* Supply Chain Management (SCM)
Supply Chain Management (SCM): buyer-supplier relationships 113–114; concepts of 110; cost-effective reductions 112; increased levels of, positive impact of 124; information flows in 117; integrated 111–112; maintaining 111; in management of festivals 110–113; national account manager 118; qualitative research on 113; semi-structured interviews 114; suppliers 112–113; sustainability 112; time and 119; *see also* purchasing; supply chain
supply risk 121–122
sustainability 112
symbolism: of French Festival 173–174; of Icelandic horses 55; of Landsmót 52–53, 57, 59

Takamatua 172
Tango Festival 36
TedTalks 104
TEQRDP *see* Regional Development Program (TEQRDP)
Te Waihora 172
theme of Housing Fair in Finland 39–42
350th anniversary in Montreal 131–136
time 119, 161
tourism: in Akaroa 172; attractiveness of 36–37; conceptual framework of 52; on Crete 5–6; events, development strategy for 130–131; in Finland 35–36; geographical issues important for 52; in Gorski Kotar, Croatia 192, 193; heritage 53; in Iceland 55; identities in 50; in Montreal, development of 133; Real Food Festival, impact on 139–140; segregation of 36; 350th anniversary in Montreal, impact on development

of 134–135; 'Tribes, Territories and Networks' 71–72
Tourisme Montréal 133
Tourism Management 6
tourist boards 194–195
tourist trap 24
tractor-pulling festival 99
traditional managerial perspective on festival success 11–13
Traveston Crossing Dam 141
'Tribes, Territories and Networks' tourism 71–72
two-mode network 70

uniqueness 52
UK Uncut 156
University of Hertfordshire, United Kingdom 1
University of Otago, New Zealand 3
University of Quebec, Canada 3
University of Rijeka, Croati 4
University of Salford, United Kingdom 3
University of Southern Denmark 2
University of Surrey, United Kingdom 1
UNTWO 41
urban development/urbanisation 37, 38–39
usual suspects phenomenon 195

value of stakeholders 67
Vantaa 38
Varimax rotation 10
VIA Rail Canada 133
Viking Market 100
visitors 58–61
volunteers involved in festival 98–99

Walters, Trudie 3
Water Aid 25, 27
we-ness 52
Westminster Abbey 164
White, Zoe 1
whole network 69–70
wildness 55
Wise, Nicholas 4
Women and Men in Finland 45
Woolworths 141
workshops, power to 143
World Championships 55
World Cup 129
World Expos 129
World's Fair 130
World Village Festival 36
wrestling of power of Real Food Festival 142–150

Zagreb 192